Health Communication and Mass Media

An Integrated Approach to Policy and Practice

Edited by
RUKHSANA AHMED
and
BENJAMIN R. BATES

GOWER

Gower Applied Business Research
Our programme provides leaders, practitioners, scholars and researchers with thought provoking, cutting edge books that combine conceptual insights, interdisciplinary rigour and practical relevance in key areas of business and management.

Published by
Gower Publishing Limited
Wey Court East
Union Road
Farnham
Surrey, GU9 7PT
England

Gower Publishing Company
110 Cherry Street
Suite 3-1
Burlington,
VT 05401-3818
USA

www.gowerpublishing.com

British Library Cataloguing in Publication Data
Health communication and mass media : an integrated
   approach to policy and practice.
   1. Health in mass media. 2. Communication in public health.
   3. Mass media in health education.
   I. Ahmed, Rukhsana. II. Bates, Benjamin R.
   362.1'014-dc23

Library of Congress Cataloging-in-Publication Data
Health communication and mass media : an integrated approach to policy and practice / [compiled] by Rukhsana Ahmed and Benjamin R. Bates.
      pages cm
   Includes bibliographical references and index.
   ISBN 978-1-4094-4713-9 (hbk) -- ISBN 978-1-4094-4714-6 (ebk)
   -- ISBN 978-1-4724-0164-9 (epub)
1. Communication in medicine. 2. Health in mass media. 3. Interactive multimedia. I. Ahmed, Rukhsana, editor of compilation. II. Bates, Benjamin R., editor of compilation.
   R118.H4327 2013
   610--dc23
                                                                                                    2012044703

ISBN 978 1 4094 4713 9 (hbk)
ISBN 978 1 4094 4714 6 (ebk – PDF)
ISBN 978 1 4724 0164 9 (ebk – ePUB)

FSC
MIX
Paper from responsible sources
FSC® C018575
www.fsc.org

Printed and bound in Great Britain
by MPG PRINTGROUP

Health Communication and Mass Media

To Amma and Abba
To Hasan and Zerin

Rukhsana

To Betsy

Ben

Contents

List of Figures and Tables

Figures

Tables

About the Editors

Rukhsana Ahmed is an Associate Professor in the Department of Communication at the University of Ottawa. She has an interdisciplinary background with a Masters in International Relations from the University of Dhaka, Bangladesh; a Masters in International Development Studies, a Masters in Communication Studies, and PhD in Health Communication from Ohio University, USA. Her research embraces the cross/trans/inter-disciplinary nature of communication scholarship with a specific focus on health care sector services for vulnerable populations and interest in media, interpersonal, intercultural, and other realms of communication including gender and development. In this scholarship, Dr. Ahmed uses rhetorical, critical, qualitative, and quantitative procedures relevant to the question she is asking and the audience she is addressing. Dr. Ahmed has published in mainstream communication journals (such as *Communication Studies and Medical Informatics*), in health studies outlets (such as *Women's Health and Urban Life* and *Journal of Cancer Education*), nursing journals (such as *Journal of Transcultural Nursing*), and in journals at the intersection of health, communication, and culture (*Intercultural Communication Studies, Journal of Cultural Diversity* and *Identity, Culture and Politics*). Dr. Ahmed is the co-editor of the book *Medical Communication in Clinical Contexts*. Currently she is co-authoring a book on health literacy in Canada. Dr. Ahmed serves on editorial boards of and reviews papers for journals in the areas of communication, media, and health.

Benjamin R. Bates is currently an Associate Professor and Director for Graduate Studies in the School of Communication Studies at Ohio University. Dr. Bates earned his PhD at the University of Georgia in Speech Communication in 2003. Since then, he has authored or co-authored more than 50 peer-reviewed publications and made more than 100 presentations to learned societies at the intersection of health, communication, and media. Specifically, he investigates communication campaigns in the context of public and environmental health and public understanding of health and healing. Dr. Bates has published in communication journals, including *Quarterly Journal of Speech, Rhetoric Review, Health Communication*, and others. Dr. Bates has also published in several journals devoted to the biomedical sciences such as *Journal of Genetic Counseling, Community Genetics, Clinical Genetics, Journal of the National Medical Association, Genetics in Medicine*, and the *American Journal of Medical Genetics*. He has also sought to explore the intersection of the humanities and medical science in publications in the *Journal of Medicine and Philosophy* and the *Journal of Medical Humanities*. Dr. Bates has also focused on journals committed to the intersection of communication and science, including *Public Understanding of Science, Medical Informatics*, and *Social Science & Medicine*, as well as other outlets. Dr. Bates has served on the editorial boards of eight different journals in communication and as a reviewer for 21 other journals in communication, health science, and medicine. He currently edits *Communication Quarterly.*

About the Contributors

Victoria Aceti is a research assistant for the Health Informatics Institute at Algoma University in Sault Ste, Marie, Ontario. She is a graduate of the Master of Arts in Communication program at the University of Ottawa. Victoria is currently working on projects which focus on applied health informatics to improve patient outcomes. She is a published author in the area of health communication, health informatics, clinical governance, and pedagogical information technology.

Vinita Agarwal (Ph.D., Purdue University, 2009) is an Assistant Professor at the Department of Communication Arts in Salisbury University, Maryland, where she teaches research methods and public relations. Dr. Agarwal's research interests include mediated and psycho-social factors in health behaviors with a special interest in women's issues and organizational processes. She was recently a recipient of a top three health communication paper award from ECA and the Faculty Research Award from the University System of Maryland Women's Foundation and has published in peer-reviewed journals including the *Western Journal of Communication, Journal of Communication Management,* and Communication Research Reports.

Theodore A. Avtgis (Ph.D., 1999, Kent State University) is Professor and Chair, Department of Communication Studies at Ashland University and Adjunct Associate Professor of Surgery at West Virginia University School of Medicine. He is currently the Editor-in-Chief of Communication Research Reports and co-founder of Medical Communication Specialists. Dr. Avtgis is author of over 40 peer reviewed articles, 15 book chapters, and 6 books based on medical communication, aggressive communication, communication theory, and organizational communication. Most recently, Avtgis co-authored the ground-breaking book *Medical Communication: Defining the Discipline*. He is currently engaged in various projects assessing trauma networks and the organizational processes that occur within them. Among other honors, Dr. Avtgis was the recipient of the 2011 Past Presidents' Award and named Centennial Scholar by the Eastern Communication Association. He was also recognized as one of the Top Twelve Most Productive Scholars in the field of Communication Studies (between 1996–2001) and recognized as a member of the World Council on Hellenes Abroad, USA Region of American Academics.

Jennifer L. Bevan (B.A., M.A., University of Delaware; Ph.D., University of Georgia) is an associate professor in the Department of Communication Studies/M.S. Program in Health and Strategic Communication at Chapman University, Orange, CA. Her research examines interpersonal and health communication processes within close relationships. Dr. Bevan has published or has in press over 30 peer-reviewed scholarly articles in such journals as *Communication Monographs*, *Human Communication Research*, *Communication Research*, *Journal of Health Communication*, and *Patient Education and Counseling*. A 2009

Communication Research Reports study determined that she was the 24th (out of 3,800) most published scholar in peer-reviewed communication journals from 2002 to 2006.

Sharon Bogan is project manager at Public Health – Seattle & King County for the Text Messaging for Public Health Emergencies research project. Her research highlights the ways new technology can be implemented in real-world, local public health settings. Ms. Bogan has developed and evaluated health communication programs in King County and internationally. She is also an affiliate instructor of Public Health at the University of Washington and teaches courses in community development and health communications. Ms. Bogan holds an MPH (2005) from the University of Washington in Community-Oriented Public Health Practice, and a Certificate in International Health.

Rowena Briones is a doctoral student and instructor of record studying public relations and health communication in the Department of Communication at the University of Maryland, College Park. She received her B.A. in Communication Studies from The College of New Jersey and received her M.A. in Communication from the University of Maryland, College Park. Rowena's research interests include the intersections of public relations, social media and the Web, and health campaigns. Her current research explores how different social media channels impact health literacy levels and behavioral intention.

Lorraine Buis is an Assistant Professor at the Wayne State University (WSU) College of Nursing, with an honorary joint appointment in the WSU Department of Communication, where her research focuses on the use of mobile communication technologies for health promotion and self-management of chronic disease. Dr. Buis received a Ph.D. in Mass Media from the Michigan State University of Department of Telecommunication, Information Studies, and Media, as well as a MSI with a specialization in Human Computer Interaction from the University of Michigan School of Information. In addition, Dr. Buis completed a post-doctoral research fellowship at the Ann Arbor Veterans Affairs Health Services Research and Development (HSR&D) Center of Excellence.

Margaret U. D'Silva (Ph.D., University of Kentucky, 1993) is Professor of Communication and Director of the Institute for Intercultural Communication at the University of Louisville. Born in India, she was educated at St. Agnes College, Mangalore, and Mysore University, India. She serves on the governing board of the International Association for Intercultural Studies. She has served as Chair of the APAC Division of NCA. She teaches Intercultural Communication and Mass Media courses. Dr. D'Silva has published several journal articles and book chapters, and co-edited two books: *HIV/AIDS: Prevention and Health Communication* and *Communicating about HIV/AIDS: Taboo Topics and Difficult Discussions*.

Heather P. Eastman-Mueller (Ph.D., University of Missouri, 2005) is an AASECT (American Association for Sexuality Educators, Counselors and Therapists) certified sexuality educator at the Student Health Center. She coordinates the sexual health program at the University of Missouri and is an affiliate faculty member of the Women's and Gender Studies Department. Dr. Eastman-Mueller's research interests include investigating the socio-cultural manifestations of a person's sexuality. She has conducted multiple presentations on sexuality in the college setting and published a comprehensive sexual health scale in the *Handbook of Sexuality-Related Measures*.

Julia Ernst graduated cum laude from Rider University in Lawrenceville, New Jersey with a Bachelor's degree in Journalism and a minor in Science for Business. After completing her undergraduate degree in three and a half years, she went on to earn her Master's degree in Health and Strategic Communication in a one-year, accelerated program at Chapman University in Orange, California. Ms. Ernst is currently working as the assistant editor of *Skin & Aging*, a monthly dermatology journal that provides practical advice about cutaneous pathologies, cosmetic procedures and practice management. Ms. Ernst also aspires to earn her Ph.D. in journalism and teach at the university level.

Jessica Francies (B.S., M.S., Chapman University) is currently collaborating with Dr. Christopher Kim and the United States Geological Survey at Chapman University to investigate the bioaccessibility and bioavailability of toxic metals in contaminated soils and sediments from abandoned mine sites in Southern California. This research ties closely to the public health education that she was exposed to during her education in the Biological Sciences. Furthermore, during her graduate education, she took an interest in the effect the patient-provider relationship has on the patient's perception of the provider as well as on the treatment outcome. Her future goal is to become a Physician Assistant.

Micheline Frenette is currently associate professor in the department of communication (Université de Montréal, Québec, Canada). She holds a doctor's degree in education (Harvard), a master's in psychology (Ottawa) and a master's in communication (Montreal). Dr. Frenette conducts research on the role of the mass media in the lives of children, adolescents and their families, on the design of health campaigns and the potential of communication technologies such as the Internet for education and socialization purposes. She has recently published a book illustrating how the social sciences and communication research are relevant for health campaigns.

Bree Holtz, Ph.D. is a Researcher at the VA Ann Arbor Healthcare System in the department of Health Services Research and Development. She holds a Ph.D. from the College of Communication Arts and Sciences from Michigan State University and a Master of Science degree in Analysis, Design, and Management of Information Systems from the London School of Economics. Dr. Holtz's broad research interest centers around understanding the adoption of information communication technologies and its impact on health care access and delivery. Her current research interests include understanding the implementation and utilization of mHealth technologies to improve health outcomes.

Hilary N. Karasz leads the Text Messaging Initiative at Public Health – Seattle & King County (PHSKC). She is project director and co-investigator for Text Messaging for Public Health Emergencies, a five-year study with the Northwest Preparedness & Emergency Response Research Center, funded by the U.S. Centers for Disease Control and Prevention. She is also a public information officer at PHSKC and a clinical assistant professor of Public Health at the University of Washington. Dr. Karasz holds a Ph.D.

(2006) in Communication from the University of Washington. Her research focuses on public health communications and mobile technologies.

Seow Ting Lee received her M.A. and Ph.D. from the University of Missouri School of Journalism. Her research focuses on understanding the role of mass communication in health behavior change and policy. Dr. Lee's research examines message efficacy in public health campaigns and pandemic response, and the management of relationships between health organizations and governments and their publics. She is particularly interested in explicating the ethical dimensions of health communication and its underlying values, presumptions and motivations. Her research in health communication has been published in the *Journal of Health Communication*, *Health Communication*, *Public Relations Review*, and the *Journal of Mass Media Ethics*.

Greg Leichty (Ph.D., University of Kentucky, 1986) is a professor in the Department of Communication Arts at the University of Louisville in Kentucky. Dr. Leichty's research interests include public relations theory, issues management, and argumentation.

Meredith Li-Vollmer is a co-investigator for the Text Messaging for Public Health Emergencies research project. She is a risk communications specialist at Public Health – Seattle & King County. In this role, she conducts audience research, develops public outreach strategies, and directs public engagement projects, focusing on reaching those most at-risk during emergencies. Dr. Li-Vollmer is also a clinical assistant professor of Public Health at the University of Washington and serves in emergency communication planning roles at the local, state, and national level. Dr. Li-Vollmer holds a Ph.D. (2002) in Communication from the University of Washington.

Rocci Luppicini, Ph.D., is an Assistant Professor in the Department of Communication at the University of Ottawa and an expert on digital technologies. He has published eight authored and edited books and over 20 peer reviewed articles and book chapters in various areas of digital technologies within organizational settings. Key book publications include: *Trends in Educational Technology and Distance Education in Canada* (2008), *Cases on Digital Technologies in Higher Education: Issues and Challenges* (2010), *Online Learning Communities* (2007), the two volume *Handbook of Research on Technoethics* (2008), and *Technoethics in an Evolving Knowledge Society: Ethical Issues in Design Research Development and Innovation* (2010). Dr. Luppicini currently acts as the editor-in-chief for the *International Journal of Technoethics*, which focuses on areas of human life and society impacted by new technologies.

Nicole Mardis is a Ph.D. student in Sociology at McGill University, where she currently holds a Joseph-Armand Bombardier CGS Doctoral Fellowship. She has a Master of Arts in Sociology from McGill University, a Bachelor of Commerce Honours in the Management of Organizations from the University of Manitoba, and a Bachelor of Arts in Sociology from the University of Winnipeg. Her current research focuses on the emergence and structure of inter-organizational problem solving networks.

Julie McCormack is Specialist Clinical Psychologist and Coordinator of Training, Research and Psychology for Princess Margaret Hospital for Children Eating Disorders

Program in Western Australia. She is co-founder and current President of Bridges Association Incorporated and Chair of the Clinical Reference Group for the National Eating Disorders Collaboration. She holds a Master Degree in Science and a Diploma in Clinical Psychology, from University of Canterbury, New Zealand. Ms. McCormack has presented papers and workshops at local, national, and international conferences. Her current research focus is service delivery for eating disorders and involving parents and families in treatment.

Rebecca J. Meisenbach (Ph.D., Purdue University, 2004) is an assistant professor in the Department of Communication at the University of Missouri. Dr. Meisenbach's research focuses on issues of ethics and identity in relation to nonprofit and gendered organizing. Current projects address stigma management in organizational and health contexts and the experiences of working moms as they return to paid work after a maternity leave. Her work has been published in outlets such as *Communication Monographs*, *Journal of Applied Communication Research*, *Management Communication Quarterly*, and *Sex Roles*.

Galit Nimrod, Ph.D., Fulbright scholar, is a senior lecturer at the Department of Communication Studies and a research fellow at the Center for Multidisciplinary Research in Aging at Ben-Gurion University of the Negev, Israel. Dr. Nimrod holds a Ph.D. degree in Mass Communication and Journalism from the Hebrew University of Jerusalem. She was also a post-doctorate Fulbright scholar at the University of Georgia, where she was hosted by the Institute of Gerontology and the Department of Counseling and Human Development Services. Dr. Nimrod studies psychological and sociological aspects of leisure among populations with special needs such as older adults and people with disabilities, and she had published extensively on these subjects. Her current research projects focus on new media and their functions for individuals and various social groups.

Candy J. Noltensmeyer is a doctoral student in the Department of Communication at the University of Missouri. Ms. Noltensmeyer received her Master of Arts degree in Communication from Pittsburg State University in 2003. Her research interests include identity practices, stigma communication, and gender.

Whitney Offenbecher is a research assistant for the Text Messaging for Public Health Emergencies research project. In this role, Ms. Offenbecher assists with the development, execution and evaluation of pilot text messaging programs and conducts qualitative data analysis. Ms. Offenbecher previously worked with the Communications Team at Public Health – Seattle & King County in an AmeriCorps VISTA position, facilitating the translation and distribution of public health and emergency preparedness materials for vulnerable populations. Ms. Offenbecher is currently a candidate for the Master of Health Administration at the University of Washington's School of Public Health.

Sara Peters is a doctoral candidate in the Communication Department at the University of Missouri. Ms. Peters received her Masters degree in Journalism from the University of Missouri. Her research interests include the study of mass media effects, mediated health campaigns, and persuasion.

E. Phillips Polack (M.D., 1971, West Virginia University, M.A. 2006: West Virginia University) is Clinical Professor of Surgery at West Virginia University. Dr. Polack's initial book, *Applied Communication for Health Professionals*, was published in 2008. He is senior author on the new ground-breaking text *Medical Communication: Defining the Discipline*. He has lectured widely on the topic of provider-patient communication, mindfulness and teamwork at major universities, at all levels of the health care hierarchy. He is past Governor of the West Virginia Chapter of the American College of Surgeons, and is an instructor in communication at the Clinical Congress of the American College of Surgeons. He has served as Visiting Professor in both residency programs and major academic institutions including the Canadian Surgical Forum in 2007. He is currently engaged in various projects assessing trauma outcomes and the relationship those outcomes have with specific communication practices. He currently practices plastic surgery at Wheeling Hospital, Wheeling, WV where he serves as Chairman of the Committee on Ethics. He is co-founder of Medical Communication Specialists.

Nicole Santora (M.S. in Health and Strategic Communication, Chapman University) is working in the Emergency Department at St. Joseph Hospital in Orange, California as a Medical Scribe. Nicole worked as the medical coordinator at Orange County Health and Wellness – Optifast, a medical weight loss clinic and has volunteered in Honduras with Global Medical Brigades. She currently volunteers at the Dick Butkus Center for Cardiovascular Wellness. She has also participated in research investigating heart disease in firefighters. Nicole has been a member of the American Medical Students Association and Psi Chi Honors Society. She has also participated in episodes for the Telly award-winning TV show Health Matters with Dr. Larry Santora.

Lisa Sparks (Ph.D., University of Oklahoma) is Foster and Mary McGaw Endowed Professor in Behavioral Sciences at Chapman University in Orange, California, where she serves as Head/Director of the M.S. program in Health and Strategic Communication in the Schmid College of Science and Technology. Dr. Sparks is a Full Member of the Chao Family/NCI Designated Comprehensive Cancer Center at the University of California, Irvine in the School of Medicine, Division of Population Sciences; Adjunct Professor in the Department of Population Health and Disease Prevention, Program in Public Health. She is a highly regarded teacher-scholar whose published work spans more than 100 research articles and scholarly book chapters, and is the author and editor of more than ten books in the areas of communication, health, and aging with a distinct focus on cancer communication science.

Beth Sundstrom received a Master of Public Health (M.P.H) from Brown University with a specialization in health communication and women's health and a B.A. from Tulane University in political science. She is a doctoral fellow and instructor in the Department of Communication at the University of Maryland, College Park. She is pursuing a Ph.D. in Health Communication and Public Relations. Beth's interests include health communication, public relations, and social marketing. Her current research focuses on women's reproductive health and contraceptive use dynamics.

Hunna Watson is a Senior Research Scientist at the Centre for Clinical Interventions and a Senior Research Psychologist at the Princess Margaret Hospital for Children Eating

Disorders Program in Western Australia. Dr. Watson's research interest is eating disorders, particularly theories of maintenance and treatment in real-world settings. She previously served as National Research Coordinator on the National Eating Disorders Collaboration project, and is a present steering committee member, and serves on the management committee of the peak eating disorders body in Western Australia. Dr. Watson is a past recipient of the Australian and New Zealand Academy for Eating Disorders Beaumont Young Investigator of the Year Award.

Tracy R. Worrell is an assistant professor in the Department of Communication at the Rochester Institute of Technology. Dr. Worrell received her Ph.D. in Communication from Michigan State University in 2006. As a researcher Dr. Worrell has predominantly focused on examining health messages and the media. Dr. Worrell has written numerous conference papers and has been published in journals such as *Health Communication* and the *Howard Journal of Communication*. Publications have explored areas such as the portrayal of illness on television and its impact on those with said illnesses to creating effective health messages to promote behavior change.

Foreword

RAFAEL OBREGON

Health Communication and Mass Media: An Integrated Approach to Policy and Practice is a timely publication for several reasons. I will focus on three key reasons that I believe connect very well with the main threads of the book. First, it will enrich our understanding of the critical role that emerging dimensions of mediated communication play in public health today, particularly web and mobile media. The social and cultural transformations brought forth by new communication technologies require little argumentation. What is needed, urgently, is a more profound examination of how these technological transformations alter people's daily lives, including health-related issues. By examining the role of theory, this volume addresses one of the major gaps in current research in mobile and web-based communication health interventions. For instance, a review of mobile communication-based interventions to change health behaviors (Riley et al., 2011) calls for greater utilization of behavior change theories to guide mobile health behavior interventions, and a greater recognition of the interactive and systemic nature of mobile communication.

The second reason, and perhaps this is the most important contribution of this volume, is the notion of media ecosystems as a critical point of departure. This concept aptly recognizes the complexity of today's communication environment, including the increasing and pervasive presence and role of mobile and web communications in people's daily experience, in addition to an already saturated "traditional" media environment. *Health Communication and Mass Media: An Integrated Approach to Policy and Practice* examines the interconnectedness of media and mediated health communication that includes a series of exemplars provided by a solid group of contributors. While the research discourse and, to a lesser extent, practice in public health has increasingly moved toward a greater focus on the social determinants of health, and on the interconnectedness of those determinants, many public health programs still tend to approach the role of media and communication from a uni-dimensional perspective. A media ecosystem approach should set the course for a renewed exploration of the role of media and communication in health communication, and this volume provides a wonderful opportunity to identify trends and emerging questions. Further, the communicative experience, from the intrapersonal, to the interpersonal, to the family and community, to the broader social environment, following an ecological approach, of individuals and collectives need to be recognized as part of a broader media ecosystem, which has important implications for policy and practice.

The third, but by no means a less important reason, is the emphasis that *Health Communication and Mass Media: An Integrated Approach to Policy and Practice* places on the ethical dimensions of health communication and media. As a scholar and practitioner whose work for more than twenty years has primarily focused in international settings, I have seen several examples of how ethical considerations are often overlooked or minimized in order to facilitate the achievement of program goals or research objectives. In addition, the focus on positive messaging and adequate portrayals of population groups (e.g., people with disability) also brings to light the ethical implications of producing content and messages that may contribute to reinforcing long-established negative stereotypes that prevent people with a particular condition to reach their full potential. In my current position as chief of communication for development at the United Nations Children's Fund (UNICEF) we have sponsored the development of a manual on communicating with children (Lemish and Kolucki, 2011), which promotes the use of a series of principles for message and content development across a variety of media and seek to ensure inclusive communication, and an assets-based approach. Often, ethical dimensions of health communication and media are not given the type of attention that they surely deserve; therefore I think this volume also contributes to filling an important gap in the literature.

Back in 2004 Vicky Freimuth and Sandra Rouse Quinn took stock of the contributions of health communication to eliminating health disparities. In their text, they summarized major breakthroughs in the growth of health communication as a field of study, and highlighted key aspects of health communication research and practice. Five years later, Thompson, Dorsey, Miller, and Parrot (2009) co-edited the *Handbook of Health Communication*, which made a significant contribution to our understanding of the theoretical and applied breadth of health communication as a subfield, with a primary focus on the U.S.A. In 2012, my colleague Silvio Waisbord and I co-edited the *Handbook of Global Health Communication*, which looked at the international and global dimensions of health communication. While research and practice in health communication is clearly a very dynamic process, and is often approached from different disciplines, the increasing attempts to map out various aspects of health communication not only demonstrate the sustained growth of scholarship in this area, but also the need to continually examine trends in this subfield. Each of the volumes listed above, though broad in scope, asked a different set questions that led to a wide range of conclusions and new questions for research and scholarly work.

When Benjamin R. Bates and Rukhsana Ahmed, both of whom I had the opportunity of knowing and collaborating with at Ohio University, Athens, OH, asked me to write the foreword of their co-edited volume, I saw it as a reaffirmation of how dynamic the health communication subfield is, and how much work is ahead of us. Benjamin Bates and Rukhsana Ahmed have impressively pulled together a broad and rich set of contributions that collectively provide an in-depth and nuanced discussion of mobile and web mediated communication and their policy and practice implications for public health. The book's focus on the intersection of web media, mobile media, communication systems, and ethics, and theory, policy and practice is a welcomed contribution to an increasingly multi-disciplinary and complex subfield, which is likely to grow in complexity as a result of the rapidly changing media and communication environment. I hope readers concur with me in finding this volume a valuable complement to the health communication literature.

References

Freimuth, V. and Rouse Quinn, S. 2004. "The contributions of health communication to eliminating health disparities". *American Journal of Public Health*, 94(12), 2053–5.

Lemish, D. and Kolucki, B. 2011. *Communicating with Children: Principles and Practices to Nurture, Inspire, Educate and Heal*. UNICEF, New York, NY.

Obregon, R. and S. Waisbord. 2012. *The Handbook of Global Health Communication*. New York: Wiley Blackwell.

Riley, W.T., Rivera, D.E, Autienza, A.A., Nilsen, W., Allison, S. and R. Mermelstein. 2011. "Health behavior models in the age of mobile interventions: Are our theories up to the task?" *Translational Behavioral Medicine*, 1(1), 53–71.

Thompson, T.L., Dorsey, A., Miller, K. and Parrott, R. 2009. *Handbook of Health Communication*. New York: Routledge.

Preface

I'm not a media scholar, but my life is quite mediated – through the Internet, of course, and radio, recorded music, and countless hours spent watching TV and films. Illness, sorrow, and perhaps especially memory are inscribed with mediated traces that are influential in sense-making and managing fundamental dialectics of living. (Sharf 2010: 628)

In this remark, health communication scholar Barbara Sharf notes how pervasive mass media are in shaping communication about health issues. Today's media-rich environment presents opportunities as well as challenges for health communicators to use the different media platforms for dissemination and interpretation of health-related messages regarding prevention, health promotion and treatment for patients, their families, health care providers, and public health policy makers. Over the past several decades, there has been a considerable growth in health communication research demonstrating how the processes and application of lessons learned from research can help in media efforts to prevent diseases, promote health, and shape public health policies and practices. Yet, we still have much to learn about the influences of mediated communication on health outcomes as well as to apply best practices from this research into public policy. There is a need to consider multiple perspectives and approaches in the study of health communication in ever-changing mass mediated contexts, including examination of mobile communication technologies, new media and the web, communication systems, and media ethics. To this end, *Health Communication and Mass Media: An Integrated Approach to Policy and Practice* brings together exemplars of current health communication research and applications in mass mediated contexts spanning across geographic regions.

Rukhsana and Ben

Acknowledgments

Rukhsana and Ben

This book has been made possible by the generous contribution of a large number of people. We owe deep gratitude to the authors for their contributions, professionalism, dedication, and peer-strengthening needed to realize the vision of this book. Their collective expertise across the broad range of issues in mass media and health communication helped us create an integrated volume to advance policy and practice. We gratefully thank Neil Jordan, Commissioning Editor at Ashgate Publishing, for his faith, feedback, and support at the proposal stage and Martin West, Commissioning Editor at Gower Publishing for his invaluable guidance in taking this book project forward and providing support along the way. We are indebted to Donna Shanks, Assistant Commissioning Editor, Chris Muddiman, Editorial Administrator, Adam Guppy, Production Editor, and the production staff at Gower Publishing for their timely feedback and needed assistance for the successful continuation and completion of this book.

Rukhsana

I am very grateful to my co-editor, Benjamin R. Bates, for the privilege and great learning opportunity to work collaboratively on new projects. His depth of knowledge and experience across the areas of health communication have stimulated my thinking and learning about mass mediated health communication. My appreciation also extends to my colleagues and students at the University of Ottawa who also inspired this project. Special thanks to the Chair at the Department of Communication, Martine Lagacé, and the Dean of the Faculty of Arts, Antoni Lewkowicz, for always providing the support to make projects like this intellectually rewarding. Finally, completion of this project would not have been possible without the commitment and sacrifice of my family members, especially my husband, our daughter, and my parents. I sincerely acknowledge and thank them for their unconditional love and steadfast support and encouragement.

Ben

Once again, I have enjoyed working with my co-editor, Rukhsana Ahmed. Her spirit of exploration in new areas of health communication and her willingness to see projects through to their completion should inspire many people in our field. The support of my colleagues at Ohio University has always been invaluable; and my School Director, Jerry Miller, and the Dean of the Scripps College of Communication, Scott Titsworth, have always been supportive of faculty writing and editing books. I will always owe a debt to Celeste Condit, my former advisor at the University of Georgia, for supporting the diversity of interests and methodologies in the fields of media and health communication. Finally, this book could not have been prepared without the support and encouragement of Betsy Morley and the rest of my family outside of academe.

1 *Introduction*

CHAPTER 1

Communicating Health through Mass Media: An Overview

RUKHSANA AHMED AND BENJAMIN R. BATES

Introduction

Health communication has been defined as the study and use of communication strategies to inform, influence, and motivate individuals, institutions, and communities in making effective decisions to improve health and enhance quality of life (U.S. Department of Health and Human Services 2005). Considering this wide scope of health communication, scholars, practitioners, and policy makers recognize the significance of health communication to public health (Rimal and Lapinski 2009, Schiavo 2007). In today's media-saturated world, the importance of research on health communication in mass mediated contexts cannot be overemphasized, especially given that mass media are important communication channels for advancing health education and promotion, disease prevention, and shaping public policy.

Much of the public's understanding of health and health policy is not from their direct experience. Instead, most of their understanding is mediated. Health and illness discourses are pervasive in the print media, television, cinema, and the Internet (King and Watson 2005). Media channels, including print journalism, advertisements, fiction films, television shows, documentaries, and computer technology affect the healthcare system and individuals' use of that system (Friedman 2004). Clearly, media representations of health and illness shape our understanding of the experience of illness, health, and healthcare and influence health beliefs, health behaviors, healthcare practices, and policy-making (Seale 2002, 2004).

In addition to shaping general understandings, mass media play an important role in promoting public health (Abroms and Maibach 2008, Atkin and Wallack 1990, Viswanath, Wallington and Blake 2009). As Wallack (2000) argued, media "can be a delivery mechanism for getting the right information to the right people in the right way at the right time to promote personal change" and that "they can be a vehicle for increasing participation in civic and political life and social capital to promote social change" (338). In today's media rich landscape, and especially with the advancements of Information and Communication Technologies (ICTs), increasing efforts are underway to incorporate mass media strategies into health education, promotion, and disease prevention practices (Melanie, Wakefield and Hornik 2010, Parker and Thorson 2009, Viswanath, Wallington and Blake 2009). At the same time, scholars have documented mass media's reach to select audiences and specific, limited, and moderate effects in influencing health knowledge, attitude, and behavior (Atkin 2001, Rice and Atkin 2009, Atkin and Salmon 2010, Salmon and Atkin 2003). To fully realize mass media's role in facilitating the pursuit of health education and promotion, and disease prevention, health communicators need to exploit multiple mass media and interactive digital media channels and carry out carefully planned media strategies to reach intended audiences.

Regardless of medium or strategy, Griffiths and Knutson (1960) argued that "three effects might occur: the learning of correct health information, the changing of health attitudes and values, and the establishment of new health behavior" (515). Scholars interested in the role of mass media in health communication have studied effects of media use on health outcomes and effects of planned use of media to achieve health outcomes in many areas (Finnegan and Viswanath 2008). Programs designed to promote changes in health behavior and prompt treatment of illness have demonstrated the effectiveness of mass media channels in health promotion and disease prevention efforts such as discouraging alcohol, tobacco, and drug use (Snyder et al. 2006, Strasburger and Wilson 2002); minimizing harmful effects of violent television (Rosenkoetter, Ozretich and Acock 2004, Rosenkoetter, Rosenkoetter and Acock 2009); addressing eating disorders (Shields 2005, 2006); promoting physical activity (Strasburger and Wilson 2002, Van den Berg, Sztainer, Hannan and Haines 2007); curbing aggressive behavior and violence (Murray 2008, Strasburger and Wilson 2002); and promoting responsible sexual decision-making (Strasburger 2005, Strasburger and Wilson 2002), among other areas.

Collectively, these studies encourage us to attend to two issues for a successful mass mediated health communication intervention: the issue of theory and the issue of medium.

THE ISSUE OF THEORY

Health communication, when delivered effectively in mass mediated contexts, has considerable potential to promote the health of individuals, communities, and populations. These mass mediated messages are more likely to be successful in affecting health knowledge, attitudes, behavior, practice, and policy if they integrate health communication theory into their design and evaluation (Atkin and Wallack 1990, Dutta-Bergman 2005, Hornik 2002, Maibach and Parrott 1995, Murray-Johnson and Witte 2003, Noar, Harrington and Helme, 2010, Palmgreen and Donohew 2010, Randolph and Viswanath 2004, Rice and Atkin 2001, Salmon and Atkin 2003, Silk, Akin and Salmon 2011, Slater 2006). Although there are many specific communication theories that can be brought to bear on mass mediated messages, three families of theoretic approaches have been most commonly used: media advocacy approaches, social marketing approaches, and entertainment – education approaches.

Media advocacy approaches include theories that involve "the strategic use of mass media for advancing a social or public policy initiative" (Stewart and Casswell 1993: 167). Although these approaches are used for public health promotion, they do so in a way that addresses institutional and governmental decision makers through indirect lobbying efforts (Wallack et al.1993). As a powerful health communication strategy, media advocacy plays an important role in engaging people in dialogue about health promotion and disease prevention, facilitating community organizing to generate demand or support for health services, and potentially influencing policy-making on critical public health issues (Marchibroda 2009, Rock et al. 2011, Wallack and Dorfman 1996). In general, such efforts are likely to draw on communication theories from the realm of rhetoric, public relations, and agenda-setting.

Social marketing approaches involve the use of marketing concepts and techniques "to design and implement programs to promote socially beneficial behavior change" (Grier and Bryant 2005: 319). Social marketing approaches – such as the Theory of Reasoned Action, the Health Belief Model, and the Transtheoretical Model – have become a popular health promotion tool to influence perceptions, beliefs, attitudes, and behaviors regarding health issues (Edgar, Volkman Logan and 2011, Paço et al. 2010). Scholars have identified social marketing as an important condition for successful public health mass media campaigns because of its potential to "create the appropriate messages for distribution and, where possible, message theory and tailoring (creative marketing and messages)" (Randolph and Viswanath 2004: 422, Huhman 2010). However, health communicators and practitioners require understanding of the theoretical underpinnings of social marketing to effectively use it to plan public health interventions (Dooley, Jones and Desmarais 2009, Grier and Bryant 2005, Walsh et al. 1993). Because most social marketing approaches seek to affect individual beliefs, attitudes, or behaviors, the theories used in social marketing tend to be derived from psychological theories of decision-making.

Entertainment-education approaches consist of:

> purposely designing and implementing a media message to both entertain and educate, in order to increase audience knowledge about an educational issue, create favorable attitudes, and change overt behavior (Singhal and Rogers 1999: xii).

Studies have documented how, through combining entertainment and education, this mass media strategy has been applied to produce behavior changes for HIV/AIDS and Sexually Transmitted Disease (STD) prevention (Glik et al. 2002, Kennedy et al. 2004), syphilis screening (Whittier et al. 2005), and condom use (Collins et al. 2003). Entertainment-education approaches emphasize partnership among entertainment media practitioners, public health and health communication professionals and academics for designing effective health promotion and disease prevention interventions (Kennedy et al. 2004). Most entertainment education approaches draw from the family of theories that emphasize social learning and social psychology.

As important as a strong theoretical basis for mass mediated health communication is, a strong theory needs an equally strong consideration of the medium to be used.

THE ISSUE OF MEDIUM

Any health communicator has a variety of media from which to choose when attempting to influence health beliefs, behaviors, and policies. These media include, but are not limited to, news media, mass mediated advertising, and new communication technologies. For different issues and different audiences, different media may be more or less effective in spreading the desired message.

Print and electronic news media are major sources of health information (Rice 2001, Winett and Wallack 1996). Health news media coverage has an important role in shaping health behaviors at the population level (Pierce and Gilpin 2001, Niederdeppe and Frosch 2009) and influencing public health policy (Tong et al. 2008, Asbridge 2004).

However, as health news coverage becomes more prevalent in the media, researchers are calling into question the quality, completeness, and validity of reporting (Cassels and Lexchin, 2008, Hayes et al. 2007, Hoffman-Goetz and Friedman 2005, Jaffery et al. 2006, Moynihan et al. 2000, Cassels et al. 2002, Larsson et al. 2003). Given the role of news media in shaping public perception of health issues and public policy agenda-setting, journalists, healthcare researchers, and professionals should work together in assuring quality, completeness, and accuracy of reporting is vital (Schwartz and Woloshin 2004, Moynihan 2003, Entwistle 1995).

Health promoting advertising is also used as a medium for health communication. As part of a multimedia campaign to promote healthy behavior, advertising on television, radio, or cinema and in print outlets can play a central role promoting public health (Peddecord et al. 2008). However, while health promotion advertisements can influence health through demonstrating health effects (Hyland et al. 2006, Siegel 1998) and raising awareness of health messages (Levy and Stokes 1987), the efficacy of health-promoting advertising has yet to be established (Lynch and Dunn 2002). Therefore, scholars call for more research to map its potential for health promotion (Fennis 2003, Lynch and Dunn 2002, Peddecord et al. 2008).

In today's media saturated environment and within a global context of bio-terrorism, infectious disease threats, and natural disasters, traditional one-way delivery of messages from a central source can be usefully complemented by more interactive platforms that allow people to engage with health issues, help them find acceptable and appropriate solutions to health problems, and encourage them to play a central role in self-care. While public health mass media campaigns traditionally rely on "television, radio, newspaper, and printed materials, especially broadcast spots, press releases, and pamphlets" (Salmon and Atkin 2003: 461), ICTs have "the potential to transform health campaigns" (468). Yet, as Kline (2003) argues, "there is considerable interest regarding the relationship between the popular media and our understanding of health issues" (575). As such, traditional communication methods have not been replaced by new media; rather there is a complex media ecosystem in which health consumers, practitioners, and regulators find themselves. And, as ICTs promise for public health increases with more people turning to the Internet to access healthcare information (Cline and Haynes 2001, Rice and Katz 2001, Shuyler and Knight 2003) and with more public health agencies using these tools for communicating public health issues (Brownstein et al. 2010, Currie 2009, Khan et al. 2010), more studies need to analyze the efficacy and efficiency of new media in this context.

Rapid advancements in mass media technologies continue to offer new and more effective ways to provide healthcare. Web and mobile technologies – including eHealth and mHealth technologies, electronic health records and other communication systems – have shown themselves to be helpful for improving health communication (Glueckauf and Lustria 2009, Whitten, Cook and Cornacchione 2011, Wright 2009). Although these, and other, communication technologies may make medical communication faster and more convenient, and may have developed alongside better medications and surgical techniques, it is important not to confuse improvements in technology with simple improvements in human health. On the one hand, new ICTs have accelerated the means for improving public health processes and healthcare delivery in terms of enhancing the dissemination of health information (Jareethum et al. 2008, Levine et al. 2008); aiding remote medical consultation, diagnosis, and treatment (Handschu et al. 2003, Hsieh et al. 2004); and facilitating communication, collaboration, and team work among and between healthcare professional and receivers (Rice and Katz 2001, Turner 2003). ICT-based health information systems and decision support systems can also help facilitate medical research and increase administrative effectiveness in medical facilities (Murphy, Ferris and O'Donnell 2007, Ortiz and Clancy 2003). On the other hand, efforts to integrate ICTs into healthcare services have given rise to newer health communication challenges. For example, not every individual has access to these technologies, thus widening the digital divide in access to health information (Hagglund, Shigaki and McCall 2009, Lorence, Park and Fox 2006). Increased availability of online health information and services places a demand on consumers to develop additional skills essential to navigate the technology used to obtain, process, understand, and apply health information (Bernhardt and Cameron 2003, Berry 2007, Zarcadoolas and Pleasant 2009). Moreover, while technology will allow more convenient communication between patients and physicians and geographically bounded medical settings, the importance of understanding the effects of technology-mediated communication on patient-doctor relationship cannot be denied (Cullen 2006, Eckler, Worsowicz and Downey 2009, Turner 2003). Hence, we need to better appreciate the ways that communication technologies assist, sometimes, and interfere, other times, with the ability to attain health goals by patients, providers, and public health agencies.

Meeting the Challenge of New Theories and New Media

In light of this rapidly developing and changing media ecosystem, there is a need for scholars and practitioners of health communication to understand multiple perspectives and approaches in the study of health communication if they are to understand the unique contributions, benefits, and challenges of different media technologies on health practices and policies. As Viswanath, Wallington, and Blake (2009: 324) argued:

> *A clearer understanding of the range of mass media delivery channels; the changing and converging media environment; the communication inequalities that exist; social, institutional, cultural, and policy influences; and new and existing theoretical and methodological frameworks are all necessary to understand the complex influence of mass media on population health. Addressing these issues, both in study and in practice, will undoubtedly help researchers and health professionals harness the best practices of communication and the mass media to improve individual and population health.*

As such, in addition to exploring the role of traditional media, such as print and television, we need to examine the role of new technologies in shaping the public's health. And, even if we understand the technologies, we also need to consider *how* we use these technologies: are we using these technologies in effective, appropriate, and ethical ways as sources of health information and advocates for health behavior? Against such a backdrop, this volume, *Health Communication and Mass Media: An Integrated Approach to Policy and Practice*, seeks to contribute to our understanding of traditional media and new media technologies in supporting health policy and practice by bringing together exemplars of current health communication research and applications in mass mediated contexts spanning across geographic regions.

To meet this goal, this volume attempts to accomplish four objectives. First, we seek to offer a broad treatment of health communication practices and theories in mass mediated contexts. We do not seek an in depth exploration of a single medium or a single technology. Instead, we seek to demonstrate the breadth of options available to health communicators to give communicators an awareness of the options for media available to them. Second, we promote a diversity of methodological approaches. Depending on the medium under investigation, and the kind of questions the researchers are asking about it, some methods will reveal more insight to inform health policy and practice than other methods will. We believe, then, that each project should use the methodology best suited to the question being asked. Third, we support an integrated approach to theory and application; we believe that the best theory can be demonstrated in health policy and practice and that the best health policies and practices are those that allow for greater understanding of larger theoretical principles. Each author has been asked to show how their theoretical understanding informs the application that they offer and how their applications result in better understandings of communication theories. Finally, we seek to include up-to-date exemplars of both completed and ongoing health communication research and applications in mass mediated contexts, including mobile communication technologies, new media and the web, communication systems, and media ethics.

We realize that the present volume is partial; it does not represent all possible media contexts analyzed with all possible methodological tools under the lens of all possible theories. This book only hints at the breadth of health communication in mass mediated contexts and we make no apology for this broad treatment. We ask you to see this volume as a starting point for your own research, policies, and practices in mass mediated health communication.

How is this Book Structured?

The collection of contributions in this volume is divided into five parts with one introductory part and four thematic parts: Introduction; Health Communication and Web Media; Health Communication and Mobile Media; Health Communication and Communication Systems; and Health Communication and Media Ethics. Part 1 serves to introduce the book, its purpose and organization. It also deals with important questions concerning types of information source and the value of theory-informed campaigns in mass mediated health communication contexts. Parts 2, 3 and 4 offer integrations of theory and applications in specific mass mediated contexts: web media, mobile media, and communication systems. Finally, Part 5 addresses the ethical ramifications of different mass media strategies and representations. Collectively, these five parts feature exemplars of current research in health communication and of practical applications of best health communication practices in mass mediated contexts.

INTRODUCTION

The first part of this book features three chapters devoted to the setting of the book and introductory perspectives. Beginning with this chapter, in Chapter 1, "Communicating Health through Mass Media: An Overview," the editors provide an overview of the book.

This chapter contextualizes the book with an aim to facilitate readers' understanding and use of the book.

Considering media as integral sources of health information, in Chapter 2, "Healthcare Reform Information Sources in Relation to Information Quality, Information-Seeking, and Uncertainty," Bevan, Sparks, Ernst, Francies, and Santora underscore the importance of examining how and where the public obtain healthcare reform information. More specifically, the chapter explores American public perception of information quality, level of information-seeking, and the degree of uncertainty experienced in relation to their use of various interpersonal and media sources to gather healthcare reform information. The online survey findings reveal participants' preference for magazines as a source to obtain quality healthcare reform information and reduce uncertainty. The findings also reveal the Internet as the most important and frequently used source of healthcare reform information. As such, Bevan and colleagues argue that policy makers should use this medium to disseminate healthcare reform information. In conclusion, Bevan and colleagues urge government officials and health communication scholars to consider their findings for developing effective ways of communicating healthcare reform information and policies to the public.

Closing this part, Frenette, in Chapter 3, "Theory-based Health Campaigns: A Winning Combination," brings our attention to health campaigns and the need for these to be theoretically grounded. Frenette argues that successful health communication campaigns are theoretically informed and successful applications, in turn, contribute to the further development of theory. More specifically, by providing examples of successful health campaigns, Frenette demonstrates how media theories are crucial, but often overlooked, components in designing and evaluating health campaigns. She shows that persuasion theories, models, and frameworks can offer a sound theoretical foundation to help increase the success of mass media health campaigns. Although the final outcome of a health campaign depends on other factors as well, Frenette insists both health practitioners and academics need to develop theoretically informed health campaigns, considering their potential to help enhance individual and public health.

HEALTH COMMUNICATION AND WEB MEDIA

The second part of this book is concerned with integration of theory and application of health communication in the web media context. The three chapters in this part are centered on the increasing use of web technologies to promote public health initiatives, carry out health education interventions, and provide social support to deal with health related issues. Chapter 4, "Disease, Representation, and Public Relations: A Discourse Analysis of HIV/AIDS Websites," Agarwal, D'Silva and Leichty examine health communication in the context of mediated HIV/AIDS issue representation. More specifically, they provide a discursive critique of the HIV/AIDS representation on three International Nongovernment Organizations websites. Findings of the discourse analysis reveal communicative challenges in international public relations programs in addressing important health promotion initiatives in an online format. Using the lenses of power and identity, Agarwal and colleagues provide a framework to understand how discursive content of the websites constructs the HIV epidemic, the affected publics, and potential solutions.

In Chapter 5, "Managing Sexual Health and Related Stigma through Electronic Learning Environments," Noltensmeyer, Peters, Meisenbach, and Eastman-Mueller discuss the development of a media health intervention, the University of Missouri's sexual health education website, known as {s}health. The website was developed with two objectives in mind: providing accurate, engaging sexual health information in a safe and secure online environment; and creating an electronic learning environment that educates students about stigma management communication. By discussing innovations of using peer-to-peer learning, implementation difficulties encountered and promotion strategies, and presenting the theoretical foundation for the design and content used on the site, Noltensmeyer and colleagues demonstrate how research, theory, and application can inform one another through an interdisciplinary approach to developing interactive, web-based sexual health attitude and behavior intervention. The chapter offers insights into the challenges in and importance of designing modules and messages that are guided by theory and demonstrates interactive yet efficient ways of engaging students in discussions of sexual health.

Finally, Nimrod, in Chapter 6, "Beneficial Participation: Lurking vs. Posting in Online Support Groups," explores the association between the type of participation in health-related Online Support Groups (OSGs) and psychological well-being. More specifically, Nimrod examines differences between "posters" (who post messages to other members of the community and/or respond to their posts) and "lurkers" (who do not interact with other members and simply read others' posts) in OSGs for people with depression. He finds that "posters" agree more than "lurkers" that the online support groups provide them with both online support and offline improvement. Nimrod argues that being actively involved in communication can improve the health and well-being of individuals. The chapter offers theoretical and practical implications regarding Internet-based communicative practices in health contexts. Nimrod concludes that, to be effective, health professionals should encourage patients to use OSGs, and that group moderators should use de-lurking strategies to enhance the lurkers' experience.

HEALTH COMMUNICATION AND MOBILE MEDIA

The third part of this book deals with integration of theory and application of health communication in mobile media contexts. The three chapters in this section are focused on the growing use and application of mobile phones to disseminate and access health information, deliver health interventions, and influence health outcomes. Holtz and Buis, in Chapter 7, "Effectively Promoting Healthy Living and Behaviors through Mobile Phones," discuss the use of mobile phones as a practical intervention delivery modality within the field of health communication. They present a case study that employed principles from social cognitive theory to test an innovative mobile phone SMS intervention for asthma management. The pilot study findings indicate the feasibility of tracking asthma symptoms and improving self-efficacy of asthma patients. In light of the rapid technological progress and mHealth as an emerging field, Holtz and Buis argue for designing and testing more theoretically based interventions to understand the full impact of mobile phone applications for managing chronic diseases.

Based on the premise that public health agencies need to understand how to develop text messaging initiatives that are most likely to be effective, Karasz, Li-Vollmer, Bogan and Offenbecher in Chapter 8, "Targeting Young Adult Texters for Public Health Emergency

Messages: A Q-study of Uses and Gratifications," investigate the uses and gratifications of text messaging for young adults in an urban area in King County, Washington. They employ uses and gratifications theory and Q-methodology to shed light on how and why young adults use texting to help health practitioners understand what will make their text messaging programs more resonant and appealing to this audience. Karasz and colleagues discuss how the findings can assist in targeting and marketing text messaging campaigns for emergency preparedness and response to young adults. They also discuss how the findings can inform the content of text messages in order to maximize the potential for influencing health outcomes in this group.

In light of the increasing use of the Internet and mobile technologies to access health information, Briones and Sundstrom close Chapter 9, "Reaching the Unreachable: How eHealth and Mobile Health Technologies Impact At-Risk Populations," by exploring how traditionally hard-to-reach health consumers use the web and mobile technology for health purposes, and why they prefer to use these channels. They show how eHealth affects medical providers, health educators, consumers, patients, and vulnerable populations. With special attention to aspects of mobile health and its relationship with at-risk populations, Briones and Sundstrom present a case example of the Text4Baby campaign in the United States. Briones and Sundstrom argue that the Text4Baby is an effective model of an mHealth communication campaign and its ability to reach targeted audiences with discrete advice and information will narrow the gap between knowledge and behavior change. Briones and Sundstrom offer suggestions for health practitioners and directions for health communication scholarly research in order to fully understand and determine the effects of the Internet and mobile technologies on health issues.

HEALTH COMMUNICATION AND COMMUNICATION SYSTEMS

The fourth part of this book comprises three chapters that demonstrate media are not just used to push information, but that networked communications technology allows us to input and participate in the creation of health information on individual and organizational scales. These studies address the growing interconnectedness of clinical, organizational, and administrative practices in technology-mediated health communication efforts. As individuals use networked communications technology for delivery of healthcare at a distance, understanding how these systems are used and engaged is growing more important. In Chapter 10, "Coming Full Circle in Rural Trauma: Chronicling the Development and Testing of Communication Systems in Rural Trauma Networks," Avtgis and Polack present a longitudinal, multi-study collaboration that seeks to improve the communication-related aspects of trauma team function, interaction, and coordination for the ultimate outcome of increased performance and patient safety within the rural trauma system in West Virginia. They find that the use of competent communication and appropriate computer mediated communication contributes to effective rural trauma network communication practices. Avtgis and Polack call for more attention to complex phenomena such as the trauma patient triage process and resulting communication and argue for interdisciplinary collaboration to identify problematic issues associated with communication and the practice of trauma medicine.

In Chapter 11, "From Patient-based Records to Patient-centered Care: Reconfiguring Health Care Systems for Interoperable Electronic Health Records," Mardis uses a Computer-Mediated Communication perspective to explore the scope, complexity, and interdisciplinary nature of interoperable Electronic Health Record EHR systems. Through an assessment of standardization practices in clinical, administrative, and technical domains, she highlights some of the unresolved conflicts-over-standards that EHR initiatives have inherited and will have to face if widespread interoperability is pursued. Mardis argues that, to make the interoperable EHR possible, healthcare systems must undergo significant transformations that can achieve uniformity in health information uses, interpretations, and collection practices.

Aceti and Luppicini, in Chapter 12, "The Role of Communication in Health Informatics Integration Success: Case Study of an Ontario Pediatric Critical Care Unit," uses a sociotechnology lens to present a case study of the integration of mHealth technologies within an Ontario pediatric critical care unit. Considering the challenges in integrating health informatics into practice, and because mistakes can disrupt clinical workflows and patient care, Aceti and Luppicini hold it necessary to understand the interaction of social and technological contexts to ensure the successful use of health informatics within an organization. Focusing on end-user experiences and organizational strategic vision, their case study illustrates key issues with and the processes involved in health informatics integration. Aceti and Luppicini report the development of an integration model which they argue can be used to assist organizations in integrating health informatics and anticipate obstacles that may possibly occur before the integration is completely derailed.

HEALTH COMMUNICATION AND MEDIA ETHICS

The fifth and final part of this book features three chapters dedicated to addressing the ethical dimensions of communicating health through mass media. The potential of mass media channels in advancing health education and promotion, and disease prevention goals raise important ethical concerns that are embedded in these activities. Lee, in Chapter 13, "Doing Good, Doing Right: The Ethics of Health Communication," opens this section by highlighting the scarcity of research on the ethics of mass mediated health communication. Lee attributes this lack to the exclusive focus on message efficacy, which, she argues, is grounded in the assumption that "doing good" is more important than doing "right." Against such a backdrop, Lee seeks to better understand the relationships between and among ethical values, message ethicality, and message efficacy in mediated health communication. Lee advocates for morally grounded health messages and the need for an ethical model of public health messages.

Continuing the argument about the importance of positive health communication messages, in Chapter 14, "Eating Disorders and Obesity: Conflict and Common Ground in Health Promotion and Prevention," Watson and McCormack bring our attention to the challenges to ensure consistency and reach of health messages about weight, bodies, and eating in light of various mediated contexts. They discuss conflicting and common ground in health promotion, prevention, and early intervention for obesity and eating disorders. By presenting cases based on a composite narrative of clinical experience, Watson and McCormack exemplify how mediated health communication messages designed to improve health knowledge and/or behaviors may result in unintended harmful effects. They offer practical key messages and strategies to exemplify integrated positive approaches to eating disorder and obesity prevention and health communication and promotion initiatives and media portrayals.

Finally, Chapter 15, "The Ethics of Disability Representations on Television," by Worrell focuses on the ethical implications of the portrayal of health issues in the media. Worrell examines the ethics of disability representation on primetime television by focusing on the portrayals of disability and the accuracy of such portrayals. Finding the under- and mis-representations of disabilities in the media to be problematic and potentially harmful, Worrell advocates for continuing research into disability portrayals. She calls for examining their potential effects of these portrayals to help generate more knowledge of their ethical implications. This knowledge can help educate individuals, policymakers, and voters regarding issues related to disability, argues Worrell.

Conclusion

WHO SHOULD READ THIS BOOK? WHY AND HOW?

We have carefully chosen the contributions in this volume so that they collectively shed light on health communication research and practice in mass mediated contexts. We hope reading this book will allow readers to access and understand multiple perspectives on mass mediated health communication. We wish readers to recognize how health communication theory, research, and practice in mass mediated contexts inform each another. Finally, we desire readers to engage applied media and communication projects that provide models for their own efforts in health communication policy and practice.

As mentioned above, the book has a broad scope, offering an integrated approach to communication theory and application in mass mediated contexts. When reading this book, we encourage readers to reflect on the topical and methodological diversity in the field. We also encourage readers to appreciate the ways that theory shapes health communication applications and how those applications inform the further construction of theory. We believe reading this book will facilitate dialogue about the nexus between health communication research and application in mass mediated contexts.

References

Abroms, L. and Maibach, E. 2008. The effectiveness of mass communication to change public behavior. *Annual Review of Public Health*, 29, 219–34.

Asbridge, M. 2004. Public place restrictions on smoking in Canada: Assessing the role of the state, media, science and public health advocacy. *Social Science & Medicine*, 58(1), 13–24.

Atkin, C.K. 1990. Effects of televised alcohol messages on teenage drinking patterns. *Journal of Adolescent Health Care*, 11(1), 10–24.

Atkin, C. and Salmon, C. 2010. Communication campaigns, in *Handbook of Communication Science*, 2nd Edition, edited by C. Berger, M. Roloff and D. Roskos-Ewoldsen. Thousand Oaks, CA: Sage Publications, 419–35.

Atkin, C. and Wallack, L. (eds) 1990. *Mass Communication and Public Health: Complexities and Conflicts*. Newbury Park, CA: Sage Publications.

Bernhardt, J.M. and Cameron, K.A. 2003. Accessing, understanding, and applying health communication messages: The challenge of health literacy, in *Handbook of Health Communication*, edited by T.L. Thompson, A.M. Dorsey, K.I. Miller and R. Parrott. Mahwah, NJ: Lawrence Erlbaum Associates, 583–605.

Berry, D. 2007. Diversity among patients, in *Health Communication: Theory and Practice*, edited by D. Berry. Maidenhead and New York, NY: Open University Press, 131–58.

Brownstein, J.S., Freifeld, C.C., Chan, E.H., Keller, M., Sonricker, A.L., Mekaru, S.R. and Buckeridge, D.L. 2010. Information technology and global surveillance of cases of 2009 H1N1 influenza. *New England Journal of Medicine*, 362, 1731–5.

Cassels, A. and Lexchin, J. 2008. How well do Canadian media outlets convey medical treatment information? Initial findings from a year and a half of media monitoring by Media Doctor Canada. *Open Medicine* [Online], 2(2). Available at: http://www.openmedicine.ca/article/view/170/131 [accessed: 13 January 2011].

Cassels, A., Hughes, M.A., Cole, C., Mintzes, B., Lexchin, J. and McCormack, J.P. 2002. Drugs in the news: An analysis of Canadian newspaper coverage of new prescription drugs. *Canadian Medical Association Journal,* 168(9), 1133–7.

Cline, R.J.W. and Haynes, K.M. 2001. Consumer health information seeking on the Internet: The state of the art. *Health Education Research*, 16(6), 671–92.

Collins, R.L., Elliott, M.N., Berry, S.H., Kanouse, D.E. and Hunter, S.B. 2003. Entertainment television as a healthy sex educator: The impact of condom-efficacy information in an episode of friends. *Pediatrics*, 112(5), 1115–21.

Cullen, R. 2006. Telemedicine and online medical services, in *Health Information on the Internet: A Study of Providers, Quality, and Users*, edited by R. Cullen. Westport, CT: Praeger Publishers, 166–88.

Dooley, J.A., Jones, S.C. and Desmarais, K. 2009. Strategic social marketing in Canada: Ten phases to planning and implementing cancer prevention and cancer screening campaigns. *Social Marketing Quarterly*, 15(3), 33–48.

Dutta-Bergman, M.J. 2005. Theory and practice in health communication campaigns: A critical interrogation. *Health Communication*, 18(2), 103–22.

Edgar, T., Volkman, J.E. and Logan, A. 2011. Social marketing: Its meaning, use, and application for health communication, in *The Routledge Handbook of Health Communication*, 2nd Edition, edited by T. Thompson, R. Parrott and J. Nussbaum. New York, NY: Routledge, 235–51.

Eckler, P., Worsowicz, G. and Downey, K. 2009. Improving physician-patient communication, in *Health Communication in the New Media Landscape*, edited by J. Parker and E. Thorson. New York, NY: Springer Publishing Company, 283–302.

Entwistle, V. 1995. Reporting research in medical journals and newspapers. *British Medical Journal*, 310(6984), 920–23.

Fennis, B.M. 2003. Advertising, consumer behavior and health: Exploring possibilities for health promotion. *International Journal of Medical Marketing* [Online], 3(4), 316–26. Available at: http://www.gmpua.com/Marketing/worldmarket/cim/10793966.pdf [accessed: 4 December 2011].

Finnegan, J.R. and Viswanath, K. 2008. Communication theory and health behavior change: The media studies framework, in *Health Behavior and Health Education: Theory, Research and Practice*, 4th Edition, edited by K. Glantz, et al. San Francisco, CA: Jossey-Bass, 361–388.

Friedman, L.D. (ed.). 2004. *Cultural Sutures: Medicine and Media*. Chapel Hill, NC: Duke University Press.

Glik, D., Nowak, G., Valente, T., Sapsis, K. and Martin, C. 2002. Youth performing arts entertainment-education for HIV/AIDS prevention and health promotion: Practice and research. *Journal of Health Communication*, 7(1), 39–57.

Glueckauf, R.L. and Lustria, M.L. 2009. E-health self-care interventions for persons with chronic illnesses: Review and future directions, in *Health Communication in the New Media Landscape*, edited by C. Parker and E. Thorson. New York, NY: Springer Publishing Company, 151–241.

Griffiths, W. and Knutson, A. 1960. The role of mass media in public health. *American Journal of Public Health*, 50(5), 15–523.

Hagglund, K.J., Shigaki, C.L. and McCall, J.G. 2009. New media: A third force in health care, in *Health Communication in the New Media Landscape*, edited by C. Parker and E. Thorson. New York, NY: Springer Publishing Company, 417– 36.

Handschu, R., Littmann, R., Reulbach, U., Gaul, C., Heckmann, J.G., Neundörfer, B. and Scibor, M. 2003. Telemedicine in emergency evaluation of acute stroke: Inter rater agreement in remote video examination with a novel multimedia system. *Stroke*, 34(12), 2842–6.

Hayes, M.V., Ross, I., Gasher, M., Gutstein, D.D., James, R. and Hackett, R.A. 2007. Telling stories: News media, health literacy and public policy in Canada. *Social Science and Medicine*, 64(9), 1842– 52.

Hoffman-Goetz, L. and Friedman, D.B. 2005. Disparities in the coverage of cancer information in ethnic minority and mainstream print media. *Ethnicity & Disease*, 15(2), 332–40.

Hornik, R.C. (ed.). 2002. *Public Health Communication: Evidence for Behavior Change*. Mahwah, NJ: Lawrence Erlbaum Associates.

Hsieh, C.H., Tsai, H.H., Yin, J.W., Chen, C.Y., Yang, J.C. and Jeng, S.F. 2004. Teleconsultation with the mobile camera phone in digital soft-tissue injury: A feasibility study. *Plastic and Reconstructive Surgery*, 114(7), 1776–82.

Huhman, M. 2010. Impacting behavior by integrating health communication and marketing. *Health Communication*, 25(6–7), 617–18.

Hyland, A., Wakefield, M., Higbee, C., Szczypka, G. and Cummings, K.M. 2006. Anti-tobacco television advertising and indicators of smoking cessation in adults: A cohort study. *Health Education Research*, 21(3), 348–54.

Jareethum, R., Titapant, V., Chantra, T., Sommal, V., Chuenwattana, O. and Jirawan, C. 2008. Satisfaction of healthy pregnant women receiving short message service via Mobile phone for prenatal support: A randomized controlled trial. *Journal of the Medical Association of Thailand*, 91(4), 458–63.

Kennedy, M.G., O'Leary, A., Beck, V., Pollard, K. and Simpson, P. 2004. Increases in calls to the CDC national STD and AIDS hotline following AIDS-related episodes in a soap opera. *Journal of Communication*, 54(2), 287–301.

Khan, A.S., Fleischauer, A., Casani, J. and Groseclose, S.L. 2010. The next public health revolution: Public health information fusion and social networks. *American Journal of Public Health*, 100(7), 1237–42.

King, M. and Watson, K. (eds). 2005. *Representing Health: Discourses of Health and Illness in the Media*. New York, NY: Palgrave Macmillan.

Kline, K.N. 2003. Popular media and health: Images, effects, and institutions, in *Handbook of Health Communication*, edited by T.L. Thompson, A.M. Dorsey, K.I. Miller and R. Parrott. Mahwah, NJ: Lawrence Erlbaum Associates, 313–29.

Larsson, A., Oxman, A.D., Carling, C. and Herrin, J. 2003. Medical messages in the media – barriers and solutions to improving medical journalism. *Health Expect*, 6(4), 323–31.

Levine, D., McCright, J., Dobkin, L., Woodruff, A.J. and Klausner, J.D. 2008. SEXINFO: A sexual health text messaging service for San Francisco youth. *American Journal of Public Health*, 98(3), 393–5.

Levy, A.S. and Stokes, R.C. 1987. Effects of a health promotion advertising campaign on sales of ready-to-eat cereals. *Public Health Reports*, 102(4), 398–403.

Lorence, D.P., Park, H. and Fox, S. 2006. Racial disparities in health information access: Resilience of the Digital Divide. *Journal of Medical Systems*, 30(4), 241–9.

Lynch, B.M. and Dunn, J. 2003. Scoreboard advertising at sporting events as a health promotion medium. *Health Education Research* [Online], 18, 488–92. Available at: http://her.oxfordjournals.org/content/18/4/488.full.pdf+html [accessed: 11 January 2011].

Lynch, B.M. and Dunn, J. 2002. Scoreboard advertising at sporting events as a health promotion medium. *Health Education Research*, 18(4), 488–92.

Maibach, E. and Parrott, R. (eds). 1995. *Designing Health Messages: Approaches from Communication Theory and Public Health Practice*. Thousand Oaks, CA: Sage Publications.

Marchibroda, J.M. 2009. Engaging consumers in healthcare advocacy using the Internet, in *Health Communication in the New Media Landscape*, edited by C. Parker and E. Thorson. New York, NY: Springer Publishing Company, 267–82.

Melanie, A., Wakefield, B.L. and Hornik, R.C. 2010. Use of mass media campaigns to change health behavior. *Lancet*, 376, 1261–71.

Moynihan, R. 2003. Making medical journalism healthier. *Lancet*, 361(9375), 2097–8.

Moynihan, R., Bero, L., Ross-Degnan, D., Henry, D., Lee, K., Watkins, J., Mah, C. and Soumerai, S.B. 2000. Coverage by the news media of the benefits and risks of medications. *New England Journal of Medicine*, 342, 1645–50.

Murero, M. and Rice, R.E. (eds). 2006. *The Internet and Health Care: Theory, Research and Practice*. Mahwah, NJ: Lawrence Erlbaum Associates.

Murphy, E.C., Ferris, F.L. III and O'Donnell, W.R. 2007. An electronic medical records system for clinical research and the EMR EDC interface. *Investigative Ophthalmology & Visual Science*, 48(10), 4383–9.

Murray-Johnson, L. and Witte, K. 2003. Looking towards the future: Health message design strategies, in *Handbook of Health Communication*, edited by T.L. Thompson, A.M. Dorsey, K.I. Miller and R. Parrott. Mahwah, NJ: Lawrence Erlbaum Associates, 473–95.

Niederdeppe, J. and Frosch, D. 2009. News coverage and sales of products with trans fats: Effects before and after changes in federal labeling policy. *American Journal of Preventive Medicine*, 36(5), 395–401.

Noar, S.M., Harrington, N.G. and Helme, D.W. 2010. The contributions of health communication research to campaign practice. *Health Communication*, 25(6), 593–4.

Ortiz, E. and Clancy, C.M. 2003. Use of information technology to improve the quality of health care in the United States. *Health Services Research*, 38(2), xi–xxii.

Paço, A.D., Rodrigues, R.G., Duarte, P., Pinheiro, P., de Oliveira, J.M. and Soares, M. 2010. The role of marketing in the promotion of breastfeeding. *Journal of Medical Marketing: Device, Diagnostic and Pharmaceutical Marketing*, 10(3), 199–212.

Palmgreen, P. and Donohew, L. 2010. Impact of SENTAR on prevention campaign policy and practice. *Health Communication*, 25(6–7), 609–10.

Parker, J.C. and Thorson, E. (eds). 2009. *Health Communication in the New Media Landscape*. New York, NY: Springer Publishing Company.

Peddecord, K.M., Jacobson, I.G., Engelberg, M., Kwizera, L., Macias, V. and Gustafson, K.W. 2008. Can movie theater advertisements promote health behaviors? Evaluation of a flu vaccination pilot campaign. *Journal of Health Communication*, 13(6), 596–613.

Pierce, J.P. and Gilpin, E.A. 2001. News media coverage of smoking and health is associated with changes in population rates of smoking cessation but not initiation. *Tobacco Control*, 10, 145–53.

Randolph, W. and Viswanath, K. 2004. Lessons learned from public health mass media campaigns: Marketing health in a crowded media world. *Annual Reviews in Public Health*, 25, 419–37.

Rice, R.E. 2001. The Internet and health communication: A framework of experiences, in *The Internet and Health Communication: Experiences and Expectations*, edited by R. Rice and J.E. Katz. Thousand Oaks, CA: Sage Publications, 5–46.

Rice, R.E. and Atkin, C.K. 2001. *Public Communication Campaigns*, 3rd Edition. Thousand Oaks, CA: Sage Publications.

Rice, R. and Atkin, C. 2009. Public communication campaigns: Theoretical principles and practical applications, in *Media effects: Advances in Theory and Research*, 3rd Edition, edited by J. Bryant and M. Oliver. New York: Routledge, 436–68.

Rice, R.E. and Katz, J.E. (eds). 2001. *The Internet and Health Communication: Experiences and Expectations*. Thousand Oaks, CA: Sage Publications.

Rimal, R.N. and Lapinski, M.K. 2009. Why health communication is important in public health. *Bulletin of the World Health Organization* [Online], 87, 247. Available at: http://www.who.int/bulletin/volumes/87/4/08-056713/en/index.html [accessed: 4 December 2011].

Rock, M.J., McIntyre, L., Persaud, S.A. and Thomas, K.L. 2011. A media advocacy intervention linking health disparities and food insecurity. *Health Education Research*, 26(6), 948–60.

Salmon, C.T. and Atkin, C. 2003. Using media campaigns for health promotion, in *Handbook of Health Communication*, edited by T.L. Thompson, A.M. Dorsey, K.I. Miller and R. Parrott. Mahwah, NJ: Lawrence Erlbaum Associates, 449–72.

Schiavo, R. 2007. What is health communication?, in *Health Communication: From Theory to Practice*, edited by R. Schiavo. San Francisco, CA: John Wiley & Sons, 3–29.

Schwartz, L.M. and Woloshin, S. 2004. The media matter: A call for straightforward medical reporting. *Annals of Internal Medicine*,140(3), 226–8.

Seale, C. (ed.). 2002. *Media and Health*. Thousand Oaks, CA: Sage Publications.

Seale, C. (ed.). 2004. *Health and the Media*. Oxford: Wiley-Blackwell.

Shuyler, K.S. and Knight, K.M. 2003. What are patients seeking when they turn to the internet? Qualitative content analysis of questions asked by visitors to an orthopaedics web site. *Journal of Medical Internet Research* [Online], 5(4), e24. Available at: http://www.jmir.org/2003/4/e24/ [accessed: 4 December 2011].

Siegel, M. 1998. Mass media antismoking campaigns: A powerful tool for health promotion. *Annals of Internal Medicine*, 129(2), 128–32.

Silk, K.J., Atkin, C. and Salmon, C. 2011. Developing effective media campaigns for health promotion, in *The Routledge Handbook of Health Communication*, 2nd Edition, edited by T. Thompson, R. Parrott and J. Nussbaum. New York, NY: Routledge, 203–19.

Singhal, A. and Rogers, E.M. 1999. *Entertainment-Education: A Communication Strategy for Social Change*. Mahwah, NJ: Lawrence Erlbaum Associates.

Slater, M.D. 2006. Specification and misspecification of theoretical foundations and logic models for health communication campaigns. *Health Communication*, 20, 149–57.

Sonya Grier, S. and Bryant, C.A. 2005. Social marketing in public health. *Annual Review of Public Health*, 26, 319–39.

Stewart, L. and Casswell, S. 1993. Media advocacy for alcohol policy support: Results from the New Zealand Community Action Project. *Health Promotion International*, 8(3), 167–75.

Tong, A., Chapman, S., Sainsbury, P. and Craig, J.C. 2008. An analysis of media coverage on the prevention and early detection of CKD in Australia. *American Journal of Kidney Diseases*, 52(1), 159–70.

Turner, J.W. 2003. Telemedicine: Expanding healthcare into virtual environments, in *Handbook of Health Communication*, edited by T.L. Thompson, A.M. Dorsey, K.I. Miller and R. Parrott. Mahwah, NJ: Lawrence Erlbaum Associates, 35–61.

Viswanath, K., Wallington, S.F. and Blake, K.D. 2009. Media effects and population health, in *The Sage Handbook of Media Processes and Effects*, edited by R.L. and M.B. Oliver. Thousand Oaks, CA: Sage Publications, 313–29.

Wallack, L. 2000. The role of mass media in creating social capital: A new direction for public health, in *Promoting Health: Intervention Strategies from Social and Behavioral Research*, edited by B.D. Smedley and S.L. Syme. Washington, DC: National Academy Press, 337–65.

Wallack, L., Dorfman, L., Jernigan, D. and Themba, M. 1993. *Media Advocacy and Public Health: Power for Prevention*. Newbury Park, CA: Sage Publications.

Wallack, L. and Dorfman, L. 1996. Media advocacy: A strategy for advancing policy and promoting health. *Health Education & Behavior*, 23(3), 293–317.

Walsh, D.C., Rudd, R.E., Moeykens, B.A. and Moloney, T.W. 1993. Social marketing for public health. *Health Affairs*, 12(2), 104–19.

Whittier, D.K., Kennedy, M.G., St Lawrence, J.S., Seeley S. and Beck, V. 2005. Embedding health messages into entertainment television: Effect on gay men's response to a syphilis outbreak. *Journal of Health Communication*, 10(3), 251–9.

Winett, L.B. and Wallack, L. 1996. Advancing public health goals through the mass media. *Journal of Health Communication*, 1(2), 173–96.

Wright, K.B. 2009. Increasing computer-mediated social support, in *Health Communication in the New Media Landscape*, edited by C. Parker and E. Thorson. New York, NY: Springer Publishing Company, 243–66.

Zarcadoolas, C. and Pleasant, A. 2009. Health literacy in the digital world, in *Health Communication in the New Media Landscape*, edited by C. Parker and E. Thorson. New York, NY: Springer Publishing Company, 303–22.

2 *Healthcare Reform Information Sources in Relation to Information Quality, Information-Seeking, and Uncertainty*

JENNIFER L. BEVAN, LISA SPARKS, JULIA ERNST, JESSICA FRANCIES AND NICOLE SANTORA

Introduction

Passed in March 2010, the Patient Protection and Affordable Care Act of 2010 (PPACA) has engendered significant, sometimes heated, debate among citizens and policymakers and will set into motion numerous, sweeping changes for the U.S. healthcare system. PPACA (hereafter referred to as healthcare reform) has the capacity to affect almost every single American by changing legislation, regulating insurance laws and employee benefits, and covering an additional 32 million individuals (The Commonwealth Fund 2010). Though there is much debate about healthcare reform and the impact it will have on the healthcare industry and the economy in the U.S. (Doherty 2010), there is little systematic knowledge regarding how the public is acquiring information about healthcare reform and the public's perceptions and understanding of healthcare reform itself.

Healthcare reform is an emerging health policy context that is relevant to health communication researchers for three reasons. First, healthcare reform can have a direct, simultaneous impact both on well individuals and those with chronic and acute health conditions. Second, information about healthcare reform includes elements of prevention, intervention, and/or treatment, based on individuals' current health status. Finally, due to healthcare reform's partisan nature, public perceptions and understandings of it could be considerably impacted by the one-sided, divisive perspectives of the political entities and organizations that have a considerable stake in the success or failure of the legislation. Thus, determining how and where the public is acquiring healthcare reform information is important in order to begin to recognize public perceptions and understandings of the legislation. This chapter thus explores the various interpersonal and media sources used by the public to gather healthcare reform information in relation to individuals' amount of information-seeking, beliefs about the provision of reliable, quality information, and level of uncertainty about healthcare reform.

Media and Interpersonal Information Sources

Information, which is "stimuli from a person's environment that contribute to his or her knowledge or beliefs" (Brashers et al. 2002: 259), can be obtained via a number of communication channels (Dutta-Bergman 2004). One reason health communication scholars and researchers have become interested in health information-seeking behavior in particular is because it is such a prevalent use of media and interpersonal sources (Burkell et al. 2006). Initially, individuals seeking health information are likely to consult interpersonal sources such as family or friends (Buller et al. 1995), though media sources such as television, newspapers, and the Internet, are subsequent, important sources for health information (Brashers et al.). Media are certainly integral health information sources, as they define illness and health, feature services and products that can help consumers manage their health, and provide a representation of others who have specific health conditions to a large number of individuals (Cotten and Gupta 2004). For example, Fox (2006) suggests 80 percent of adults surveyed have searched for health information online, and 53 percent indicated they used the information they found to make health decisions.

Dutta-Bergman (2004) examined interpersonal and media health information sources that included TV, radio, newspapers or magazines, hotlines, the Internet, and family or friends. He found that individuals who utilized active sources such as newspapers, magazines, and the Internet, which encourage the gathering of information and require participants to communicate with others while obtaining information, were more likely to have strong health beliefs and to be health conscious than those employing passive sources such as TV and radio. Dutta-Bergman's study examined a random sample of Americans, which presumably included both individuals who were healthy and those with health conditions; this is a population similar to those who we believe will be impacted by healthcare reform and thus will seek information about it. As such, we also utilize these information sources in this chapter to understand how the public acquires and evaluates information about healthcare reform.

In related research on health information sources, Pecchioni and Sparks (2007) found that patients' family members reported being significantly more satisfied with the Internet as a health information source, whereas patients themselves reported more satisfaction with doctors and nurses as health information sources. Madden and Fox (2006) also found that 58 percent of caretakers reported the Internet was an important tool for making health decisions. Time constraints, competing demands for attention, and a lack of training in effective communication impair physician's communication with patients (Sparks et al. 2007), which most certainly influences patient health information-seeking behaviors (Sparks and Villagran 2010), and can greatly impact medical adherence and decision-making for patients (Tinley et al. 2004).

In addition to being related to multiple aspects of individuals' health beliefs, use of various information sources are also of interest because they can be linked to specific health behaviors. For example, Buller et al. (1995) found that the more individuals sought skin cancer information from print media (that is, newspapers, magazines, newsletters, or pamphlets), the more they engaged in skin-protection behaviors. Further, use of healthcare providers and magazines or newspapers as information sources, as opposed to the Internet and toll-free phone numbers, was positively related to requesting a specific prescription medication (Lee 2009). Lee also determined that using the Internet as an information source facilitated consumers to discuss specific prescription medication with their health providers, an effect that grew substantially between 1999 and 2002. As such, using various media and interpersonal sources for obtaining health information has a number of potentially important implications, particularly when considering that behaviors related to healthcare reform can involve any combination of prevention, intervention, and/or treatment. We thus examine these sources in relation to information-seeking, information quality, and uncertainty.

INFORMATION-SEEKING

Information-seeking is defined as "the purposive gathering of information" that is intentional and goal-directed (Hogan and Brashers 2008: 50). Passively attending to healthcare reform coverage when it is encountered, especially in a media environment where health information is readily available and difficult to avoid (Brashers et al. 2002), would also constitute information-seeking in this chapter. This perspective also aligns with Hogan and Brasher's principle of uncertainty management which states that there are multiple information sources and forms.

In terms of health information-seeking, individuals employ a variety of sources. In a study of breast cancer patients, high monitors (that is, active information seekers) were more likely to use newspapers and magazines as cancer information sources than low monitors (Cowan and Hoskins 2007). Further, individuals with diabetes reported frequently turning to their friends and family for information, as well as passively acquiring information from sources such as newspapers and television (Longo et al. 2010). The Internet was a popular source for prescription medication information (DeLorme et al. 2011).

According to Buller et al. (1995), individuals who are faced with risky, uncertain health situations where multiple courses of action are possible will actively search for information. Though healthcare reform was followed very closely by 51 percent of the American public in 2010 (Pew Research Center for the People and the Press 2010), many individuals could not accurately or confidently describe the specifics of the legislation (Knowledge Networks 2010). Thus, it is likely that many citizens sought information about healthcare reform and employed a variety of mediated and interpersonal sources to do so. We next consider how they evaluate the information that they seek.

INFORMATION QUALITY

The quality of health information involves individuals evaluating the information they seek by way of the following components: how current or recent the information is; how relevant it is to what the individual is searching for; how reliable and accurate the information is believed to be; how comprehensive and inclusive the information is; and, how useful the individual finds it to be in meeting his or her needs (Eysenbach and Kohler 2002, Sheppard et al. 1999). Burkell et al.'s (2006) sample of spinal cord injury participants indicated that, though online information was seen as more accessible, it was also perceived to be less accurate, current, and specific. Participants also expressed some concerns about magazines or newsletters, with information from this mediated periodical source viewed as more current, but less accessible and specific. Nevertheless, periodicals were a source of spinal cord injury information that was employed by a large proportion of participants. In another context, HIV/AIDS patients rated their healthcare professionals as being most likely to provide quality, reliable information (Hogan and Palmer 2005). Though other interpersonal information sources were ranked next, Hogan and Palmer noted that this source was not very strong in terms of quality and reliability.

Similar to interpersonal sources, prior research has shown that the Internet produces an overload of information that is not regulated for quality and, thus, could potentially be unreliable and harmful (Christensen and Griffiths 2008, Cowan and Hoskins 2007). Despite this limitation, perceived usefulness of the Internet as an information source positively predicted individuals seeking prescription drug information online (DeLorme et al. 2011). Information quality thus seems to be of particular concern when the Internet is a primary information source. Overall, there is conflicting research evidence about the extent to which online health information is perceived to be of high quality, and little empirical indication about whether the quality of health information varies by other media and interpersonal health information sources. As a broad health topic that affects both well and ill consumers and provides information for health prevention, maintenance, and treatment, healthcare reform is thus an ideal context for examining information quality differences by information source.

UNCERTAINTY

According to Brashers (2001), uncertainty occurs "when details of the situation are ambiguous, complex, unpredictable, or probabilistic; when information is unavailable or inconsistent; and when people feel insecure in their own state of knowledge or the state of knowledge in general" (478). In the health context, uncertainty is so integral to information-seeking that Cotten and Gupta (2004) define health information-seeking as searching for and receiving messages that assist in uncertainty reduction about one's health status. Uncertainty can also be linked to information quality. For example, information about a subject that is found to be unreliable or inaccurate, dated, irrelevant, and/or incomplete will likely mean that the individual is uncertain about the topic. Indeed, in the long-distance caregiving context, uncertainty shared a significant small-to-moderate, positive relationship with information quality (Bevan et al. 2011). Though uncertainty and information processes are inextricably linked (for example, Hogan and Brashers 2008), no known research has examined whether levels of uncertainty differ by health information source. However, Gill and Babrow (2007) found that themes of uncertainty and ambivalence were dominant in magazine articles about breast cancer, suggesting that uncertain messages are present in (and may differ by) health information sources.

As healthcare reform significantly alters a health care system that is already challenging and complex (Johnson 2011) and how the legislation will actually unfold and be implemented is unknown (Doherty 2010), it should be a highly uncertain situation for consumers and thus an ideal context for comparing uncertainty levels in relation to different information sources. Further, healthcare reform is a health topic that is of interest both to those who are well and ill and involves prevention, intervention, and treatment messages. Thus, healthcare reform differs from many specific health conditions or illnesses in an integral way: individuals cannot rely on health professionals as a reliable information source. For example, research regarding information sources for health topics such as skin (Buller et al. 1995) and breast (Cowan and Hoskins 2007) cancer, diabetes

(Longo et al. 2010), HIV/AIDS (Hogan and Palmer 2005), and spinal cord injury (Burkell et al. 2006) identified health professionals as frequent, reliable sources of information for participants about their conditions. However, physicians themselves are uncertain about healthcare reform (Doherty 2010) and if that influential information source is not available, individuals are likely to experience uncertainty about the legislation. Further, this uncertainty could differ by both the sources that are employed and viewed as most important.

Research Questions

Healthcare reform is a health issue that has been extensively covered by media sources such as the Internet, television, magazines, and newspapers. Indeed, it was one of 2010's top news stories (Crary 2010, Pew Research Center for the People and the Press 2010, Tharoor 2010). Despite the extensive news coverage, individuals were frequently wrong about what was and was not contained in the healthcare reform bill, and were also fairly uncertain about their judgments (Knowledge Networks 2010). As such, investigating which sources were used and preferred by the American public for healthcare reform information in relation to information-seeking, information quality, and uncertainty is valuable for understanding which sources are perceived as useful and which are not about this important, far-reaching topic.

Healthcare reform is clearly a new and unique form of health policy and is a broad health topic. As such, it is unlike much health information-seeking research topics that focus on a specific illness or condition. We thus ask the following three exploratory research questions in the context of healthcare reform:

RQ1: Does level of information-seeking vary by (a) whether or not a particular information source was used and (b) what the most important source of information was?

RQ2: Does level of information quality vary by (a) whether or not a particular information source was used and (b) what the most important source of information was?

RQ3: Does level of uncertainty vary by (a) whether or not a particular information source was used and (b) what the most important source of information was?

Method

PARTICIPANTS AND PROCEDURES

Researchers at Chapman University collected these data, as part of a larger study on public perceptions of healthcare reform. An online questionnaire on SurveyMonkey. com was employed. All individuals had to meet two criteria to participate: (1) be 18 years or older; and (2) be an American citizen. Participants ($N = 389$) were recruited in three ways. First, Facebook and Twitter posts and emails to the researchers' extended social and professional contacts were employed. Initial participants recruited via this method were also asked to forward the study link to others who they thought may want to participate. Second, study information was posted under Craislist.org's Community: Volunteers section in six randomly selected cities: Kansas City, MO; New York, NY; Dallas, TX; Butte, MT; and Baltimore, MD. Third, information about the study was announced in Chapman University undergraduate communication studies classes, and the survey link was given to interested students. Upon consenting to participate, individuals were told that the study investigated individuals' perceptions and understanding of healthcare reform, defined as "the Patient Protection and Affordable Care Act (PPACA) that was signed into law in March 2010." Participation took approximately 10–15 minutes, was voluntary, anonymous, and without compensation.

The survey was open from September 24, 2010 to October 30, 2010, a date range that was chosen for three reasons:

1. to ensure that enough time had passed since March 2010, when healthcare reform became law, so that participants could seek information and form opinions about it;
2. to correspond with heightened healthcare reform media coverage accompanying the implementation of the initial set of benefits of the law that took place on September 23, 2010; and
3. to finish collecting data before the November 2, 2010 national midterm elections so participant responses would not be impacted by the election results.

Participants averaged 41 years of age (*range* = 18–78, SD = 16.06), were primarily male (n = 239, female n = 98), and classified themselves as White/Caucasian (n = 280, Asian n = 25, Hispanic/Latino n = 24, other n = 22, Black/African American n = 3, American Indian or Alaska native n = 2, Hawaiian or Pacific Islander n = 1). Respondents' highest completed education level included no degree (n = 2), high school/GED (n = 41), Associates degree (n = 27), Bachelor's degree (n = 113), Master's degree (n = 94), Ph.D./Ed.D. (n = 33), MD (n = 8), and other (n = 11). Participants were currently employed in full-time (n = 177) or part-time (n = 75) positions, or were unemployed (n = 72). Annual household income ranged from under \$10,000 (n = 11), \$11,000–20,000 (n = 13), \$21,000–\$30,000 (n = 11), \$31,000–\$50,000 (n = 31), \$51,000–\$75,000 (n = 45), \$76,000–\$100,000 (n = 51), \$101,000–\$150,000 (n = 67), to over \$150,000 (n = 53, prefer not to answer n = 47). Most participants (n = 204) voted for Barack Obama for president in the 2008 election (did not vote for Obama n = 88, did not vote n = 34) and were Democrats (n = 168, Republican n = 54, Independent n = 77, other n = 25).

The majority of participants currently had health insurance (yes n = 352, no n = 37), and those who were insured indicated it was sufficient for their healthcare needs (yes n = 295, no n = 57) and was moderately-to-highly satisfying (M = 5.37, SD = 1.53, 1 = strongly disagree, 7 = strongly agree). Via a series of non-exclusive items, a minority of participants reported being members of groups that were particularly likely to be impacted by healthcare reform (that is, parents with children without insurance n = 23, those with jobs that do not provide health insurance n = 62, who cannot get insurance due to a pre-existing condition n = 23, who cannot afford health insurance n = 56, who are employed in the healthcare field n = 74, are small business owners/self-employed n = 46, or are seniors on Medicare n = 18). Via three 7-point items, participants moderately:

1. supported healthcare reform (M = 4.71, SD = 2.09); believed that
2. healthcare reform will personally impact their health (M = 4.54, SD = 1.68); and
3. that healthcare reform will be an improvement over the U.S.'s prior method of handling healthcare (M = 4.47, SD = 2.01).

In addition, a 7-point item found that participants were paying a moderate-to-high amount of attention to healthcare reform (M = 5.03, SD = 1.59).

MEASURES

Information sources   Information source about healthcare reform was measured using items adapted from Dutta-Bergman (2004). Seven dichotomous yes/no items asked whether participants had used each source for healthcare reform information and then were asked via a single item to choose which source was most important (see Table 2.1). The following information sources were included: TV, radio, newspaper, magazines, Internet, family or friends, and other.

Information-seeking   Healthcare reform information-seeking was adapted from Kahlor et al.'s (2006) 2-item scale. Higher values indicate more information seeking (1 = Strongly disagree, 7 = Strongly agree; When healthcare reform comes up, I try to learn more about it; M = 4.88, SD = 1.36, a = .69).

Information quality   The healthcare reform information quality scale was adapted using eight Likert-type items from the 2003 Health Information National Trends Survey (HINTS) that measured cancer information quality (1 = Strongly disagree, 7 = Strongly agree). As this adapted scale has not been used in a health policy context such as healthcare reform, we conducted an exploratory principal component analysis with varimax rotation. Criteria for factor selection were a .65 primary loading with all other loadings under .35, an eigenvalue of at least 1, and at least two items per factor. Two factors meeting these criteria emerged: (1) a 4-item *satisfaction with information quality* factor (for example, You were satisfied with the information you learned about healthcare reform; eigenvalue =

Table 2.1   Media and Interpersonal Information Source Frequency and Importance

Information source	Use: Yes/No	Most important
TV	285/79	42
Radio	208/136	46
Newspaper	258/92	62
Magazines	151/172	10
Internet	304/54	149
Family or Friends	236/98	35
Other	51/169	26

Note: N = 389.

1.19, 11.93 percent of the variance explained; $M = 4.34$, $SD = 1.33$, a = .77); and (2) a 6-item *difficulty obtaining information* factor (for example, It took a lot of effort to get the information you needed about healthcare reform; eigenvalue = 4.55, 45.52 percent of the variance explained; $M = 3.80$, $SD = 1.33$, a = .81). Higher items indicate greater information quality satisfaction and difficulty.

Uncertainty   Uncertainty regarding healthcare reform was assessed by way of seven items from Mishel's (1981) health-related uncertainty measure (1 = Strongly disagree, 7 = Strongly agree; It is not clear to me what is going to happen with healthcare reform). Higher values indicate greater uncertainty ($M = 4.39$, $SD = 1.27$, a = .85).

Results

The three research questions were tested via a series of univariate ANOVAs. For RQs 1a, 2a, and 3a, univariate ANOVAs examined levels of the information and uncertainty variables according to whether or not each information source was used. For RQ1a, those who employed each of the healthcare reform information sources except for family/friends engaged in greater information-seeking than those who did not use these sources. For RQ2a, those who read magazines were more satisfied and had less difficulty with healthcare reform information quality than those who did not. In addition, those consulting family/friends were less satisfied and had more difficulty with healthcare reform information quality than those who did not. For RQ3a, individuals who used magazines as an information source for healthcare reform were more certain than those who did not. In contrast, those who acquired healthcare reform information from family/ friends experienced more uncertainty than individuals who did not employ this source of information. No other information source differences were observed for information-seeking, information quality, and uncertainty (see Table 2.2 for means and F values).

For RQs 1b, 2b, and 3b, the four information and uncertainty variables were examined in relation to the fixed factor of most important healthcare reform source. Tukey HSD *posthoc* tests were employed. Only information-seeking (RQ1b) significantly differed according to most important information sources: when newspaper or other sources were rated as most important, there was more information-seeking than when family/ friends was the most important source with no other sources differing from one another. No other most important information source differences were observed for information quality (RQ2b) or uncertainty (RQ3b; see 2.3 for means and F values).

Discussion

Our exploratory study detected a number of interesting trends regarding participant sources of information about the topic of healthcare reform in relation to differing levels of information quality, information-seeking, and uncertainty. Participants who used each information source, except for friends/family, reported seeking more information about healthcare reform (RQ1a). If magazines were used or family/friends were not used as information sources, the quality of information was satisfying to participants, and this information was also viewed as less difficult to obtain (RQ2a). If participants did not use magazines or did use family/friends as an information source, they were more uncertain about healthcare reform (RQ3a). Results showed those who indicated that newspaper or other channels were their most important information source engaged in more information-seeking than those who identified family/friends as most important, with no differences observed by most important information source for uncertainty or information quality (RQ1b, 2b, and 3b). What these findings mean for understanding the utility of various information sources for acquiring healthcare reform information is discussed below.

Participants' use or non-use of a particular information source was found to be significantly related to each of the information and uncertainty variables. In particular, when magazines were employed as a source of healthcare reform information, participants

Table 2.2   *F* **Values and Means for Media and Interpersonal Information Sources by Information-seeking, Information Quality, and Uncertainty**

	Satisfaction with information quality	Difficulty obtaining quality information	Information-seeking	Uncertainty
Information Source	*F*	*F*	*F*	*F*
TV	.69	.27	4.78*	.90
Yes *M*	4.29	3.85	4.94ᵃ	4.45
No *M*	4.43	3.76	4.56ᵇ	4.30
Radio	.48	1.27	8.45**	1.00
Yes *M*	4.31	3.74	5.07ᵃ	4.35
No *M*	4.41	3.91	4.63ᵇ	4.50
Newspaper	.05	2.25	18.84***	.02
Yes *M*	4.33	3.74	5.08ᵃ	4.41
No *M*	4.37	3.99	4.38ᵇ	4.43
Magazines	8.08**	9.92**	16.98***	9.27**
Yes *M*	4.57ᵃ	3.54ᵃ	5.22ᵃ	4.18ᵇ
No *M*	4.15ᵇ	3.01ᵇ	4.60ᵇ	4.62ᵃ
Internet	.01	.81	13.03***	1.33
Yes *M*	4.34	3.77	5.01ᵃ	4.37
No *M*	4.33	3.95	4.27ᵇ	4.59
Family or Friends	5.65*	10.48**	1.49	14.27***
Yes *M*	4.22ᵇ	3.97ᵃ	4.78	4.59ᵃ
No *M*	4.60ᵃ	3.46ᵇ	4.98	4.00ᵇ
Other	.10	1.59	15.68***	.23
Yes *M*	3.56	3.56	5.55ᵃ	4.17
No *M*	3.51	3.83	4.73ᵇ	4.28

Note: For each column, values with different subscript letters significantly differ at $p < .05$.

* $p < .05$ ** $p < .01$ *** $p < .001$.

Table 2.3   *F* Values and Means for Most Important Media and Interpersonal Information Sources by Information-seeking, Information Quality, and Uncertainty

Information Source	Satisfaction with information quality	Difficulty obtaining quality information	Information-seeking	Uncertainty
F	1.10	1.53	5.17*	1.05
TV	4.01	3.94	4.33[a, b]	4.55
Radio	4.39	3.60	5.02[a, b]	4.18
Newspaper	4.42	3.73	5.23[a]	4.36
Magazines	4.32	4.12	4.25[a, b]	4.15
Internet	4.44	3.76	5.04[a, b]	4.38
Family or Friends	4.01	4.33	4.07[b]	4.81
Other	4.56	3.51	5.25[a]	4.23

Note: For each column, values with different subscript letters significantly differ at $p < .05$.
* $p < .01$.

engaged in information-seeking, felt that this information was less difficult to obtain and satisfy, and felt more certain about healthcare reform. Further, when newspapers were rated the most important healthcare reform information source, participants sought more information. These findings are generally consistent with Dutta-Bergman's (2004) research, which found that those who obtained health information from newspapers or magazines were more health-oriented than individuals who did not.

Both newspapers and magazines can provide active, cognitively involved, in-depth coverage of a health issue and can also be archived for future information-seeking (Dutta-Bergman 2004). These qualities may make magazines, and to a lesser extent, newspapers, particularly appealing as an information source for individuals who are learning about healthcare reform and may thus explain this pattern of findings. Further, compared to television and newspapers, magazines may be viewed as a less partisan or biased form of media for health information, which may explain why participants viewed information from this particular media source as being of relatively higher quality and providing more certainty about healthcare reform. Magazines may have also been viewed as providing information that is easier to obtain because they can be available in multiple forms (for example, both in paper form and online through the magazine's website). Further, magazines provide a great deal of information, which to our participants may have translated into less difficulty obtaining information because they did not have to consult additional information sources. In addition, the growth of magazines as a health information source (Gill and Babrow 2007) means that this media channel has the potential to be an invaluable resource for individuals seeking healthcare reform information.

In contrast, when healthcare reform information was obtained from interpersonal sources such as family/friends, participants felt that this knowledge was less satisfying, more difficult to obtain, and felt more uncertain about healthcare reform than those who did not. Further, when family or friends was selected as the most important healthcare reform information source, less information-seeking occurred. Our results are potentially problematic when considering that university students recently indicated they used family and friends most frequently as a source of health information (Percheski and Hargittai 2011). This pattern of findings also differs from Dutta-Bergman's (2004) results, which viewed family/friends as a useful source of information. However, our findings suggest our participants may be aware that family or friends can be an inaccurate and detrimental source of health information, as cautioned by Buller et al. (1995).

In addition, the topic itself may explain the inconsistency between our findings and Dutta-Bergman's (2004) regarding the family/friends information source, such that the ubiquity of healthcare reform may have meant our participants found themselves as passive, even unwilling, participants in interpersonal interactions about the issue. This pattern of non-use also would clarify why use of the family/friends information source was the only one for which information-seeking levels did not significantly differ. Further, the controversy of the topic may also assist in understanding these findings – the politically charged, partisan atmosphere surrounding healthcare reform may have meant that discussing the topic with family or friends was not perceived by participants as helpful. In fact, if discussed with those who have differing, extreme opinions and if the conversation is primarily one-sided in nature, healthcare reform could be a polarizing, frustrating, and conflict-inducing topic. Overall, our pattern of findings suggests that magazines, and to a lesser extent, newspapers, seem to be a useful form of healthcare reform information, whereas learning about healthcare reform from family and friends can potentially be problematic.

Though not a specific focus of our investigation, we also found that the Internet was both the most-used healthcare reform information source and the most important channel for our participants. Though this finding may to some extent be an artifact of our online data collection method, it is consistent with previous research (for example, DeLorme et al. 2011, Eysenbach et al. 2002, Fox 2006). Our results may partially be explained by Pecchioni and Sparks' (2007) research, which found that family caregivers were more satisfied with the Internet as a source of health information.

As the Internet is an active information source that is used by individuals who are health conscious, have strong health orientations, and take part in healthy activities (Dutta-Bergman 2004), that this source is preferred by our participants for acquiring healthcare reform information makes sense. However, the general lack of quality control regarding online health information (for example, Cline and Haynes 2001, Eysenbach and Kohler 2002) means that information obtained about healthcare reform via the Internet could be inaccurate, misleading, or biased. These limitations of the Internet seem to be of particular concern for our participants, who did not discern that information quality differed according to whether or not the Internet was used or was their most important source of healthcare reform information.

Implications for Academics

Academic research can extend and be informed by our findings in two ways. First, our information quality variable emerged as a multidimensional concept. The satisfaction with the quality of information dimension involved confidently being able to find information about healthcare reform and viewing information as useful, satisfying, and trustworthy. Conversely, the difficulty in obtaining quality information variable included frustration, trouble, and effort in locating and comprehending information about healthcare reform. Using the same 2003 cancer information HINTS items, these same information quality dimensions were also observed in long-distance caregiving research (Bevan et al. 2011). Information quality has been measured unidimensionally, but our findings suggest that information quality is multidimensional. Future research may want to consider these nuances and how quality of information is assessed in multiple ways.

Second, a variety of future research ideas for scholars interested in healthcare reform emerge from our findings. Longitudinal studies that trace public information-seeking and understanding of healthcare reform until and beyond its full implementation in 2014 would provide an ongoing examination of how the public seeks and consumes knowledge about this important topic. Another healthcare reform research topic is to compare information management and usage behaviors of individuals who are healthy to those with acute and chronic health conditions. Relatedly, the extent to which healthcare reform information-seeking and usage behaviors may differ when attempting to prevent or treat specific health conditions or simply to remain well would also be informative.

Implications for Health Practitioners

The PPACA is a new and evolving national health policy that will affect millions of Americans. Which sources for healthcare reform information are used and viewed as most important can assist health practitioners in designing messages that alleviate uncertainty and difficulty in obtaining information, while promoting information-seeking practices and satisfaction with the quality of information obtained. We thus offer a number of implications of our findings for health practitioners.

First, healthcare reform campaign messages may want to recommend active, in-depth information media sources such as magazines to individuals who are interested in acquiring quality healthcare reform information. However, individuals who are not health-oriented may be less likely to employ active media sources such as magazines and newspapers, and doing so exclusively in campaigns may create a knowledge gap, especially if a unique population is of particular interest (Dutta-Bergman 2004). Tailoring different healthcare reform messages for passive media sources, such as TV and radio, may also target individuals with a low health orientation (Dutta-Bergman).

Conversely, designers of health campaign messages may want to caution individuals about acquiring information from their family or friends about healthcare reform. Though this source of health information has been considered valuable in previous research (for example, Buller et al. 1995, Dutta-Bergman 2004), the partisan and controversial nature of healthcare reform means these interpersonal sources are likely to be less useful in this context. Finally, the Internet is generally thought of as a valuable and frequently employed health resource (for example, Rains 2007). In this context, however, health communicators should understand that the Internet, though the most frequently used and preferred healthcare reform information source for our sample, was also perceived by our participants as no more or less a useful or certain information source than TV, radio, or newspapers. As such, determining ways to assure consumers that they can be certain about online healthcare reform information from specific sources such as www.healthcare.gov, the official government website, and that it is of high quality, would allow health campaign designers to make the best use of this media source for disseminating healthcare reform information.

Conclusion

A number of limitations exist in this study. Our convenience sample does not truly represent the perspectives of the entire U.S. population about healthcare reform. That this study was conducted online also likely inflated the number of individuals who used and preferred the Internet as a healthcare reform information source. However, from September 23–26, 2010, during the start of our data collection, healthcare was the second most followed news story by the American public (Pew Research Center for the People and the Press 2010), suggesting that many of our participants were likely seeking healthcare reform information via a variety of sources at that time. Nonetheless, future research should attempt to include a larger sample size with individuals from a broader range of backgrounds (for example, SES, race/ethnicity, age, gender, and so on) using multiple data collection methods.

In conclusion, all aspects of healthcare reform are new – the actual guidelines of the legislation, the interpretation and enactment of the laws, media coverage, and even the response and feedback of individuals who are most affected by it. As the provisions of healthcare reform continue to take effect and are challenged in federal and state courts, individuals are going to desire more certainty about the legislation as well as more quality information. Our exploratory findings suggest that magazines are the preferred source for such quality healthcare reform information and decreased uncertainty. However, the Internet, as the most frequently used and important source of healthcare reform information by our sample, should also be considered by those who are invested in the continuation and success of the healthcare reform legislation. Overall, government officials and health communication scholars can use our findings to devise the most concise and effective way of communicating healthcare reform information and policies to the public.

Acknowledgement

The authors acknowledge the contributions of Flora Bahadoran Feiz, Nicole Lieppman, and Nasim Mirkiani Thompson to this project. An earlier version of this chapter was presented as a poster at the 2011 DC Health Communication Conference.

References

Knowledge Networks. 2010. *Health Care Reform Survey* [Online, 21 September]. Available at: http://surveys.ap.org/data/KnowledgeNetworks/Health%20Reform%20Topline%20for%20Posting.pdf [accessed: September 30, 2010].

Bevan, J.L., Jupin, A. and Sparks, L. 2011. Information quality, uncertainty, and quality of care in long distance caregiving. *Communication Research Reports*, 28(2), 190–95.

Brashers, D.E. 2001. Communication and uncertainty management. *Journal of Communication*, 51(3), 447–97.

Brashers, D.E., Goldsmith, D.J. and Hsieh, E. 2002. Information seeking and avoiding in health contexts. *Human Communication Research*, 28(2), 258–71.

Buller, D.B., Callister, M.A. and Reichert, T. 1995. Skin cancer prevention by parents of young children: Health information and sources, skin cancer knowledge, and sun-protection practices. *Oncology Nursing Forum*, 22(10), 1559–66.

Burkell, J.A., Wolfe, D.L., Potter, P.J. and Jutai, J.W. 2006. Information needs and information sources of individuals living with spinal cord injury. *Health Information and Libraries Journal*, 23(4), 257–65.

Christensen, H. and Griffiths, K. 2008. The Internet and mental health literacy. *Australian and New Zealand Journal of Psychiatry*, 34(6), 975–9.

Cline, R.J. and Haynes, K.M. 2001. Consumer health information seeking on the Internet: The state of the art. *Health Education Research*, 16(6), 671–92.

The Commonwealth Fund. 2010. What will happen under health reform – and what's next? *Columbia Journalism Review*, 1–12.

Cotten, S.R. and Gupta, S.S. 2004. Characteristics of online and offline health information seekers and factors that discriminate between them. *Social Science and Medicine*, 59(9), 1795–806.

Cowan, C. and Hoskins, R. 2007. Information preferences of women receiving chemotherapy for breast cancer. *European Journal of Cancer Care*, 16(6), 543–50.

Crary, D. 2010. Gulf oil spill voted top news story of 2010. *Associated Press* [Online, December 21]. Available at: http://www.ap.org/pages/about/whatsnew/wn_122110b.html [accessed: July 25, 2011].

DeLorme, D., Huh, J. and Reid, L.N. 2011. Source selection in prescription drug information seeking and influencing factors: Applying the comprehensive model of information seeking in an American context. *Health Communication*, 16(7), 766–87.

Doherty, R. 2010. The certitudes and uncertainties of health care reform. *Annals of Internal Medicine*, 152(10), 679–82.

Dutta-Bergman, M.J. 2004. Primary sources of health information: Comparisons in the domain of health attitudes, health cognitions, and health behaviors. *Health Communication*, 16(3), 273–88.

Eysenbach, G. and Kohler, C. 2002. How do consumers search for and appraise health information on the World Wide Web? Qualitative study using focus groups, usability tests and in-depth interviews. *British Medical Journal*, 324(7337), 573–7.

Eysenbach, G., Powell, J., Kuss, O. and Sa, E.R. 2002. Empirical studies assessing the quality of health information for consumers on the World Wide Web: A systematic review. *Journal of the American Medical Association*, 287(20), 2691–700.

Fox, S. 2006. Online Health Search 2006 [Online: Pew Research Center's Internet and American Life Project]. Available at: http://www.pewinternet.org/PPF/r/190/report_display.asp [accessed: November 27, 2010].

Gill, E.A. and Babrow, A.S. 2007. To hope or to know: Coping with uncertainty and ambivalence in women's magazine breast cancer articles. *Journal of Applied Communication Research*, 35(2), 133–55.

Hogan, T.P. and Brashers, D.E. 2008. The theory of communication and uncertainty management: Implications from the wider realm of information behavior, in *Uncertainty, Information Management, and Disclosure Decisions: Theories and Applications*, edited by T.D. Afifi and W.A. Afifi. New York: Routledge, 45–66.

Hogan, T.P. and Palmer, C.L. 2005. Information preferences and practices among people living with HIV/AIDS: Results from a nationwide survey. *Journal of the Medical Library Association*, 93(4), 431–9.

Johnson, M.O. 2011. The shifting landscape of health care: Toward a model of health care empowerment. *American Journal of Public Health*, 101(2), 265–70.

Kahlor, L., Dunwoody, S., Griffin, R.J. and Neuwirth, K. 2006. Seeking and processing information about impersonal risk. *Science Communication*, 28(2), 163–94.

Lee, A.L. 2009. Changing effects of direct-to-consumer broadcast drug advertising information sources on prescription drug requests. *Health Communication*, 24(4), 361–76.

Longo, D.R., Schubert, S.L., Wright, B.A., LeMaster, J., Williams, C.D. and Clore, J.N. 2010. Health information seeking, receipt, and use in diabetes self management. *Annals of Family Medicine*, 8(4), 334–40.

Madden, M. and Fox, S. 2006. Finding Answers Online in Sickness and in Health [Online: Pew Research Center's Internet and American Life Project]. Available at: http://pewinternet.com/~/media/Files/Reports/2006/PIP_Health_Decisions_2006.pdf.pdf [accessed: August 21, 2010].

Mishel, M.H. 1981. The measurement of uncertainty in illness. *Nursing Research*, 30(5), 258–63.

Percheski, C. and Hargittai, E. 2011. Health information-seeking in the digital age. *Journal of American College Health*, 59(5), 379–86.

Pecchioni, L.L. and Sparks, L. 2007. Health information sources of individuals with cancer and their family members. *Health Communication*, 21(2), 143–51.

Pew Research Center for the People and the Press. 2010. *Top Stories of 2010: Haiti Earthquake, Gulf Oil Spill* [Online, December 21: Pew Research Center Publications]. Available at: http://pewresearch.org/pubs/1837/top-news-stories-2010-public-interest-haiti-earthquake-gulf-oil-spill [accessed: July 25, 2011].

Rains, S. 2007. Perceptions of traditional information sources and use of the World Wide Web to seek health information: Findings from the Health Information National Trends Survey. *Journal of Health Communication*, 12(7), 667–80.

Sheppard, S., Charnock, D. and Gann, B. 1999. Helping patients access high quality health information. *British Medical Journal*, 319(7212), 764–6.

Sparks, L. and Villagran, M.M. 2010. *Patient and Provider Interaction: A Global Health Communication Perspective*. Cambridge: Polity Press.

Sparks, L. Villagran, M.M., Parker-Raley, J. and Cunningham, C.B. 2007. A patient centered approach to breaking bad news: Communication guidelines for healthcare professionals. *Journal of Applied Communication Research*, 35(2), 177–96.

Tinley, S.T., Houfek, J., Watson, P., Wenzel, L., Clark, M.B., Coughlin, S. and Lynch, H.T. 2004. Screening adherence in BRCA1/2 families is associated with primary physicians' behavior. *American Journal of Medical Genetics A*, 125A(1), 5–11.

Tharoor, I. 2010. Top 10 U.S. news stories. *Time* [Online, 9 December]. Available at: http://www.time.com/time/specials/packages/article/0,28804,2035319_2035315,00.html [accessed: July 25, 2011].

3

Theory-based Health Campaigns: A Winning Combination

MICHELINE FRENETTE

Introduction

Mass media health campaigns are designed to encourage people to adopt behaviors that favor their well-being. However, bringing about such changes usually requires a great deal of effort and persuading people to engage in them is quite a challenge. Although the design of a successful campaign includes many important steps such as understanding the stakeholders and documenting the problem at hand (that is, understanding the probable causes and relevant solutions as well as the characteristics of the population of concern) (see Frenette 2010), the purpose of this chapter is to underscore the importance of theoretical models as the cornerstone of any good communication strategy. Theory, in the context of health promotion, may be defined as a conceptual framework that serves to understand, explain, and predict human behavior; theory draws our attention to variables such as beliefs and attitudes that studies have shown to be linked to how a person will behave in a particular situation and provides an explanation for the relationships among these variables (Cameron 2009, Rimer and Glanz 2005). Theories are useful because they allow us to go beyond our intuition and personal experience to build a broader and more explicit understanding of human behavior and to become familiar with a variety of approaches to the challenging task of guiding people toward better health habits. In that light, it is astonishing to observe the extent to which a large number of health campaigns are not theoretically grounded. For instance, Jones and Donovan (2004) conducted a survey of health promotion practitioners to investigate the extent to which they were aware of, understood, and utilized the major health promotion theories and models derived from research in the areas of psychology and communication. To their dismay, they found that fewer than half of practitioners used any of the standard theories and models taught in health promotion courses in their work.

In developing the argument that we should keep insisting on the necessity for health campaigns to be theoretically anchored, this chapter intersects with two major themes of the book. First, it clearly echoes the principle that the best health communication campaigns are theoretically grounded and it also supports the idea that, in turn, theory development is best guided by successful applications. To that end, it will be argued that, in fact, two sets of theories are needed to increase the probability of successful mass media health campaigns. The first set of theories comprises the multiple persuasion models developed to help us understand what moves people to change their behaviors so as to better their health (or why they resist doing so) in order to translate the campaign objectives into effective communication strategies. Such strategies may be applied in a variety of contexts (that is, interpersonal, organizational, mass media, and so on). As health communication practitioners increasingly use media as vehicles of dissemination, it is argued that we need another set of theories: those that have evolved over the years to help us understand how media function within society and how they may be harnessed to influence individual and collective behaviors. I will demonstrate the relevance of the two ensembles of theories by offering examples of successful health campaigns in each case.

Persuasion Models

There are many persuasion models and the reader will find a useful overview in Cameron (2009). Space constraints allow the presentation of only two of the best known ones, the Health Belief Model and the Stages of Change (or Transtheoretical) model. They will serve as examples of how theories can lead to a better understanding of the issues and subsequently, translate into concrete suggestions for the design of campaigns on a diversity of health problems.

THE HEALTH BELIEF MODEL

The Health Belief Model (HBM) (Becker 1974, Janz and Becker 1984) identifies, in its earliest incarnation, four factors that, together, determine the probability that a person will change her/his behavior in order to minimize risks to her/his health. The first factor is the person's own *perceived vulnerability*, which depends on the perceived level of risk ("How likely is it that I have this problem if I persist in my ways?") and on the severity of the problem ("How harmful would the consequences be?"). The second factor is related to the assessment of the *costs and benefits of the recommended solution*: the person must be convinced that the recommended behavior will solve the problem and that its benefits will outweigh the costs and drawbacks entailed by its adoption. Third, the person must be *confident in her/his ability* to put the solution into action. Fourth, the HBM suggests that the presence of *environmental incentives* that push the individual to act could tip the scales (for example, the pressure from a friend, services offered in the neighborhood and so on).

Campaigns inspired by the Health Belief Model generally seek to increase the targeted population's perception of the risk, which is not always easy: logical demonstrations may leave people indifferent, while emotional messages like the ones using fear must be handled cautiously. For example, messages presenting people with disability following a traffic accident certainly illustrate the serious potential consequences of speeding, but individuals living with disabilities may feel that the message stigmatizes them as somehow deserving of their disability. In addition to increasing risk perception, there are many other angles of approach suggested by the HBM. Based on the analysis of the problem as experienced by the audience, it is possible to either highlight the benefits of the solution (that is, being more in control of one's health, better weight management, and so on) or to demystify the perceived disadvantages of the latter (that is, explaining preventive medical tests, suggesting ways of preparing vegetables, and so on). For complex problems such as drugs and gambling addictions, self-confidence may be the most important factor to consider, in which case the best option for the campaign could be to direct people towards the appropriate resources. The HBM has proved a valuable guide for interventions related to various health problems. Let us consider three of them briefly.

Wong and Tang (2005) explored the factors specified by the Health Belief Model relating to the practice of habitual and volitional health behaviors against Severe Acute Respiratory Syndrome (SARS) among Chinese adolescents. These factors included perceived threat of SARS, perceived benefits and barriers in practicing SARS preventive health behaviors, cues to action, knowledge of SARS, and self-efficacy. Perceived health threat (as reported in the media) and environmental cues to action (such as posters and disinfection stations) were salient correlates of the practice of SARS preventive health behaviors. Wong believed that adolescents (as well as the general population) perceived preventive health behaviors against SARS (such as facemask-wearing and hand-washing) as having more benefits than costs, since local health authorities often emphasized their effectiveness and simplicity. In this case, self-efficacy did not contribute significantly to the understanding of SARS preventive health behaviors compared to other components of the HBM, mainly because they were relatively easy to perform. In short, the HBM offered an explanation of why the interventions to counter SARS were effective. Such knowledge is valuable because it provides guidelines for the analysis of similar problems in the future.

A more complex situation involves adolescents who engage in a wide variety of high-risk behaviors for contracting hepatitis B because they perceive the risk to be low. Slonim et al. (2005) examined this problem from the perspective of the HBM, which led them to identify the barriers that prevented the adoption of protective behaviors such as vaccination. The biggest barrier by far, mentioned by 94 percent of interviewees, was that "most adolescents do not like getting shots" (180) and fear of needles was the most frequently listed potential barrier to vaccine acceptance (30 percent). Suggestions as to how campaigns could help overcome such barriers included increasing perceived susceptibility (for example, "provide everyday examples of how hepatitis B is contracted" (182), "emphasize that the virus lives on surfaces for at least seven days" (182), "tell them that hepatitis B is 100 times more contagious than HIV" (182)); increasing perceived severity (for example, "hepatitis B may lead to cirrhosis – scarring of the liver, liver cancer, liver transplants, or even death" (183)); or, increasing response-efficacy (for example, "the three-dose vaccine series prevents hepatitis B" (183), "hepatitis B is the only STD you can get vaccinated against" (183), "a shot is less painful than getting a tattoo or ears pierced" (183)). In this case, the HBM suggested it was necessary to intervene simultaneously on various aspects of the situation to help bring about change. In the next example, a different picture of the situation is derived from the same model.

To support breast cancer prevention among adolescent girls and their mothers, Silk et al. (2006) conducted focus groups and analyzed them with a coding scheme based on the Health Belief Model. With regard to susceptibility, adolescent girls were able to identify age and heredity as risk factors, but they were somewhat confused about what heredity really means. A campaign might then acknowledge and define the role of heredity (for example: "If your mother or aunt had breast cancer, later in life you might be at risk too. Here are some things you should know" (Silk et al. 2006: 3133). The researchers also suggested addressing myths as a way to attract teenagers' attention and increase the salience of the issue. For instance, adolescents erroneously believed that being hit in the breast might increase your chances of breast cancer later in life.

A message that incorporates casual, familiar language that they commonly use could address "hits to the chest" and focus instead on relevant factors that do reduce risk (for example, to avoid alcohol and to exercise regularly). Indeed, both mothers and daughters reported strong beliefs about eating fruit and vegetables and exercising regularly as essential factors for good health, but they did not clearly link such lifestyle factors to breast cancer prevention. Due to the high levels of perceived severity of breast cancer by both mothers and daughters, the authors felt it was unnecessary for a campaign to insist on the potential severity of the disease. In this case, the HBM drew attention to the fact that the major obstacles to change lay in the erroneous beliefs about susceptibility and the lack of knowledge of preventive factors.

THE STAGES OF CHANGE (OR TRANSTHEORETICAL) MODEL

Another well-known theoretical model for health campaigns is Prochaska and DiClemente's (1983) Stages of Change model, later renamed the Transtheoretical Model of Change (TMC) (Prochaska, Johnson and Lee 1998). The TMC defines six stages and ten processes of change. The stages of change are defined as occurring over time and consist of:

a) precontemplation;
b) contemplation;
c) preparation;
d) action;
e) maintenance; and
f) termination.

Precontemplators are identified as people who see no problem with their current behavior and express no intention of changing. Individuals in the contemplation stage convey awareness of a behavior problem, and are seriously thinking about overcoming it within the next six months. Preparation defines the stage within which people intend to take action shortly, usually in the next 30 days, and have begun to make some small behavioral changes. Action is the stage in which individuals have modified their behavior, experience or environment in the last six months, to change or overcome a problem. The maintenance stage involves preventing relapse and can last from six months to as long as five years. Finally, termination is the stage in which individuals express no temptations to return to their former behavior and have 100 percent self-efficacy. Progression through these stages is not necessarily linear and regression is always a possibility.

Processes describe how people go about making changes and include five experiential ones and five behavioral ones. The experiential processes of change consist of *consciousness raising, dramatic relief, environmental reevaluation, social liberation,* and *self-reevaluation*. The behavioral processes of change include *helping relationships, stimulus control, counterconditioning, reinforcement management,* and *self-liberation*. The processes of change and the stages of change are interrelated, with the former acting as precursors to/ facilitators of the latter (Prochaska, Johnson and Lee 1998). The number and complexity of processes used to make change increase as people move from precontemplation to maintenance. Two additional constructs used with the Transtheoretical Model of Change are reminiscent of the Health Belief Model: "decisional balance" and "self-efficacy"

(Prochaska, Johnson and Lee 1998: 71). Decisional balance refers to the ways people perceive the benefits and barriers associated with making changes. Self-efficacy refers to the degree of confidence a person has in being able to make or maintain change in various situations. People who are in the precontemplation or contemplation stage typically perceive barriers as strongly outweighing benefits. They also often have low self-efficacy. The opposite is usually seen for those in the action or maintenance stages. For tailored materials to be effective, the components of decisional balance, self-efficacy, and processes of change must be relevant to the people targeted based on which stage they are in.

Over the years, studies have confirmed the relevance of the TMC to foster a wide range of healthy behaviors, such as exercising and eating vegetables as well as preventive behaviors to avoid injury and skin cancer. For example, Tai-Seale (2003) identified the proportion of citizens in rural counties at different stages of change for regular physical activity. Almost half of the population was in the precontemplation stage – suggesting a population at great risk for diseases with physical inactivity as a risk factor. Further, barriers and triggers differed by stage of change and demography. The author concluded that specific groups in this population may benefit from a campaign aiming to increase self-efficacy, the availability of time for activity, and the awareness of associated benefits.

Ruud et al. (2005) designed newsletters containing stage-matched messages based on the TMC to increase motivational readiness to increase fruit and vegetable intake among young adults. While participants in all stages wanted to know how to add more fruits and vegetables to their diets, their needs and interests varied somewhat according to what stage they were in. Although participants from all stages liked the recipes, time and ease of preparation were especially important to participants in the precontemplation or contemplation stage. Participants in the preparation stage particularly focused on the pictures and graphics, indicating they provided a good cue for trying the item pictured. They also appreciated tips on making simple substitutions to common foods. On the other hand, if they were in the action or maintenance stage, respondents enjoyed the more creative recipes in addition to the simple ones. Participants in the precontemplation or contemplation stage were also interested in how to prevent spoilage, while those in the preparation and action or maintenance stage wanted more information about serving sizes. Those in the precontemplation or contemplation stage made stronger statements about how the taste of vegetables influenced their intake. Thus, they may benefit from stage-tailored messages that focus not only on how to add more vegetables to the diet but also on ways to enhance their flavor.

Kidd et al. (2003) used the TMC to improve injury prevention interventions because they felt it allowed greater sensitivity in detecting where along the change process an intervention might be more effective to move a person to think about injury prevention or to function as a "booster" in supporting movement from action to maintenance of hazard avoidance. Among the participating high school agriculture students selected for follow-up farm visits one year later, 86 percent had made safety behavior changes in their work. For their part, Cho and Salmon (2006) conducted a pilot study to investigate the effects of fear appeals for the promotion of skin cancer preventive behavior among college students in different stages of change. After being exposed to fear appeals, individuals who were in the precontemplation stage indicated a greater likelihood of thinking defensively and fatalistically regarding the facts on health risk than those who had intended to engage in or who had previously engaged in preventive behavior. Concurrently, after being exposed to fear appeals, those who were in the precontemplation stage reported less favorable attitudes toward message recommendations, weaker intentions to engage in the recommended behavior, and less performance of preventive behavior than those who had contemplated or had previously engaged in preventive behavior. This study is a good example of how the stages of change TMC may be advantageously combined with different persuasion techniques, thereby enhancing the effectiveness of the latter.

Nonetheless, like any theoretical tool, the TMC does not offer a foolproof solution. For example, one shortcoming was pointed out by Rutter and Quine (2002); they contested the premise that barriers are identical from one person to another, and yet believed that this shortcoming is easy to circumvent by knowing the specific barriers for any given circumstance. Furthermore, interactive media can compensate for this weakness by offering individuals the opportunity to select the information that directly concerns them, or by sending reminders or reinforcements through emails or text messages. Another legitimate objection that applies to all persuasion models deplores the fact that they tend to focus on individual responsibility and to ignore the wider social determinants of health such as laws and regulations, school systems, workplaces, social and medical services, community cohesion, and so on (Dutta-Bergman 2005). Indeed, a campaign on healthy eating for young people is an empty gesture if a school's cafeteria and vending machine offer low quality food. As a result, a significant portion of the energy spent on health promotion may be better oriented towards structural changes of this kind. Nonetheless, health practitioners still need to address individual citizens and they are likely to do so through the media. To enhance the effectiveness of the persuasion models hopefully used in the design of health campaigns, proper consideration should also be given to the ways in which the media themselves influence people.

Media Influence Theories

When a health campaign is launched in the media, it accounts for only a minuscule part of the content competing for the public's attention. In addition, the message will reach people while their interest is directed toward other activities, such as listening to the news or enjoying a movie with family members. Therefore, it seems necessary to understand how the campaign's influence will be amplified, reduced or cancelled by the media dynamics within which it is inserted. To illustrate this point, I will discuss two theories that are promising for planning health campaigns: Uses and Gratifications (U&G) and Cultural Studies (CS). There are several other theories about media influence and the interested reader will find a complete presentation in McQuail (1994).

THE USES AND GRATIFICATIONS THEORY

Following initial attempts to document the supposedly powerful effects of media, researchers eventually focused instead on what uses people made of the media (for example, listening to the news, watching movies, and so on) and how these uses gratified certain needs (for example, feeling connected to society, relaxing and so on) (Katz, Gurevitch and Haas 1973, McQuail 1994). The studies conducted within the tradition of "uses and gratifications" (or U&G) provide at least three valuable observations that can be kept in mind when trying to augment the potential success of a health campaign.

First, the central component of uses and gratifications theory, that is, the very idea that people actively seek out particular contents with the aim of satisfying certain needs, is also quite relevant for health campaigns. In fact, there are two ways to incorporate the concept into one's thinking about health campaigns. One is to consider how the campaign can merge with the uses the individual is engaged in when she/he becomes aware of the message. Indeed, it is easy to overlook the fact that a health campaign aired in the mainstream media is not sought out by the individual, but occurs when she/he is watching the news, listening to music or entertaining herself/himself through a story. Another researcher also believes this to be significant; Dutta-Bergman (2005: 9) writes:

> take, for instance, the case of audience exposure to a fear-inducing advertisement right after watching a positive, emotion-inducing television program (a situation comedy). The viewer might simply be likely to avoid the message to maintain his or her positive emotional state.

Ideally, one would choose a program that would naturally blend in with the campaign's content, but this is rarely possible. Instead, special attention can be devoted to the campaign's format to make it as consonant as possible with the public's listening or viewing experience (unless the avowed goal is to be provocative). The second way of taking into account the uses and gratifications concept for health campaigns is to consider what uses and gratifications the message lends itself to. Is it emotionally gratifying and/or aesthetically appealing? Does it provide practical advice? Does it point to resources in the environment, such as a helpline or website? DeBar et al. (2009) studied website use and behavioral outcomes in a multi-component lifestyle intervention promoting healthy diet and exercise for adolescents and found that the most visited website pages had content related to incentive points, caption contests, and fun facts. They concluded that web elements of a multi-component intervention may promote retention and engagement in target behaviors, as long as they blend fun and behavioral elements, rather than exclusively focusing on behavioral changes, to make them more acceptable to adolescent participants.

The second lesson to be learned from this perspective is to be mindful of the natural *resistance to change*. Indeed, members of the public, far from being easily malleable, spontaneously tend to choose content that will be in line with their needs, tastes, and opinions. Cognitive filters based on prior interests and views lead to selective exposure to media content, then to selective perception, and finally, to selective memorization. This selection is especially true for messages that go against the personal views of the individual; these messages are more likely to be filtered in order to avoid psychological discomfort, a phenomenon known as "cognitive dissonance." Dutta-Bergman (2005: 11) is one of the few researchers to have acknowledged the value of this concept for campaign planners:

> Selective exposure theory documents that individuals selectively orient their attention to those stimuli in their environments that match their existing predispositions, values, and behaviors. Therefore, campaign materials that propose to alter the belief structure of the receiver of the message are not likely to be adhered to. Instead, those individuals who are already interested in the issue end up learning from the message.

An example of such a cognitive filter comes from a study by Déry and Renaud (2007) who found that adolescents who already had an active lifestyle were more interested than their peers in the content on physical activity presented within an educational program.

As the reader may have noticed, the concept of resistance to change developed within the U&G tradition is reminiscent of the Health Belief Model's admonition to overcome barriers to change. However, it precedes the HBM in that it acts as a reminder that the best designed campaign may be easily ignored not only because a campaign is a minute portion of media content, but especially because a campaign's core message usually contrasts with media content centered on entertainment, excitement, story-telling, consumerism, and pleasures of all sorts. However, campaign planners can come to terms with this reality as illustrated by the following two examples. In a study on sexual risk reduction, Horner et al. (2008) found a way to capitalize on the story-telling potential of the media. They used a culture-centered approach for developing messages to promote sexual risk reduction in urban African American adolescents. Analysis focused on two barriers to sexual risk reduction: (a) social pressure for early initiation of sexual intercourse and (b) perceptions that condoms reduce sexual pleasure. They demonstrated how competing narratives identified in the analysis could be featured in radio and television messages advocating healthy behavior by modeling risk-reducing negotiation skills. Working on a sun protection campaign, Potente et al. (2011) had to contend with the fact that the sun is more often presented in the media as a source of beauty and pleasure rather than a risk factor. They used ethnographic methods to produce insights into sun protection behaviors and attitudes of Australian adolescents and revealed the complexity of the factors that influence sun protection behaviors, such as peers, lifestyle, environments, social norms, and fashion. Sun protection was imbued with associations of negativity, dullness, and irritation which were dissonant with adolescents' buoyant, dynamic and fun filled experience of the sun. Key barriers to sun protection were found to stem from the perceived impact of sun protection behavior on peer acceptance, negative perceptions around what sun protection communicates about the user, the tone of existing sun protection communication, in sharp contrast with the spontaneous, unplanned nature of the adolescent lifestyle. As a consequence, a successful campaign on sun protection would need to acknowledge adolescent concerns in both its persuasive strategy and its format.

A third powerful idea for health campaigns that emerges from the uses and gratifications theory is the fact that media messages do not reach an individual who lives in isolation but one who instead is embedded within overlapping social circles (that is, family, friends, fellow students and/or coworkers, and so on). Indeed, some campaign planners tend to overlook the fact that media messages are often discussed in social circles, whether on the spot or later on, and that these discussions are likely to alter the individual's perception of the campaign. As Dutta-Bergman (2005) points out:

> A college student watching a message alone in a dorm room will perhaps respond very differently to the message as opposed to being exposed to the message amidst a group of friends at the student union (9).

This difference was in fact observed by Helme et al. (2011). Her study team conducted interviews with young adults about conversations that took place in the context of a large, televised safer sex mass media campaign. Results indicated that Public Service Announcements (PSAs) were often viewed in the company of friends and significant others, and that it was not uncommon for conversations about the PSAs to take place. Three broad categories of these conversations involved discussions about PSA realism, the seriousness of the message, and humor. While in some cases, conversations seemed to advance the goal of the campaign (for example, participants discussed the risk of sexually transmitted infections [STIs] and condom use), in other cases they did not (for example, participants discussed the lack of realism in a particular PSA).

Consequently, health practitioners might plan to harness the interpersonal component of media reception instead of leaving the outcome to chance. Van den Putte et al. (2011) point out that interpersonal communication can serve at least two functions in the context of health campaigns: (a) to stimulate change through social interaction and (b) to further disseminate message content in a secondary diffusion process. Van den Putte and colleagues' study of smokers found that mass media messages (antismoking campaigns and news coverage relevant to smoking cessation) have an indirect effect on smoking cessation intention and behavior via interpersonal communication. Exposure to campaigns and news coverage prompts discussion about the campaigns, and, in turn, about smoking cessation. Interpersonal communication regarding smoking cessation then influences intention to quit smoking and attempts to quit smoking. In addition, a substantial number of smokers who were not directly exposed to the antismoking campaigns were nevertheless indirectly exposed via communication with people who had seen these campaigns. These results imply that the encouragement of interpersonal communication can be an important campaign objective.

The U&G theory we have just discussed is centered on individual needs and habits that guide media practices while the next theory directs our attention toward broader cultural issues pertaining to peoples's experiences with the media.

THE CULTURAL STUDIES THEORY

Researchers in the tradition of cultural studies, among which Stuart Hall (1977, 1980) is considered as a founder, approach media in a different way. From their point of view, media are carriers of an ideology, understood as a system of meanings and practices that reflect the values of a social group (Curran, Morley and Walkerdine 1996). Media would tend to reproduce the society's dominant ideological field and to make it look as natural and universal. In other words, the media are seen to function primarily as public meeting places that reinforce consensus by favoring a certain vision of the world, both in the news coverage and in works of entertainment. From this angle, the cultural studies approach leads us to question health campaigns from an ethical point of view, regarding the underlying values they embody. For example, do they attribute responsibility for the problem to individuals in the first place? Do they promote solutions that benefit the pharmaceutical industry? Do they act as a simple relay for established figures of authority?

Moreover, the cultural studies tradition has emphasized the interpretive capacities of members of the audience (Morley 1980, 1992). They are viewed as active participants in the communicative exchange who will strive to make meaning from whatever message they encounter. Cultural studies researchers also argue that, when faced with ideologically charged media content, persons may display various reactions. They can accept the worldview that is presented (hegemonic mode), partially accept it (negotiated mode), or reject it outright (oppositional mode). Although the "text" (that is, the campaign message) directs people toward a preferred reading, the decoding of the text can go in a number of directions since the process is grounded in several characteristics of the individual, including knowledge and experience, but most notably, culture, values, and social context. Several examples may be found of how health messages lend themselves to different interpretations.

For instance, Richer and Renaud (2007) found that an imaginary character (the "blue man") that was part of a campaign promoting physical activity was perceived differently by girls and boys. While boys were focused on his behavior and accepted him as an "athlete" who displayed skills they could imitate, girls saw him as an unattractive mascot that did not inspire them. In other words, girls overlooked the character's message because his appearance did not appeal to them. The researchers argued that girls are socially conditioned to maintain high expectations of appearance, even when it threatens to interfere with their personal development. Cultural affiliations, even within a given society, also lead to different interpretations of health messages. For example, Miller-Day and Barnett (2004) examined ways in which ethnic identity and perceptions of cultural norms were linked to adolescent drug use attitudes. A cultural approach to adolescent drug use behavior entails investigating and describing a culture's normative beliefs and the perceptions of members of that particular ethnic culture toward those beliefs as tied to cultural practices. Arguments for this framework suggest that drug prevention information presented in ways that are meaningful and culturally relevant to the targeted population is more likely to be retained and used than information presented in ways that do not reflect group values or norms. The most interesting difference that emerged in the stories of the Black respondents was that Blacks did more drugs than other races although demographics did not support this view. The Whites generally did not perceive drug use to be normative among other Whites. Miller-Day and Barnett (2004) argued for increased health campaign prevention efforts directed at erroneous perceptions of ethnic cultural norms.

Finally, let us consider another example that underscores the need to design media campaigns with the intended audience's cultural beliefs in mind. In a study with young African teenagers, Ragnarsson, Onya and Aaro (2009) found that participants had limited knowledge about HIV from a biomedical perspective. Instead, their understanding and interpretations of HIV and other sexually transmitted diseases were largely informed by traditional and religious belief systems. Based on these interpretations, they also expressed distrust towards the medical health system, and distrust influenced where they said they would go for care, support, and treatment. The study demonstrated that some ways of understanding HIV/AIDS and other sexually transmitted illnesses may weaken efforts of health education interventions based solely on a medical and modern notion of disease. Consequently, the authors emphasized the importance of exploring traditional and religious belief systems and taking these into account when planning and designing behavior change interventions such as media campaigns.

In short, the Cultural Studies approach brings forward a very important idea: no unique meaning is inscribed within a message; rather, different interpretations, guided in great part by cultural affiliations, are likely to take place. As a consequence, the persuasive strategies of health campaigns should strive to be culturally meaningful. The preceding examples are meant to illustrate how media theories can merge with persuasion theories to help make health campaigns as relevant as possible. Such theoretical tools are valuable assets for both academics and practitioners.

Implications for Academics

There are at least four ways in which academics may contribute to building theoretically sound health campaigns. First, they have an important role to play in helping health practitioners take advantage of the full range of theories by developing an integrated or "polymorphic" approach to campaign design. According to Dutta-Bergman (2005):

> *A polymorphic approach to theorizing and application development focuses on locating and harnessing the multiplicities of communication, on integrating the rich body of communication theories, and simultaneously retaining their diversity (16).*

This recommendation supports the suggestion to work toward an integrative framework that would include both persuasion models and media influence theories. The evaluation of health campaigns is also worthy of academics' attention. In addition to measuring results, the theoretical bases of campaigns should also be examined so that we may continuously improve our theoretical constructs. Furthermore, an exciting challenge for researchers is to study the extent to which current theoretical models may be adapted for the design and evaluation of campaigns now taking advantage of the multiple applications of interactive communication technologies. Finally, it behooves researchers to find productive ways of sharing academic knowledge with health practitioners through traditional avenues such as workshops and publications while simultaneously exploring the creative possibilities of personalized media and social networks to such ends.

Implications for Health Practitioners

Throughout this chapter, several examples of how theoretical concepts were helpful in designing media health campaigns were presented. In closing, I would like to offer counter examples of campaigns that have sold themselves short for lack of proper attention to a theoretical foundation. After analyzing a set of smoking cessation messages to identify their underlying communication strategies, Cohen, Shumate and Gold (2007) found that message designers tended to favor certain strategies, hence abandoning other promising ones, because they knew little or nothing about theoretical models. The researchers further argued that, "These data might also indicate that message designers have difficulty producing theoretically grounded health communication messages" (Cohen, Shumate and Gold 2007: 100).

Another example comes from Lombardo and Léger (2007) who examined the Canadian *Think Again* social marketing HIV/AIDS prevention campaign, encouraging gay men to rethink their assumptions about their partners' HIV statuses and the risks of unsafe sex. They found that while its design was clearly guided by social marketing principles, the campaign was not explicitly informed by any specific health behavior change theory and that theoretical concerns appeared to be an after-the-fact consideration. And yet, reviews and meta-analyses consistently show that effective HIV/AIDS interventions are theory driven and incorporate skill and self-efficacy-building aspects. In the researchers' view, the *Think Again* campaign's effectiveness may have been limited by its assumption of the ideal scenario of a man making rational choices in a situation under his full volitional control which bore little resemblance to most situations encountered in real life.

Conclusion

The purpose of this chapter was to argue that a sound theoretical foundation should be a fundamental component of mass media health campaigns and to illustrate how both persuasion and media theories are necessary in this regard. Persuasion theories help us understand how people deal with a variety of health problems, how they resist change and how they may be more likely convinced to bring improvements to their lifestyle. Media theories are often overlooked in the process of designing and evaluating health campaigns and yet, they are a complementary theoretical asset to be used in conjunction with persuasion theories. Indeed, they help us understand how media function in society and how they may best be harnessed to reach individuals in the most meaningful manner possible. Clearly, there is no guarantee of success since the ultimate outcome of a health campaign depends on many other factors, some of which are not under the control of health practitioners. Nonetheless, a solid theoretical base remains the cornerstone of an optimal campaign and should be a primary concern for both health practitioners and academics. The efforts necessary to develop theoretically anchored health campaigns appear justified, given their potential to assist people in improving their individual and collective well-being.

Acknowledgement

This chapter benefited from the collaboration of Maxime Boivin, Candidate, M.Sc. Communication, Université de Montréal.

References

Becker, M.H. 1974. The health belief model and personal health behavior. *Health Education Monographs*, 2, 324–73.

Cameron, K.A. 2009. A practitioner's guide to persuasion: An overview of 15 selected persuasion theories, models and frameworks. *Patient Education and Counseling*, 74, 309–17.

Cho, H.O. and Salmon, C.T. 2006. Fear appeals for individuals in different stages of change: Intended and unintended effects and implications on public health campaigns. *Health Communication*, 20(1), 91–9.

Cohen, E., Shumate, M. and Gold, A. 2007. Anti-smoking media campaign messages: Theory and practice. *Health Communication*, 22(2), 91–102.

Curran, J., Morley, D. and Walkerdine, V. 1996. *Cultural Studies and Communications*. London: Arnold.

DeBar, L.L., Dickerson, J., Clarke, G., Stevens, V.J., Ritenbaugh, C. and Aickin, M. 2009. Using a website to build community and enhance outcomes in a group, multi-component intervention promoting healthy diet and exercise in adolescents. *Journal of Pediatric Psychology*, 34(5), 539–50.

Déry, V. and Renaud, L. 2007. Perception par les adolescents de messages portant sur l'activité physique, in *Les Médias et le Façonnement des Normes en Matière de Santé*, edited by L. Renaud. Québec: Presses de l'Université du Québec, 205–12.

Dutta-Bergman, M.J. 2005. Theory and practice in health communication campaigns: A critical interrogation. *Health Communication*, 18(2), 103–22.

Frenette, M. 2010. *La Recherche en Communication: Un Atout pour les Campagnes Sociales*. Québec: Presses de l'Université du Québec.

Hall, S. 1977. Culture, media and the ideological effect, in *Mass Communication and Society*, edited by J. Curran, M. Gurevitch and J. Woollacott. London: Arnold, 315–48.

Hall, S. 1980. Encoding/decoding, in *Culture, Media, Language*, edited by S. Hall. London: Hutchison, 128–38.

Helme, D.W., Noar, S.M., Allard, S., Zimmerman, R.S., Palmgreen, P. and McClanahan, K.J. 2011. In-depth investigation of interpersonal discussions in response to a safer sex mass media campaign. *Health Communication*, 26(4), 366–78.

Horner, J.R., Romer, D., Vanable, PA., Salazar, LF., Carey, M.P., Juzang, I., Fortune, T., DiClemente, R. and Farber, N. 2008. Using culture-centered qualitative formative research to design broadcast messages for HIV prevention for African American adolescents. *Journal of Health Communication*, 13(4), 309–25.

Janz, N. and Becker, M.H. 1984. The health belief model: A decade later. *Health Education Quarterly*, 11, 1–47.

Jones, S.C. and Donovan, R.J. 2004. Does theory inform practice in health promotion in Australia? *Health Education Research*, 19(1), 1–14.

Katz, E., Gurevitch, M. and Haas, H. 1973. On the use of mass media for important things. *American Sociological Review*, 38(2), 164–81.

Kidd, P., Reed, D., Weaver, L., Westnear, S. and Rayens, M.K. 2003. The transtheoretical model of change in adolescents: Implications for injury prevention. *Journal of Safety Research*, 34(3), 281–8.

Lombardo, A.P. and Léger, Y.A. 2007. Thinking about *"Think Again"* in Canada: Assessing a social marketing HIV/AIDS prevention campaign. *Journal of Health Communication: International perspectives*, 12(4), 377–97.

McQuail, D. 1994. *Mass Communication Theory: An Introduction*. London: Sage.

Miller-Day, M. and Barnett, J.M. 2004. *"I'm not a druggie"*: Adolescents' ethnicity and (erroneous) beliefs about drug use norms. *Health Communication*, 16(2), 209–28.

Morley, D. 1980. *The Nationwide Audience: Structure and Decoding*. London: British Film Institute.

Morley, D. 1992. *Television, Audiences and Cultural Studies*. London: Routledge.

Potente, S., Coppa, K., Williams, A. and Engels, R. 2011. Legally brown: Using ethnographic methods to understand sun protection attitudes and behaviours among young Australians "I didn't mean to get burnt – it just happened!". *Health Education Research*, 26(1), 39–52.

Prochaska, J.O., Johnson, S. and Lee, P. 1998. The transtheoretical model of behavior change, in *The Handbook of Health Behavior Change*, 2nd Edition, edited by S.S. Shumaker and E.B. Schron. New York: Springer, 59–84.

Prochaska, J.O. and DiClemente, C.C. 1983. Stages and processes of self-change in smoking: Toward an integrative model of change. *Journal of Consulting and Clinical Psychology*, 51(3), 390–95.

Ragnarsson, A., Onya, H.E. and Aaro, L.E. 2009. Young people's understanding of HIV: A qualitative study among school students in Mankweng, South Africa. *Scandinavian Journal of Public Health*, 37(2), 101–6.

Richer, Y. and Renaud, L. 2007. Perception de la campagne *"Vers un Québec en santé"* par des jeunes québécois de 12 à 14 ans, in *Les Médias et le Façonnement des Normes en Matière de Santé*, edited by L. Renaud. Québec: Presses de l'Université du Québec, 213–23.

Rimer, B.K. and Glanz, K. 2005. *Theory at a Glance: A Guide for Health Promotion Practice*, 2nd Edition. Washington, DC: National Cancer Institute and U.S. Department of Health and Human Services.

Rutter, D. and Quine, L. 2002. *Changing Health Behaviour*. Buckingham: Open University Press.

Ruud, J.S., Betts, N., Kritch, K., Nitzke, S., Lohse, B. and Boeckner, L. 2005. Acceptability of stage-tailored newsletters about fruits and vegetables by young adults. *Journal of the American Dietetic Association*, 105(11), 1774–8.

Silk, K.J., Bigsby, E., Volkman, J., Kingsley, C., Atkin, C., Ferrara, M. and Leigh-Anne Goins, L.-A. 2006. Formative research on adolescent and adult perceptions of risk factors for breast cancer. *Social Science & Medicine*, 63, 3124–36.

Slonim, A.B., Roberto, A.J., Downing, C.R., Adams, I.F., Fasano, N.J., Davis-Satterla, L. and Miller, M.A. 2005. Adolescents' knowledge, beliefs, and behaviors regarding hepatitis B: Insights and implications for programs targeting vaccine-preventable diseases. *Journal of Adolescent Health*, 36, 178–86.

Tai-Seale, T. 2003. Stage of change specific triggers and barriers to moderate physical activity. *American Journal of Health Behavior*, 27(3), 219–27.

Van den Putte, B., Yzer, M., Southwell, B.G., de Bruijn, G.J. and Willemsen, M.C. 2011. Interpersonal communication as an indirect pathway for the effect of antismoking media content on smoking cessation. *Journal of Health Communication*, 16(5), 470–85.

Wong, C. and Tang, C.S. 2005. Practice of habitual and volitional health behaviors to prevent severe acute respiratory syndrome among Chinese adolescents in Hong Kong. *Journal of Adolescent Health*, 36(3), 193–200.

Health Communication and Web Media

4 Disease, Representation, and Public Relations: A Discourse Analysis of HIV/AIDS Websites

VINITA AGARWAL, MARGARET U. D'SILVA AND
GREG B. LEICHTY

Introduction

While approximately 8,200 people from developing countries die of HIV/AIDS daily, each day there are 13,500 new HIV infections (ActionAid 2010). AIDS has no cure. Because of the enormity of the crisis, several International Non Government Organizations (INGOs) offer a wide range of HIV/AIDS-related information on their websites. Based on the premise that HIV/AIDS-related health communication is integrally constituted by the discursive representation of disease, in this chapter, we provide a discourse analysis of HIV/AIDS representation on three INGO websites – ActionAid, AIDS Alliance (Alliance), and Avert. Our analysis focuses on an examination of how the INGOs represent HIV/AIDS on their websites with respect to their target publics. We investigate how the organization communicates with affected stakeholders and publics. We also examine how the websites construct the identities of those infected with HIV/AIDS and their communities. The goal of the analysis is to develop solutions that are both ethical and culturally sensitive.

International NGO websites strive to fulfill organizational goals through maintaining relationships with diverse publics that cross national borders. Stakeholders in such relationship-building processes include not only those affected, but also their families, the community within which these practices are embedded, INGOs, activist groups, pharmaceutical companies, corporate stakeholders, service organizations, governments, and policymakers. A key challenge in issue representation on an international website is to present the issues in a manner that is sensitive to both the local context and the multiple stakeholders. For example, researchers have examined the HIV/AIDS pandemic from the perspective of communicative relationship building with stakeholders with the goals of disease prevention and fostering context-friendly practice (Bardhan 2002). Examining relationships with international publics, however, involves the challenges of bringing into the mainstream marginalized voices while simultaneously remaining true to local cultural and social norms (Sriramesh and White 1992). INGOs dealing with HIV/AIDS need to build relationships with marginalized publics that are sensitive to local norms, beliefs, and practices.

Our chapter examines health communication in the context of mediated HIV/ AIDS issue representation. We analyze international public relations discourse on INGO websites. In offering a discursive critique of the HIV/AIDS representation of three INGOs, the chapter identifies communicative challenges in international public relations programs addressing vital health promotion initiatives in an online format. We examine HIV/AIDS issue representation using the lenses of power and identity. These lenses enable us to investigate how publics and potential solutions for the HIV epidemic are framed. We begin with a discussion distinguishing INGOs from NGOs and their role in issue representation in initiatives involving health promotion and social change.

INGOs and Issue Representation on Websites

Although INGOs function like NGOs, INGOS have a wider scope of activity. They operate globally while NGOs function within a particular nation. NGOs are defined as "private, voluntary, nonprofit groups whose primary aim is to influence publicly some form of social change" (Khagram, Riker and Sikkink 2002: 6). In extending this definition of NGOs to the international sphere, INGOs can be defined as international nonprofit groups working in more than one country to influence or bring about social change.

In recent years, as INGOs have grown dramatically in number, size, and networks (Keck and Sikkink 1998), so has their impact on the causes they represent. Their impact has been aided, in particular, by the use of information and communication technologies (ICTs) such as organizational websites. ICTs have increased membership across geographical regions and promoted media coverage received by the issue (Shumate and Pike 2006). ICTs also assist INGOs in achieving other goals such as fostering social change, connecting stakeholders and building a policy consensus around an issue (Shumate, Fulk and Monge 2005).

Although the potential of ICTs for promoting social change globally is promising, ICTs also have limitations in that they can impede meaningful transformations that seek to integrate disempowered voices into the mainstream. Disempowered publics often do not have Internet access and hence cannot participate in framing the issue or in disseminating communications about the issue. These asymmetries limit an INGO's capacity to bring about desired social, economic, and political change where it is needed most.

International Public Relations and INGO Website Discourse

International public relations has been defined as the examination of the theory and practice of public relations across borders (Curtin and Gaither 2007) even as others have wondered if there is any form of public relations that is not global anymore (Sriramesh and Vercic 2003). International public relations endeavors are encumbered by environmental variables that are specific to particular contexts such as those of political ideology, economic system, activism, culture, and media (Sriramesh and Vercic 2003). Given the diversity in these variables, culture has emerged as one of the most important facets of international public relations practice (Huang 2000, Taylor 2001, Zaharna 2000,

2001) and is recognized as central to the act of meaning production in society (Curtin and Gaither 2007, Hall 1980, Williams 1961).

As a form of global media discourse, websites of large INGOs strategically construct both the identities of those represented as well as the international organization itself (Appadurai 2001). The discourse on the websites of the international organizations engages both in (a) communicative relationship building with its stakeholders and (b) in identity construction of the publics and the organization. It is therefore important to consider the implications of online forms of communication on shifting traditional notions of power and access (Holtz 1996).

Despite the challenges of the digital divide where a large number of those affected in developing contexts may not have access to the Internet or the information presented on the Internet, it is still important to examine the impact of INGO websites on HIV/AIDS for their communicative engagement with stakeholders and in framing the identity of affected publics. We believe such an examination opens a discursive forum to represent issues of identity and stigma in a manner that recognizes local cultural meanings of gender, sexual practices, and disease while constructing solutions based on the epidemiology of the pandemic.

Method

Examining the discourse for the micro-practices of representation implies viewing discourse as "not just of representing the world, but of signifying the world in meaning" (Fairclough 1992: 64). Not only does discourse serve to represent, but it also imbues the issues, publics, or relationships, it represents with meaning. To analyze the HIV/AIDS discourse on the websites, we drew upon Fairclough's (1992) three-level approach to discourse analysis. The first level of analysis examines textual information for the rhetorical devices employed and the manner in which they position the speaker within the discourse. The second level of analysis considers the type of discourse and how it is articulated (for example, dominant discourse, contradictory discourse, silent discourse) and its location in the text. The third level of analysis locates the discourse within larger social, historical, and cultural contexts (Fairclough 1992). Our analysis focuses particularly on the representation of the goals of the INGOs on their websites along these three levels.

We chose the websites for analysis using the principle of maximum variation sampling. This approach selects cases that differ significantly on a dimension of critical interest (Flyvvbjerg 2006). We selected INGO websites that differed significantly in how they framed their mission with respect to HIV/AIDS. This sampling approach enables the researcher to identify common patterns that hold across the different sampled units. It also allows a researcher to identify unique variations on the general pattern (Patton 2001). We expected this strategy to provide information-rich cases that would capture some of the variation in HIV/AIDS issue representation on INGO websites. Using this principle, we selected the following: ActionAid, AIDS Alliance, and Avert.

BRIEF DESCRIPTION OF THE THREE INGO WEBSITES

ActionAid   ActionAid depicts HIV/AIDS as an issue of social justice. HIV/AIDS is one of many social justice and equity issues that the organization addresses. ActionAid (www.

actionaid.org) has over 1500 full-time staff worldwide. It has programs and partnerships in approximately 40 countries, particularly in Africa and South Asia (Yearbook of International Organizations 2009a).

AIDS Alliance (The Alliance)   The Alliance (www.aidsalliance.org) focuses solely on HIV/AIDS along multiple dimensions, especially as it relates to community organization. The Alliance has a full-time staff of more than 300 people and has programs in nearly 25 countries in Africa and South Asia (Yearbook of International Organizations 2009b).

Avert   Avert (www.avert.org) is a small NGO that explicitly defines itself as the "most popular AIDS website" on the Internet. Avert is a small organization that is primarily focused on its educational mission via its website. It only has 11 full-time staff that primarily maintains its website. The site had more than 11 million visitors in 2008. Avert partners with community organizations in South Africa, but its international presence is quite modest (Whitehill 2009).

Analysis and Findings

We examined the dialogic representation of the dominant and silent stakeholders, cultures, and solutions. INGO websites may inadvertently reproduce or challenge the hegemonic sociocultural and political conditions. INGOs have an existence outside of the local sociocultural, political, and economic conditions in which HIV/AIDs occurs. As a result, INGO websites may be able to generate new discourses that oppose the dominant local narratives surrounding HIV/AIDS. These narratives could illuminate underlying assumptions, and challenge essentializing discourses around HIV/AIDS. Because of their international scope, INGO websites may also constitute persuasive frames that reify difference as for example, through marginalization of publics, or (re)envisioning alternative solutions that challenge disempowering discourses.

ANALYSIS OF POWER

The discourse of power is significant because it illuminates how INGO websites shape strategic initiatives through mainstreaming the issue, regulating access, or promoting relational dialogue. We begin with an analysis of ActionAid's website.

ActionAid Website   ActionAid's website is oriented toward lobbying, providing preventive care, campaigning, and communicating with international institutions. For example, the web page states that in Africa, ActionAid is "working with the governments [to] establish National AIDS Commissions and community support groups that act as lifelines in hard-hit regions" (ActionAid 2010) as well as helping to create a program where individuals find agency by devising solutions to address their own needs.

Prominent on ActionAid's HIV/AIDS web page are documents for institutional stakeholders such as annual reports and policy documents for financing universal access. These documents provide information for government and the institutional targets of public lobbying initiatives; they thereby facilitate integrative engagement with other members of the community (see also Buzzanell 1994). Other links on the web page's left margin exemplify the tactics of large-scale issue mobilization for HIV/AIDS through events such as the World AIDS Day and Global AIDS Week (both for 2007, 2008), as well as academic and empirical endeavors (ActionAid Fellowship Program).

ActionAid's strategy of bridging the individual and the collective, the margins and the mainstream, on a common platform is exemplified by the membership that includes those in positions of political power as well as those at the margins of the discourse. For example, a procession organized by a nominated member of the Parliament, Ms Njoki Ndungu, "call(ed) on the government to review its policies on the links between violence against women and girls and HIV and AIDS" (ActionAid 2010). Participants highlighted issues of cultural and legal discrimination and the need to create awareness among those in legislative power so that "if they can see the injustices that we are going through, only then will they create laws to protect us" (ActionAid 2010). Further, ActionAid's use of governmental and state actors legitimizes the issue through an official recognition of the pandemic; one that offers protection to those victimized by the legal system. Its strengths lie in creating an inclusive platform for collective articulation. In this regard, empowerment through collective mobilization can be envisioned as a form of cooperative enactment in organizing to bring about meaningful social and political change through supporting a form of participatory politics.

However, in its framing of the issue, one limitation of the mobilization efforts is that women are constituted as discriminated against, as seeking institutional protection and guidance. Ultimately the voices of ordinary women represent a silent discourse and lack agency in a framework where women are represented as embodying meaningful agency seemingly only within a governmental logic. While oriented toward collective agency, ActionAid must strive to balance the constraints of a "control system that orients and constrains member behavior" (Harter, Edwards, McClanahan, Hopson and Carson-Stern, 2005: 420). In other words, it should embody the strengths of collective agency without silencing the individual voices of those receiving assistance or those who are at the margins (Papa, Auwal and Singhal 1997).

Alliance Website   The Alliance represents HIV/AIDS as a dominant discourse that is embedded in community narratives and universal access to large-scale structural initiatives. The Alliance focuses its strategies on strengthening the individual-community relationship: "It may be because the drugs are not available. Or it may be that you're scared to ask for the help you need" (AIDS Alliance 2010). At the same time the Alliance strategies also focus on the core principle of universal access to structural resources. For example, on its website the Alliance recognizes the importance of taking a community and infrastructural approach such that "the actions taken by all stakeholders in the coming years will determine [how] many lives are saved (or not) as a result" (AIDS Alliance 2010).

The Alliance website thus includes both the dominant power structures and the community context that defines those infected with HIV/AIDS. Toward that end, the Alliance's website utilizes strategies of institutional collaboration such as publishing a report along with UNAIDS focusing on universal access, policy deliberations, and funding (AIDS Alliance 2010). This set of strategies illustrates the Alliance's concern with mainstreaming the issue and targeting publics through integrating collective action at the global level with corresponding tactics at the local and community level.

One way the public relations function can achieve its ethical goals of creating a more equitable, democratic society is by analyzing the manner in which the public relations function selectively represents power discourses for articulating the voices of those most affected yet not traditionally included in the stakeholder-publics framework of INGOs (Motion and Weaver 2005). An illustration of this ethical framework can be found under "How We Work," (AIDS Alliance 2010). There, the Alliance writes, "We know from our experience that the most successful responses to HIV are built on local leadership, commitment and responsibility" (AIDS Alliance 2010). The Alliance site also states, "We emphasise the importance of working with people most likely to affect or be affected by the spread of HIV. These are often people from marginalised groups, who are the most vulnerable and hardest to reach" (AIDS Alliance 2010). As exemplified by both these instances, the Alliance website discursively constructs micro-level power relationships between local leadership and the marginalized publics.

Avert Website   Avert's website presents a primarily informational strategic approach, wherein the framing of target publics and solutions empowers by offering knowledge countering prevalent stigmatizing discourses and empowerment through mainstreaming the marginalized. For example, the *smart card* initiative (launched by Ashodaya, an NGO in Karnataka, a state in India) is described on Avert's website thus:

> As well as encouraging sex workers to look after their health, this initiative raises sex workers' self-esteem by integrating them into mainstream culture. [T]his can help them to take a firmer stance on condom use when negotiating with clients (Avert 2010).

The *smart card* contains medical details of the holder (that is, the sex worker) and must be presented at a health check-up at least once in three months to remain valid. A valid *smart card* can be used by sex workers to get discounts on essential amenities. As a public relations tactic, we find that the *smart card* performs two vital functions: (a) that of providing knowledge of their epidemic and the systemic causes; and, (b) that of empowerment, in simultaneously leveraging power in favor of those marginalized.

Similarly, other initiatives on Avert's website offer innovative strategies for articulation of an empowered role-identity for the sex workers. The most well known of these programs is the Sonagachi program in Kolkata, India. This program conjoins peer educators, madams (brothel-owners), and pimps in educational initiatives and training in a way that targets the constraints of their lived experience (such as client resistance to using a condom, dependence on clients for subsistence and wages) productively through leveraging power in partnership with the local (institutional) law enforcement. Avert's presentation of successful solutions help to identify these strategies and empower individuals in these interstitial discursive public spaces.

ANALYSIS OF IDENTITY CONSTRUCTION AND STIGMA

The discourse of identity illuminates the manner in which the identity or public face of social justice contradicts local struggles through locating stigma as a means of reproducing social difference. Stigma is defined as the socially constructed identification of a particular social group or groups of people that is based on a physical, behavioral, or social trait that diverges from prevalent group norms (Goffman 1961, 1963). A relational interrogation of the beliefs and social processes underlying construction of stigma reveal how stigmatization discursively reproduces embedded hegemonic societal norms that victimize or de-legitimize those most affected by the epidemic. For example, research shows that stigma negatively affects sexual behaviors, care-seeking behaviors, and adherence to antibiotic regimens to disadvantage those at-risk (Farmer 1994, Fortenberry, McFarlane, Beakley, Bull, Fishbein, Grimley et al. 2002, Herek, Capitanio and Widaman 2002, Scott 2009). By investigating identity constructions surrounding HIV/AIDS we hope to reveal alternative ways of constructing identity that envisage meaningful change at both the community levels and individual levels (Parker and Aggleton 2003). By interrogating stigma in identity construction we frame the social inequalities underlying HIV/AIDS-related practices through the lens of an informed biosocial understanding. This understanding can lead to interventions addressing relationships between those affected and the communities they are a part of, their institutional structures, and the inter-organizational network of INGOs to have an integrative and meaningful social, political, and cultural impact.

Because HIV/AIDS is a sexually transmitted disease, its meaning attaches to a number of taboo topics related to gender and sexuality. Hence, local constructions of gender and stigma must be overtly invoked and subverted in order to undermine existing dominant elements of HIV/AIDS narratives. We now compare and contrast INGO website representation of stigma in conjunction with gender representation.

ActionAid Website   ActionAid recognizes stigma implicitly in its discursive construction of the implications of living with HIV/AIDS. It states, for example, that "people living with HIV and AIDS are denied many of their basic rights such as employment, safety, sexual and family life and to living free from violence" (ActionAid 2010). It primarily addresses stigma by pointing to the need to redress gendered forms of poverty. ActionAid also notes that stigma is a cause of poverty: "women and girls are the poorest of the poor because of the extreme forms of discrimination that persist in many parts of today's world" (ActionAid 2010).

Furthermore, ActionAid's discursive framing of strategies targeting HIV/AIDS focuses attention on violence against women while being mindful of the micro-operations of power in localized contexts. For example, the website states: "Women are more vulnerable to HIV infection because they are not able to insist on protected sex, even when they know their partner is infected. Men often use physical violence to reinforce their power over women and girls" (ActionAid 2010). ActionAid seeks to address the micro-operations of gender relations through targeting the localized mechanisms of social construction of sexuality and control.

Alliance Website   On its website, the Alliance describes itself as "a network of national, independent, locally governed and managed *linking organisations*" (AIDS Alliance 2010). One of its core principles is that "everyone has the right to access the HIV treatment they need, without stigma" (AIDS Alliance 2010). The programmatic intervention strategies of Alliance target victimizing identity norms, specifically: "harmful sexual and gender norms and structural factors that fail to promote a legal and policy environment that fully supports the human rights of people living with HIV and those who are most at risk of infection" (AIDS Alliance 2010). Although treatment through antiretroviral therapies enable HIV infected individuals to live longer, those infected continue to be stigmatized. Stigma is a powerful social label (Goffman 1959, 1963). A stigmatized group can be defined as "a pejorative category of people who are devalued, shunned, or otherwise lessened in their life chances and in access to the humanizing effect of free and unfettered social intercourse" (Alonzo and Reynolds 1992: 4). A human rights approach acknowledges and targets the fundamentally gendered premise of the issue: "The destruction wrought by HIV/AIDS is fuelled by a wide range of human rights violations, including sexual violence and coercion faced by women and girls" (AIDS Alliance 2010). The Alliance's approach for HIV prevention, treatment and care includes "bringing people with HIV, community stakeholders and health providers together to develop partnerships, address gaps and difficulties, and support families and individuals" (AIDS Alliance 2010). The Alliance's website's discursive representation presents gender as negatively constituted by essentializing discursive practices. It also represents women as empowered agents with potential for resistance and looks for innovative strategic solutions that arise from the juxtaposition of contradictory subject positions and practices. Although local discourses work toward maintaining existing hegemonic relations, by encouraging community participatory strategies in their approach, the Alliance website effectively co-opts the normalizing community response and envisions positive solutions.

The Alliance website includes examples of stigma-reduction programs in El Salvador, Mexico, and individual sub-Saharan African countries. The programs described on the Alliance website train the trainers with government support. Our analysis reveals that detailed information on stigma-reduction programs, if made available, would benefit those who access the site for information. For example, at the time of the analysis, by working with a partner organization, such as CISHAN (a linking organization comprised of 2000 partners of the International HIV/AIDS alliance in Nigeria), the Alliance had succeeded in putting a stigma and discrimination bill before the National Assembly of Nigeria. Unlike Avert, the Alliance website takes an international strategic approach by targeting government publics and performing a supportive role (such as planning and grant management) for its linking organizations.

Avert Website   Of the three websites we examined, Avert explicitly targets its strategies toward those infected with HIV/AIDS. Avert represents AIDS as a disease of epidemic proportions. Its predominant strategy is to provide information on HIV/AIDS including: the history of AIDS, the science of HIV testing, treatments, and continent-specific information. The section on Africa, for instance, provides information on the continent and specific country-based information. The website's discursive style reflects an integration of context and culture. As a discursive strategy, the site furnishes extensive general knowledge about human sexuality, questions and answers about sex, including a section about how to have sex that emphasizes contraception and disease prevention.

Recognizing that young people need sex-related information, the site extensively discusses preventive measures for teenagers. It addresses prevention by explaining that HIV/AIDS can be transmitted in multiple ways including sexual activities, blood, and mother-to-child transmission. The site thus avoids essentializing HIV/AIDS as a sexual disease. HIV/AIDS infections also are represented in a gender-neutral manner as diseases experienced by both sexes and transmitted in both heterosexual and homosexual relations. While the website itself stays clear of any stigmatizing comments, it raises awareness of stigma through extensively discussing factors that contribute to stigma, the social-cultural levels at which stigma is experienced, and the effects of stigma.

Fundamentally a social justice sensibility evokes a call to action that questions the status quo, and "entails a moral imperative to act as effectively as we can to do something about structurally sustained inequalities" (Frey, Pearce, Pollack, Aartz and Murphy 1996: 111). The intersection of power and identity concerns enables practitioners and scholars to understand "lived experience [through] which the embodiment of difference in spatially constitutive social practices reveals multiple sites of social restructuring" (Agarwal and Buzzanell 2008: 333).

Discussion

Our textual examination of the HIV/AIDS representation on the websites of three INGOs demonstrates that meaningful dialogic communication is needed to build viable relationships with relevant stakeholder groups. Issues of power are addressed by countering the stigmatizing and marginalizing discourses representing the disease and those affected. Issues of identity are addressed through reconstituting the disease-identity and the identity of its stakeholders (the people living with HIV/AIDS, the institutional, organizational, and community-based stakeholders). As we search for equitable and effective solutions to deal with the global pandemic, grassroots organizations and INGOs play a critical role in the discursive representation of the disease and those affected.

Organizationally, the three INGOs are consistent in how they target their publics and in the objectives that they construct for their publics. ActionAid's website focuses on a wide spectrum of issues and appears to target issue activists with a concern for social justice. The Alliance website focuses on community mobilization and participatory action by appealing to volunteers and those interested in engaging with HIV/AIDS within their communities. Avert's website is informational and targets a range of publics from those affected by HIV/AIDS to researchers, policy makers, and organizers. Below we (a) examine the INGOs textual discourse critiqued along the two themes and (b) identify specific strengths and challenges for each INGO.

POWER

Avert's website represents HIV/AIDS as an issue of structural power defined by an imbalance of information and knowledge among vulnerable populations. In contrast, the Alliance website represents HIV/AIDS as a problem of insufficient (infrastructural) community development. ActionAid's website constructs HIV/AIDS as an issue of social justice. The Avert website reveals the lowest display of power as a social justice issue while the Alliance website implicitly acknowledges power as a social justice issue but downplays the need for structural changes through direct political action and power redistribution. Predominantly, the focus on community solidarity and community mobilization serves to normalize the discourse and push social justice concerns to the periphery of the community, thus marginalizing these concerns. The Alliance website targets multiple stakeholders to articulate locally created knowledge frameworks. It is particularly sensitive to the global/local tensions among diverse (international or national) stakeholder groups as well as the individual (local, community) opinion leaders. Avert's strategies are primarily informational, but the discourse on the website eschews binary constructions of victimization.

Alliance's focus on community mobilization and solidarity is a good start, but it papers over many of the pathologies associated with HIV/AIDS that originate in the inequitable power distribution within local communities. Indeed its focus on community mobilization may silence the various kinds of advocacy, confrontation, and conflict that are needed to change the community and reduce power- and social-inequality. Focusing on community solidarity can direct attention away from inequitable power distributions that are the source of many HIV/AIDS problems. Part of the challenge might be to balance social activism and communitarianism to achieve social equity within communities. For Alliance's website, emancipatory power lies in its ability to engage the tensions of calling upon individual mobilization and political action. Its challenge is to critically scrutinize its tactics and ensure that they embody meaningful agency for women and empower them within the context of their lived experiences.

IDENTITY

Although ActionAid recognizes the role of identity in constituting stigmatizing differences, in defining the parameters of the issue, the site also situates women in disempowering gender roles. Its website acknowledges that society marginalizes the infected who often "suffer social discrimination and distancing. They also shoulder the blame for the infection while their families are ostracized" (D'Silva, Futrell, Jayasri and Gohain 2008: 78). The infected become characterized as the untouchables of our age (Nardi 1990). In ActionAid's case, it would be helpful to articulate strategies that address the social forces that reify gendered identities such that women can exercise control over their own sexual relations.

For Alliance's website, mitigating the detrimental impact of identity and differences on prevention, treatment, care, and support is a fundamental part of the solution. By emphasizing the role of culture in addressing the international dimensions of HIV/AIDS discourse, Alliance's strategic approach recognizes that while discriminatory practices prevalent in society are an endemic problem, their existence is also a site for re-envisioning strategic solutions.

For Avert's website, identity is represented through the lens of stigmatizing differences. While several pages are devoted to discussing AIDS-related stigma, we find that the site, however, does not effectively cover laws and countries that criminalize homosexuality, thereby silencing the voices of (and stigmatizing) homosexuals and those infected. Since its framework does not critique the ideological foundations manifesting in stigma, the Avert website is voiceless about the legal, governmental discourse surrounding this key marginalized public. This silence is one challenge the website could address.

Implications for Academics

Our study is an exemplar of how a comparative analysis of mediated strategic communications can contribute to building effective models for health communication research and practice. Furthermore, our INGO website analysis suggests that the lenses of power and identity can be usefully applied in future research regarding the public health context of HIV/AIDS. This chapter contributes to international public relations scholarship by providing insights that can be applied in future studies involving cross-cultural stakeholder management and issue representation. Given the relevance of new media and web-based platforms as well as mobile communication technologies in public health initiatives in developing countries and regions such as India, future research can focus on extending these findings to mobile communications in a range of contexts such as rural regions, marginalized or stigmatized populations. It can also build discourses that counter and contradict harmful community norms (for example, in female infanticide, child marriage, and maternal health).

Implications for Health Practitioners

Our textual analysis of HIV/AIDS representation identifies individual strengths and shortcomings of mediated strategic communication on the INGO websites. We offer the following recommendations to health practitioners that combine the strengths and address limitations of the websites analyzed. First, ActionAid's website embraces a wide range of issues that raise the concern of issue competition where different issues compete for the attention of activist publics. Practitioners, especially NGOs that are ideological and not issue-based, should design objectives and strategies that keep the clarity and specificity of focus in representing issues relating to HIV/AIDS.

Second, our study cautions that the strength of the dominant discourse of community mobilization and participatory action on Alliance's website should not become an excuse for shying away from raising issues related to power and identity imbalances within communities. Communities strongly prefer consensus and harmony. This preference can impede addressing critical power related issues. We suggest that practitioners recommending community-based and participatory strategies should be conscious of the need to integrate tactics of conflict and activism to illuminate disempowering community narratives. Third, Avert's website targets active and aware publics with comprehensive information on HIV/AIDS through tactics ranging from interactive quizzes to personal stories. We recommend that practitioners represent objective, biomedical information on HIV/AIDS with subjective, lived experiences that speak toward meaningful empowerment to successfully integrate objective and subjective forms of knowledge that articulate empowered forms of role-identity for individuals in their communities.

Conclusion

This examination of HIV/AIDS issue representation on INGO websites utilizing the themes of power and identity provide a framework to understand how discursive content of the websites constructs the epidemic, the affected publics, and ultimately, its solutions. Through the analysis of the three INGOs, our chapter foregrounds how political, socio-cultural, and economic conditions are imbued in the micro-practices of power and identity that define the communicative relationship building tactics presented on the websites of the INGOs. Future studies can extend the generalizability of our findings through multiple methods including interviews, observations, and surveys with practitioners, website designers, and key stakeholders sampled across a range of INGOs. Our chapter adds to the body of literature addressing HIV/AIDS as a cultural phenomenon that demands that the various contexts of the pandemic be explored at both the global and the local levels (Airhihenbuwa, Makinwa and Obregon 2000). Indeed, our analysis contributes to and extends the call to apply international and intercultural perspectives in public relations toward relationship-building strategies so as to find synergies in dialogue between stakeholders (Sriramesh and Vercic 2003) that help us formulate inclusive and dialogic forms of communicative action.

References

ActionAid. 2010. *Delivering the 2010 Target: Financing Universal Access to HIV and AIDS Treatment.* Available at: http://www.actionaid.org/assets/pdf/delivering2010target.pdf [accessed on February 20, 2010].

Agarwal, V. and Buzzanell, P.M. 2008. Trialectics of migrant and global representation: Real, imaginary, and online spaces of empowerment in Cyber*mohalla*. *Western Journal of Communication*, 72, 331–48.

Airhihenbuwa, C.O., Makinwa, B. and Obregon, R. 2000. Toward a new communication framework for HIV/AIDS. *Journal of Health Communication*, 5(supplement), 101–11.

Alliance. 2010. *Resources*. Available at: www.aidsalliance.org [accessed on February 20, 2010].

Alonzo, A.A. and Reynolds, N.R. 1992. *Stigma, HIV & AIDS: An Exploration and Elaboration of the Illness Trajectory Surrounding HIV Infection and AIDS.* Available at http://www.eric.ed.gov/ERICDocs/data/ericdocs2sql/content_storage_01/0000019b/80/13/f5/90.pdf [accessed on February 20, 2010].

Appadurai, A. 2001. *Globalization.* Durham, NC: Duke University Press.

Avert. 2010. *AIDS and HIV Information.* Available at: www.avert.org [accessed on February 21, 2010].

Bardhan, N. 2002. Accounts from the field: A public relations perspective on global AIDS/HIV. *Journal of Health Communication*, 7, 221–44.

Curtin, P.A. and Gaither, T.K. 2007. *International Public Relations: Negotiating Culture, Identity, and Power.* Thousand Oaks, CA: Sage.

D'Silva, M.U., Futrell, A., Jayasri, A. and Gohain, Z. 2008. Communicating HIV/AIDS through folk theater and art: Examples from India. In M.U. D'Silva, J.L. Hart and K.L. Walker (eds.), *HIV/AIDS: Prevention and Health Communication.* Tyne: Cambridge Scholars Publication, 78–91.

Fairclough, N. 1992. *Discourse and Social Change.* Cambridge: Polity Press.

Farmer, P. 1994. AIDS-talk and the constitution of cultural models. *Social Science and Medicine*, 38, 801–9.

Flyvvbjerg, G. 2006. Five misunderstandings about case-study research. *Qualitative Inquiry*, 12, 219–43.

Fortenberry, J.D., McFarlane, M., Bleakley, A., Bull, S., Fishbein, M., Grimley, D.M., Malotte, C.K. and Stoner B.P. 2002. Relationships of stigma and shame to gonorrhea and HIV screening. *American Journal of Public Health*, 92, 378–81.

Frey, L., Pearce, B., Pollack, M., Aartz, M. and Murphy B. 1996. Looking for social justice in all the wrong places: On a communication approach to social justice. *Communication Studies*, 47, 110–27.

Goffman, G. 1959. *The Presentation of Self in Everyday Life.* New York, NY: Doubleday.

Goffman, G. 1961. *Asylums: Essays on the Social Situation of Mental Patients and Other Inmates.* Garden City, NY: Anchor Books.

Goffman, G. 1963. *Stigma: Notes on the Management of Spoiled Identity.* New York, NY: Doubleday.

Hall, S. 1980. Cultural studies: Two paradigms. *Media, Culture, and Society*, 2, 57–72.

Harter, L.M., Edwards, A., McClanahan, A., Hopson, M.C. and Carson-Stern, E. 2004. Organizing for survival and social change: The case of streetwise. *Communication Studies*, 55, 407–24.

Herek, G.M., Capitanio, J.P. and Widaman, K.F. 2002. HIV-related stigma and shameto gonorrhea and HIV screening. *American Journal of Public Health*, 92, 378–81.

Holtz, S. 1996. *Communication and Technology: The Complete Guide to Using Technology for Organizational Communication*. Chicago, IL: Lawrence Ragan Communication.

Huang, Y. 2000. The personal influence model and Gao Guanxi in Taiwan Chinese public relations. *Public Relations Review*, 26, 216–39.

Keck, M.E. and Sikkink, K. 1998. *Activists Beyond Borders*. Ithaca, NY: Cornell University Press.

Khagram, S., Riker, J.V. and Sikkink, K. 2002. From Santiago to Seattle: Transnational advocacy groups restructuring world politics. In S. Khagram, J.V. Riker and K. Sikkink (eds), *Restructuring World Politics: Transnational Social Movements, Networks, and Norms*. Minneapolis, MN: University of Minnesota Press, 3–22.

Motion, J. and Weaver, K.C. 2005. A discourse perspective for critical public relations research: Life sciences network and the battle for truth. *Journal of Public Relations Research*, 17, 49–67.

Nardi, P.M. 1990. AIDS and obituaries: The perpetuation of stigma in the press. In D.A. Feldman (ed.) *Culture and AIDS*. New York: Praeger, 29–44.

Papa, M.J., Auwal, M.A. and Singhal, A. 1997. Organizing for social change within concertive control systems: Member identification, empowerment, and the masking of discipline. *Communication Monographs*, 64, 219–49.

Parker, R. and Aggleton, P. 2003. HIV and AIDS-related stigma and discrimination: A conceptual framework and implications for action. *Social Science and Medicine*, 57, 13–24.

Patton, M.Q. 2001. *Qualitative Research and Evaluation Methods*, 3rd Edition. Thousand Oaks, CA: Sage.

Scott, A. 2009. Illness meanings of AIDS among women with HIV: Merging immunology and life experience. *Qualitative Health Research*, 19, 454–65.

Shumate, M., Fulk, J. and Monge, P.R. 2005. Predictors of the international HIV/AIDS INGO network over time. *Human Communication Research*, 31, 482–510.

Shumate, M. and Pike, J. 2006. Trouble in a geographically distributed virtual network organization: Organizing tensions in continental direct action network. *Journal of Computer-Mediated Communication*, 11, 802–24.

Sriramesh, K. and Vercic, D. 2003. A theoretical framework for global public relations research and practice. In K. Sriramesh and D. Vercic (eds), *The Global Public Relations Handbook*. Mahwah, NJ: Lawrence Erlbaum Associates, 1–19.

Sriramesh, K. and White, J. 1992. Societal cultural and public relations. In J.E. Grunig (ed.), *Excellence in Public Relations and Communication Management*. Hillsdale, NJ: Lawrence Erlbaum, 597–614.

Taylor, M. 2001. International public relations: Opportunities and challenges for the 21st century. In R.L. Heath (ed.), *Handbook of Public Relations*. Thousand Oaks, CA: Sage, 629–38.

Whitehill, H.C. 2009. *Avert Trustees Report and Accounts for the Year Ended March* 31, 2009. Available at: http://www.avert.org/media/pdfs/AVERT-Accounts-2009.pdf [accessed March 9, 2010].

Williams, R. 1961. *The Long Revolution*. London: Chatto and Windus.

Yearbook of International Organizations 2009a. ActionAid. In *Yearbook of International Organizations*, Vol. 1A, Union of International Associations.

Yearbook of International Organizations 2009b. International HIV/AIDS Alliance. In *Yearbook of International Organizations*, Vol. 1A, Union of International Associations.

Zaharna, R.S. 2000. Intercultural communication and international public relations: Exploring parallels. *Communication Quarterly*, 48, 85–100.

Zaharna, R.S. 2001. "In-awareness" approach to international public relations. *Public Relations Review*, 27, 135–48.

5 *Managing Sexual Health and Related Stigma through Electronic Learning Environments*

CANDY J. NOLTENSMEYER, SARA PETERS, REBECCA J. MEISENBACH AND HEATHER EASTMAN-MUELLER

Introduction

The University of Missouri (MU) sexual health education website, known as {s}health, (see shealth.missouri.edu) was a challenging media health intervention to develop. We begin this chapter by providing background information about the sexual health climate in which this project was produced. Next, we delve into development of the {s}health website by introducing:

a) innovations using peer-to-peer learning;
b) implementation difficulties encountered; and
c) promotion strategies used.

Once the challenges of website construction have been revealed, we present a theoretical framework for providing sexual health knowledge and resources to college students, an overview of the measures developed to assess stigma-related attitudes toward Sexually Transmitted Infections (STIs) after exposure to the website, as well as preliminary findings. Then, implications for academics and health practitioners are offered. Finally, future directions are discussed such as mobile applications, diversity initiatives, and further research on tools to teach media literacy through deconstruction examples.

This chapter works to demonstrate some of the ways in which research, theory, and application can inform one another through an interdisciplinary approach to developing interactive, web-based attitude and behavior interventions. In addition, the project discussed in this chapter represents an in-progress exemplar of current communication and health research being used to enhance sexual health attitudes and practices of university students.

According to the Centers for Disease Control and Prevention (CDC 2009), sexually active adolescents aged 15–19 years and young adults aged 20–24 years are at a higher risk of acquiring STIs than are older adults. This risk in part is due to a combination of behavioral, biological, and cultural issues younger people encounter while attending college. College students are in the midst of what Arnett (2000) defines as emerging adulthood, a period of extended adolescence that individuals in their late teens through their twenties go through in which they encounter profound change. During this emerging adulthood life stage, college students are more likely to engage in a variety of sexual experiences, including unprotected sex, due to diminished parental surveillance and increased independence from normative expectations (Arnett 2000). Investigating risky sexual behaviors in college students is a priority given the high rates of newly diagnosed STIs and unintended pregnancies (Centers for Disease Control and Prevention [CDC] 2009, Kost, Henshaw and Carlin 2010).

In a study frequently cited by a CDC-funded public awareness campaign, as many as one in two sexually active persons will contract an STI by age 25 (Weinstock, Berman, and Cates 2004). In particular, the US state of Missouri is at or below the national averages for most STI categories (Cates et al. 2004). In a 2009 survey of MU students, 70 percent (n=863) reported engaging in sexual activity in the last 30 days, and of those, 42 percent did not use a barrier method (Eastman-Mueller 2009). The {s}health website was created by MU students and faculty to address this sexual-risk taking environment.

STIs at a University

The University of Missouri is centrally located between Kansas City and St. Louis in Columbia, Missouri. With a city population of 100,733, the University annually provides higher education to more than one-third of the state's college-bound high school graduates. In Fall 2010, the University had a record enrollment of more than 32,000 students, representing every Missouri county, every state, and more than 100 countries. Additionally, 11 colleges and universities are within a 50-mile radius.

In Fall 2009, the fourth author surveyed 935 MU students, ages 18 to 24, about sexual health issues. Results showed moderate to high levels of STI knowledge; specifically, 93 percent (n = 721) agreed alcohol consumption is associated with higher rates of STIs among this population, 82 percent (n = 636) reported STIs, if left untreated, can cause some forms of cancer, and 87 percent (n = 670) agreed that at least half of new HIV infections in the United States are contracted by individuals under the age of 25. Additionally, 93 percent (n = 608) felt it was important to know a partner's sexual history, and 88 percent (n = 567) reported that a partner's sexual history would influence their decision to engage in sexual activity with the partner.

Although students seemed to understand the seriousness of contracting an STI, 31 percent (n = 204) of students did not feel comfortable asking their partner if they had been tested for an STI. When asked what concerns students had when deciding to obtain STI testing, 66 percent (n = 425) reported fear of receiving positive test results as the number one barrier to their decision to get tested. Additionally, 51 percent (n = 330) were afraid of what people might think, 48 percent (n = 311) were concerned about test result confidentiality, and 46 percent (n = 300) reported the testing expense was a contributing factor in their behavior choices. Of all the students surveyed, 84 percent reported they had engaged in consensual sexual activity at some point in their life. Forty-two percent (n = 274) of sexually active respondents reported having been tested for STIs, excluding HIV; only 28 percent had been tested for HIV. The results suggest the need for improved sexual health education regarding testing procedures and a reduction in STI stigma among the MU population to promote the normalization and increased acquisition of STI testing.

Development of an Intervention Website

Despite plenty of evidence about the presence and negative consequences of STIs, the sexual health knowledge, rates of barrier method use, and STI testing among college students remain unsatisfactory, both across the US and at MU. When investigating where MU college students seek health information, 79 percent of students reported using the Internet (Eastman-Mueller 2009). In an effort to capitalize on this finding, a website was conceptualized that would not only promote student learning surrounding sexual health but also build interdisciplinary collaborations campus-wide among students and faculty in order to better address these issues.

Some universities have created websites that provide sexual health information to students; however, most outsource the construction of their websites. One of the best examples of a university-based website is the broadly focused goaskalice.columbia. edu website at Columbia University. The professionally staffed, university-run website answers questions submitted by site visitors about all health issues; one section of the website answers sexual health questions. Much more common are text-focused web-links associated with university student health centers (for example, the human sexuality pages at UNC-Chapel Hill, see also http://campushealth.unc.edu/index.php?option=com_con tent&task=view&id=425&Itemid=94). Some common non-university sexual health sites include sexualhealth.com, teensource.org, and Iwannaknow.org. A hybrid option would be for a university to outsource the creation of its sexual health resources. While this choice can create a very professional look and design, it is very expensive and likely bypasses the opportunity for a peer-to-peer learning environment online.

PEER-TO-PEER LEARNING

The project team wanted to implement interdisciplinary collaborations among both students and faculty. If students are involved in constructing and maintaining the website, they can benefit from synthesizing, evaluating, and communicating information, which in turn promotes a deeper understanding of the subject area (Christiansen and Bell 2010). Thus, having students not only create the content and text of a sexual health website, but also encouraging them to determine the best strategy to present the material to their peers, reinforced learning outside of the classroom. Peer-to-peer learning is well-documented in the literature as a cost-effective learning tool in health promotion practices, as it allows learners to take sociocognitive responsibility for their own learning (Scott et al. 2009) and promotes transferable teamwork and interpersonal skills (Keppell et al. 2006). Sociocognition involves learning through social interaction. Thus, interactivity of the website creates a social environment that promotes the construction of knowledge and could impact a change in behavior, values, and expectations.

Developing an interactive website to support the sexual health needs of college students required a wide range of skills and talents from a team of student-peers and faculty member. Our original team consisted of faculty members from the Department of Communication, University Extension Services, and the Student Health Center, graduate students from the Departments of Computer Engineering, Communication, and Rural Sociology, as well as undergraduates from a wide range of academic majors. These students and faculty members were selected due to their interests, expertise, and skills in web design, statistical analysis, sexual health, stigma theory, and health promotion.

While our overall goal was to communicate sexual health information to students, it was the interactive peer-to-peer design of the website that was to be a unique feature. In basic communication terms, the team was aiming for a transactional process of communication from peer to peer, more so than a one-way transfer of information from the research team to the university students. However, with this transactional process came a number of challenges when it came to actual implementation.

IMPLEMENTATION DIFFICULTIES

As might be expected, creating an interactive web environment using only faculty members and students' talents involved a number of challenges that had to be addressed. First, the high level of student involvement in developing the website generated several issues, including professionalism, time available to work on this project outside of class work, and student knowledge levels. The students that participated in this project were exceptional students who dedicated a lot of time to the project; however, this project was not their primary focus. Most of the undergraduate students were members of a sexual health class called Sexual Health Advocacy and Service Learning. As part of the class they designed various initial modules for the website. In addition, a graduate research assistant was assigned to oversee the undergraduate students' work. Getting these students to attend the larger team meetings to convey their ideas outside of class was challenging. There were times when particular team deadlines were set and not fulfilled due to student coursework and schedules. Most undergraduate students seemed to view their work on the project as class work and did not perceive it as something requiring workforce professionalism. Alternately, this project may have been many students' first experience with a professional project. Managing the project's timetable was sometimes problematic for the many students involved, especially when the project schedule became time sensitive as deadlines drew near. In addition, the undergraduates in the sexual health course were not trained in communication theories and the majority ended up creating traditional reports of information with bullet points that mirrored offerings on other university run websites rather than highly interactive modules.

Furthermore, having a project that focuses on sex was its own difficulty. The website name, "{s}health" was deliberately selected to avoid being blocked by security software and firewalls that block access to sites that have the word "sex" in the title. While we understood that this word gets millions of hits and searches through Google every year, we avoided creating another barrier to accessing accurate information with our somewhat ambiguous title.

Student knowledge levels also impacted the technical website development. We had a number of computer science graduate students applying to work on the project, and we were very fortunate in who we were able to hire with the limited grant funding we received. Yet, understandably, as the interactive elements of the project were developed, the team often would request tasks and outcomes that the graduate students had not yet learned to accomplish. Making the time to learn these new skills significantly slowed down the research project and sometimes resulted in modules that did not look the way the students and faculty had initially designed them. Alternately, sometimes team members changed their minds after seeing designs implemented. Hiring a professional company to (re)generate these elements would have been more efficient, but our project lacked the funding and remained committed to providing learning opportunities for our team members.

On the technical level, our team had unexpected issues getting all Internet browsers to work equally well with the programming of the web page and integrating design we wanted with what was possible. In the initial programming phase our website was functional in one browser (Chrome), however, it did not translate across browser platforms without visual distortions due to the nature of the initial programming. Our graduate student programmers spent a good deal of time trying to make the interactive elements of the web page display and function the same across browsers. These difficulties in display and function may not be unique to {s}health; many professional website designers intentionally "optimize" their programming to work with a particular browser, as the way that different browsers interpret the same computer code results in different looks and feels of a website. During the two years we have been developing this website, smartphone web surfing has become much more common among college students. Mobile phone viewing of websites also impacts the formatting of websites and will likely change many of the ways such websites are programmed.

Finally, we had to manage the constraint of needing our website to be sustainable after our initial start-up grant funding was spent. Elements of the website, such as the Ask Us forums, need to be monitored and updated. Responses to the discussion board were made on a regularly scheduled bi-weekly basis to ensure timeliness and still maintain a reasonable workload for staff. Furthermore, it was clear that managing the html content required a formidable set of skills that the main researchers did not possess. After investigating a variety of options in consultation with university technology staff, the researchers decided to transfer the webpage into a new, easy to use, open source program known as Joomla. The team hopes that in this format, individuals who are not web-design experts will feel comfortable making regular updates to the site. However, the simpler programming may limit the innovative designs. Design experts will still need to be hired occasionally if more complicated new modules are conceptualized.

PROMOTION

In addition to the construction of the website, students had their hands in the promotion of the website as well. While the initial version of the website was being tested, undergraduate students in a communication capstone course were designing proposals for promoting the website to all undergraduate students at the university. Five teams of four to seven undergraduate students each applied communication and public relations theory to create their communication campaign proposals for the website team's consideration. Representatives from the website research team, the university's Sexual Health Advocate Peer Education (SHAPE) program, the Department of Residential Life, and a non-profit community HIV prevention organization listened to formal proposal presentations from the student teams and helped select which proposal to implement. In the end, two of the proposals were selected as winners and portions of each were implemented in the final marketing plan to promote the website. This method benefitted both the students in the capstone course and the website project. The students gained the experience of designing a plan that actually could be implemented on their own campus, integrating classroom theories with real world applications. Simultaneously, the research team got the advantage of having its publicity campaign for the website being designed by members of its target audience–MU undergraduate students.

Such a plan increases student involvement in the project, but again also potentially could limit the final product based on the level of relevant knowledge the students had acquired through their program of study. In addition, the Student Health Center selected the elements that were used from the two winning campaigns in isolation from the communication researchers on the project. This practice of allowing clients to select winning campaigns on their own has been the standard procedure of the capstone course instructor, but by being involved in the implementation of the winning campaigns, the instructor now recognizes the value of having the course instructor consult with the client to guide campaign selection and implementation. In this case, the winning proposals focused heavily on one-time events with some ideas for generating sustained student awareness of the website throughout the academic year. A launch party event generated the most traffic for the website, but return visits were much less frequent. Greater focus on sustained visibility practices in contrast to one-time events is advisable.

Theoretical Framework and Preliminary Findings

With the background of the {s}health website's construction and promotion in place, this chapter now will provide discussion on the theoretical foundation for the design and content used on the site and provide preliminary findings regarding student users' stigma-related attitudes toward STIs and sexual health knowledge. The purpose of the site was to develop an interactive, engaging, evidence-based sexual health website for college students to promote critical analysis and open communication on a variety of sexual health topics and related stigmas.

SEXUAL HEALTH ENGAGEMENT

Development of the learning modules was based on the Theory of Reasoned Action (TRA) by Fishbein and Azjen (2010). A theoretical basis is an important element in the success of an intervention and TRA is one of the more functional models used to depict relationships among behavior, intent, and social norms (Roberto et al. 2007).

According to TRA, an individual's knowledge and attitudes impact both behavioral intentions and actual behavior. Behavior is primarily determined by one's intentions, although other factors such as skills and ability to follow one's intentions also impact behavior (Bleakley et al. 2009). Intention is based on the attitudes and perceptions of what others think and do with regard to performing the behavior (that is, perceived norms), and beliefs about one's ability to perform the behavior when faced with adversity (that is, self-efficacy) (Bleakley et al. 2009). An assumption of this theory is that people make decisions deliberately by taking in information, considering the consequences of engaging in a particular behavior, and reflecting on what they believe their peers' expectations are as the appropriate course of action. In contrast to many other social behavior models, such as the Theory of Planned Behavior (Azjen 1985), the TRA suggests that people do not act spontaneously but are assumed to be rational participants in their decision-making process. Many researchers have argued that when applied to younger adults and risky behavior, this theory does not take into account the influence of emotion (temperament), family, and impulsivity common among this age-group (Gerrand et al. 2008).

However, much of the literature supports the use of TRA to help explain sexual behavior. For example, research has found that social norms and beliefs impact the onset of sexual behavior (Carvajal et al. 1999, Flores, Tschann, and Marin 2002, Gillmore, Archibald and Morrison 2002) and abstinence from sexual intercourse (Collazo 2004). Alternatively, Robinson et al. (1998) showed that attitudes and efficacy expectations predicted engaging in sexual intercourse. Unger, Molina and Teran (2000) found that perceived consequences influenced individuals' desire to engage in sexual risk behaviors. We enlisted TRA to test the efficacy of an interactive website on young adults' sexual behavior and STI stigma attitudes. Based on this theory, interactive modules were created to encourage students to critically investigate their sexual health values and stigma attitudes, and acquire accurate health information in a confidential manner to promote desirable health outcomes.

Much of the content on the {s}health website contains information on a variety of topics and message delivery. For example, the site has an instructional video on how to properly use a protective barrier device. Virtual maps allow users to retrieve directions to and information about local STI testing centers, free safety products locations on campus, and resources for health education and advocacy programs. The fast facts and the interactive games sections were designed to promote knowledge acquisition in a fun, user-friendly manner. Research supports the efficacy of internet- and cell phone-based or computerized interventions (Moskowitz, Melton and Owczarzak 2009, Lightfoot, Comulada and Stover 2007, Ybarra and Bull 2007, Noar, Black and Pierce 2009). In addition to interactions possible through the website, we have transferred many of the above-mentioned modules into a mobile application. This feature allows individuals to text anonymous questions to the site and determine their real-time proximity to the nearest sexual health resource in the Columbia area.

To address the attitudinal construct within the TRA model, the site hosts the "Sex Word of the Day" campaign (SWD). This campaign enlisted peer educators to develop words that begin with the stem "sex." Each word corresponds with a sex positive, empowerment message. For example, *sex*pression is communicating with your partner about barrier protection, testing, and sexual boundaries. These SWD messages were designed to promote cultural acceptance of open communication surrounding sex. To further promote messaging normalcy, the SWD Campaign materials include photographs of our community and campus.

Peer expectations and perception of social norms were gauged by providing individuals the opportunity to pose a question to a peer educator/healthcare professional. In a randomized control study of computerized interventions for HIV prevention, adolescents who were exposed to interventions using their computers were significantly less likely to engage in sexual activity and have fewer sexual partners than both individuals involved in small group interventions and the control group (Lightfoot et al. 2007). Another study supporting the use of innovative technology to promote sexual health was a study conducted by Moskowitz et al. (2009) where counselors used instant messaging (IM) to counsel a random sample of men who have sex with men in real-time through a sexual health website. Results showed that approximately 90 percent of the 279 message sessions

Figure 5.1   Interactive Zone Webpage of {s}health
Source: Screenshot Courtesy of University of Missouri Student Health Center.

contained sexual health information with 43 percent of the IM sessions containing information about HIV/STI testing and 39 percent addressing risk-taking behaviors. On our website, real-time chats with a student blogger and video peer testimonials about different sexual health topics are features designed to normalize and de-stigmatize sexual health communication through similar technology.

The Interactive Zone or "Choose Your Own Adventure" module was designed by college students to enable their peers to navigate through realistic, potentially stigmatizing scenarios (for example, alcohol use, communicating about barrier methods, getting a positive STI test) and to experience potential consequences of their decisions without taking the risk in the real world (see Figure 5.1). Our hope is that, if we expose students to realistic outcomes, they can then weigh the benefits and consequences to determine the best plan of action to overcome challenges faced in their daily lives. These interactive modules provide a communicative bridge in which students can actively participate in stigmatizing scenarios through a preferred medium.

It is important to note that the concept of interactivity has been disputed in terms of where to locate interactivity itself. Some researchers position interactivity in the user as it is dependent on the users' skill to manipulate it (Bucy 2004); others place interactivity within the medium (Sundar 2004). However, we argue that interactivity should reside in the communication process. Interactivity is thus built upon connection between the user and the medium and the resulting interactions (Kim and Stout 2010). This definition guided the overall design of the sexual health website and more specifically, the content.

STIGMA MANAGEMENT COMMUNICATION

Although the site was primarily developed using university students' preferences for seeking sexual health information electronically as an effective route to increase sexual health knowledge and to promote dialogue surrounding perceived STI risk, a secondary goal was to educate students about stigma management communication (SMC). Our hope in developing the interactive zone scenarios was to not only provide students with opportunities to learn from realistic stigmatizing sexual health situations but to also analyze students' decisions in these situations.

Research shows that stigma is a very powerful deterrent to acquisition of STI screening, getting STI treatment, and communicating with partners about sexual history (Fortenberry et al. 2002, Kalichman and Simbayi 2003). Barriers to testing and communication may contribute to the high prevalence of STIs among this population (Fortenberry et al. 2002). The association of STIs with moral judgments and shame has been clearly documented in the literature (Lichtenstein 2003). As a result, patients frequently report fear of being stigmatized in the event of receiving a positive STI diagnosis, which in turn creates a high level of anxiety of being labeled and socially ostracized (Lichtenstein 2003).

Therefore, our research team wanted to increase the knowledge of STI prevention and risk reduction/STI stigma management techniques by exposing college students to the {s}health website. To do so, some website modules focused particularly on making site visitors aware of a variety of stigma management strategies discussed in Meisenbach's (2010) SMC model and positive messages about getting tested. The SMC model is being used as a framework to investigate how students' exposure to the website may influence their stigma-related STI attitudes. The model posits that individuals' attitudes toward (a) accepting or challenging public understanding of the stigma and (b) accepting or challenging that the stigma applies to them personally will predict what strategies they will use to manage a stigma message. Communication strategies used to manage stigma include accepting, avoiding, evading responsibility, reducing offensiveness, denying, and ignoring/displaying the stigmatizing characteristic.

Two measures were developed to measure stigma-related attitudes: the self-stigma acceptance scale and stigma activism scale. These measures were created in response to a lack of existing scales that account for, (a) whether an individual chooses to accept or challenge if the stigma applies to them personally and (b) whether an individual chooses to accept or challenge the public's understanding of the stigma. An 11-item self-stigma acceptance scale and a ten-item stigma activism scale were tested for reliability in a pilot study of 171 students. Both measures were found to have strong reliability (five items of the self-stigma acceptance scale had a Cronbach's alpha of .75; the stigma activism scale had a Cronbach's alpha of .84 with all ten items included).

The STI self-stigma acceptance scale reflects an individual's attitude about the extent to which they perceive that an STI stigma applies to them. For the measures, stigma is defined for research participants as being discredited or demeaned by others because of a particular characteristic. The measure uses a 4-point Likert-type scale (Strongly Agree, Agree, Disagree, or Strongly Disagree) and includes statements such as: "I would feel stigmatized if I had an STI," "I would want to challenge anyone who might suggest that I am somehow dirty if I have an STI," and "I would accept that others might see me as having poor morals if I had an STI."

The STI stigma activism scale indicates an individual's attitude toward accepting or challenging others' perceptions of STI stigma. Stigma activism focuses on how an individual perceives others' views of STIs as well as their level of activism. The measure uses a 4-point Likert-type scale (Strongly Agree, Agree, Disagree, or Strongly Disagree) and includes statements such as: "I think it is appropriate for the general public to view having an STI as an indication of poor morals," and "I want to stop people from treating someone with an STI as being unworthy of respect" (reverse coded).

The research team is currently testing the predicted relationships among self-stigma acceptance, stigma activism, and stigma management communication strategies. The team is also testing the impact of exposure to the website's stigma management content on these variables and relationships. The pilot study findings revealed that individuals' attitudes toward a stigma's public applicability to them (self stigma) and their attitude toward challenging or maintaining others' perceptions of the stigma (stigma activism) predicted their use of the following SMC strategies: accepting $F(2, 183) = 19.56$, $p < .001$, evading responsibility for $F(2, 183) = 5.52$, $p < .05$, and denying $F(2, 183) = 8.14$, $p < .001$. Analysis found that the more a person strongly challenges self stigma and public stigmatizing of STIs, the less likely the person will use the accepting strategy, $F(2, 183) = 19.56$, $p < .001$. Likewise, the more a person strongly disagrees with self stigma, the less likely the person will attempt to evade responsibility for the stigma; however, the more a person strongly agrees with public STI stigmatizing the more likely the person will choose the evading responsibility strategy, $F(2, 183) = 5.52$, $p < .05$. As for the denying strategy, the more a person strongly accepts self stigma and publicly challenges stigma, the more likely the person will use a denial strategy, $F(2, 183) = 8.14$, $p < .001$. The pilot study also showed that individuals who challenge public STI stigma have a greater self efficacy in practicing safe sex, $r(186) = .291$, $p < .001$, $r^2 = .08$. Thus, a person who is more likely to strongly challenge others' stigma attitudes will be more confident in their ability to practice safe sex.

The research team is currently analyzing data collected from the main experiment in which undergrad students were randomly assigned to intervention and control conditions, where the intervention condition was working through 15–20 minutes of modules on the {s}health website. These participants completed a survey including the SMC measures, self-esteem measures, and a variety of sexual knowledge, attitude, and behavior measures immediately following the experiment and again approximately one month later. The results should provide valuable initial information about the impact of the website on sexual health and stigma attitudes and behaviors.

Summary of Lessons Learned (thus far)

This project began with a coincidence of the fourth author's interest in capitalizing on student preference for the Internet as a source of sexual health information with the third author's desire to find real world opportunities for her students to implement communication theory in practice and to test her theory of stigma management communication. As such, the interdisciplinary project team has been learning along the way. In particular, we have learned to expect the unexpected with technology. Although web design may sound technical, in our experience it is equal parts art and science, and as such is difficult to predict and manage without unanticipated setbacks. Theoretically, we have learned the challenges in and importance of designing modules and messages that are guided by theory. Many of the undergraduate students who were designing initial modules were familiar with the sexual health content, but were not well trained in

TRA or SMC theory. Keeping the theories in the forefront as each interaction is designed is essential to effective projects. We will continue learning lessons as we move forward.

Implications for Academics

Beyond our lessons learned, the project has several implications for academics. From an instructor perspective/standpoint, student learning occurred throughout the entire process by challenging students on the project team to research reputable sexual and reproductive health information and to convert it into an interactive, theory guided format to promote learning among their peers. Skills students refined as a result of working on this project included critical thinking, problem solving, communication, team work, and negotiation. This model can be applied to service learning projects or to a problem-based learning module in the classroom. The project itself can and is already being used by instructors at several higher education institutions as an example of activism and social media or as a route for teaching students in a sexual health course the content they need to know.

The project findings are preliminary, but they do have some implications for research. Most specifically, the pilot test data suggests that fuller testing will provide support for the modeled relationships between self stigma and stigma advocacy attitudes and the stigma management communication strategies articulated in SMC theory (Meisenbach 2010). It also suggests a relationship between challenging public STI stigmas and safe sex related self efficacy. The project team has gathered further data to further examine these preliminary findings and in particular to determine whether exposure to website modules has an impact on stigma attitudes and SMC strategy use.

Implications for Health Practitioners

This project could also be applied to the healthcare setting. Healthcare practitioners such as mental health and primary care professionals could incorporate the website as a supplementary or additional patient education resource tool. Frequently, and throughout the healthcare system, providers are very limited in time and resources. A healthcare provider could use this resource to answer sexual health questions the client/patient may have after their appointment by assessing the anonymous question posting section. Furthermore, we hope that the website demonstrates interactive yet efficient ways of engaging students in discussions of sexual health. We hope that other sexual health providers will use this project as a springboard for their own innovative websites.

Future Directions

We propose to develop and expand our university's sexual health education website, {s}health, in various directions in the future. The next steps in expanding the website include assessing the effectiveness of the existing modules; designing additional planned interactive applications, providing individualized feedback to site visitors, incorporating ways to reach more diverse audiences, supplying multiple learning tools for media literacy and, lastly, proposing evaluation tools to improve the website in the future.

MOBILE APPLICATIONS

The biggest current innovation that complements the {s}health website is the development of a mobile phone application (app) interface. In today's changing media landscape, students are among the most frequent users of smart phones, as almost half of all iPhone users are under the age of 34 (Kellogg 2010). This platform will also allow for the student user to easily send the {s}health website's content to their friends. For example, using the mobile app, student users could forward their friends the "Sex Word of the Day" and could locate the closest sexual health services, including where free condoms are available, where to access emergency contraception, and STI and pregnancy testing centers while out in the community making choices about their sexual health. The {s}health app was made available to students in January, 2012.

DIVERSITY INITIATIVES

Another future endeavor in the expansion of the {s}health website will be to incorporate content features that will appeal to a culturally diverse audience. One of the ways to accomplish this task is to allow the user to select the language the website content is formatted in. Having this language choice is important on a college campus such as MU given that 1,948 international students attended Mizzou in 2010, representing over 100 different countries (International Center University of Missouri 2010). Previous research has also shown that making health information adaptable to international students is important because they may vary in their degree of sexual communication and level of disclosure as compared to domestic students. For instance, sex is a taboo topic in traditional Chinese culture (Gao, Lu, Shi, Sun and Cai 2001); thus, discussions regarding sexual matters with family members are a rare occurrence. Instead, Chinese students tend to rely on the public media as their primary source of sexual health information, a finding consistent in other nations as well (Porter 1993).

MEDIA LITERACY

Lastly, we propose providing media literacy opportunities on the site by posting mainstream sexual media messages that users can analyze. Website visitors will watch a video or listen to a song and then be asked a series of questions that will pop up onto the screen following the media message, encouraging them to think critically about the messages contained within the particular video or song they recently saw or heard. By using multiple modes to display sexual messages, we hope to reach a more diverse scope of learners and educate them on how to better identify the sexual messages and values contained within the popular media they are likely to be exposed to on a regular basis.

It will also be important to evaluate the website using tools such as a frequency counter to tally how often the website is accessed and which pages generate the most traffic. Likewise, a feedback button allowing direct comments from site visitors could help improve the website.

Conclusion

This chapter began by providing information about the sexual risk-taking environment that inspired this project. Then, we explained the development of the {s}health website by introducing innovations of using peer-to-peer learning, implementation difficulties encountered, and promotion. We then presented our theoretical framework for providing sexual health knowledge and resources to college students, an overview of the measures developed to assess stigma-related attitudes toward STIs after exposure to the website, and some preliminary research findings. Finally, implications for academics and health practitioners and future directions were discussed.

Overall, it is our hope that using interactive technology to promote sexual health among college students will effectively engage them in learning about and understanding their own sexual health practices. We as researchers also hope that this project and specifically this chapter will help us and others develop similar and improved electronic learning environments focused on issues of health communication and practice.

References

Arnett, J.J. 2000. Emerging adulthood: A theory of development from the late teens through the twenties. *American Psychologist*, 55(5), 469–80.

Azjen, I. 1985. From intentions to actions: A theory of planned behavior. In J. Kuhl and J. Beckman (eds), *Action Control from Cognition to Behavior*. Heidelberg: Springer.

Bleakley, A., Fishbein, M., Hennessy, M. and Jordan, A. 2009. How sources of sexual information relate to adolescents' beliefs about sex. *American Journal of Health Behavior*, 33(1), 37–48.

Bucy, E.P. 2004. Interactivity in society: Locating an elusive concept. *The Information Society*, 20, 373–83.

Carvajal, S.C., Parcel, G.S., Basen-Engquist, K., Banspach, S.W., Coyle, K.K., Kirby, D. and Chan, W. 1999. Psychosocial predictors of delay of first sexual intercourse by adolescents. *Health Psychology*, 18(5), 443–52. doi: 10.1037/0278-6133.18.5.443

Cates, J.R., Herndon, N.L., Schulz, S.L. and Darroch, J.E. 2004. *Our Voices, Our Lives, Our Futures: Youth and Sexually Transmitted Diseases*. Chapel Hill, NC: University of North Carolina at Chapel Hill School of Journalism and Mass Communication.

Centers for Disease Control and Prevention. 2009. *Sexually Transmitted Disease Surveillance* [Online: Centers for Disease Control and Prevention]. Available at: www.cdc.gov/std/stats09/adol [accessed: 31 August 2011].

Christiansen, A. and Bell, A. 2010. Peer learning partnerships: Exploring the experience of pre-registration nursing students. *Journal of Clinical Nursing*, 19, 803–10.

Clayman, M.L., Manganello, J.A., Viswanath, K., Hesse, B.W. and Arora, N.K. 2010. Providing health messages to Hispanics/Latinos: Understanding the importance of language, trust in health information sources, and media use. *Journal of Health Communication*, 15(3), 252–63.

Collazo, A.A. 2004. Theory-based predictors of intention to engage in precautionary sexual behavior among Puerto Rican high school adolescents. *Journal of HIV/AIDS Prevention in Children and Youth*, 6, 91–120.

Eastman-Mueller, H. 2009. *Sexual Health Survey*. Unpublished manuscript, Student Health Center, University of Missouri, Columbia.

Fishbein, M. and Ajzen, I. 2010. *Predicting and Changing Behavior: The Reasoned Action Approach*. New York: Psychology Press.

Flores, E., Tschann, J.M. and Marin, B.V. 2002. Latina adolescents: Predicting intention to have sex. *Adolescence*, 37, 659–79.

Fortenberry, J.D., McFarlane, M., Bleakley, A., Bull, S., Fishbein, M., Grimley, D.M., Malotte, C.K. and Stoner, B.P. 2002. Relationships of stigma and shame to gonorrhea and HIV screening. *American Journal of Public Health*, 92, 378–81.

Gao, Y., Lu, Z.Z., Shi, R., Sun, X.Y. and Cai, Y. 2001. AIDS and sex education for young people in China. *Reproduction, Fertility and Development*, 13, 729–37.

Gerrard, M., Gibbons, F.X., Houlihan, A.E., Stock, M.L. and Pomeroy, E.A. 2008. A dual-process approach to health risk decision-making: The prototype willingness model. *Developmental Review*, 28, 29–61.

Gillmore, M.R., Archibald, M.E. and Morrison, D.M. 2002. Teen sexual behavior: Applicability of the theory of reasoned action. *Journal of Marriage and Family*, 64, 885–97.

International Center University of Missouri. 2010. Fast facts on MU international students. University of Missouri website. [Online: International Center University of Missouri]. Available at: http://international.missouri.edu/documents/students.pdf [accessed: 20 July 2011].

Kalichman, S.C. and Simbayi, L.C. 2003. HIV testing attitudes, AIDS stigma, and voluntary HIV counseling and testing in a black township in Cape Town, South Africa. *Sexually Transmitted Infections*, 79(6), 442–7.

Kellogg, D. 2010, June. iPhone vs. Android. The Nielsen Company. Available at: http://blog.nielsen.com/nielsenwire/online_mobile/iphone-vs-android [accessed: 20 July 20 2011].

Keppell, M., Au, E., Ma, A. and Chan, C. 2006. Peer learning and learning-oriented assessment in technology-enhanced environments. *Assessment & Evaluation in Higher Education*, 31(4), 453–64.

Kim, H. and Stout, P.A. 2010. The effects of interactivity on information processing and attitude change: Implications for mental health stigma. *Health Communication*, 25, 142–54.

Kost, K., Henshaw, S. and Carlin, L. 2010. *U.S. Teenage Pregnancies, Births and Abortions: National and State Trends by Race and Ethnicity*. New York: Guttmacher Institute.

Kumparak, G. 2010, October. Apple sold 14.1 million iPhones last quarter, over 70 million since launch. *MobileCrunch*. Available at: http://www.mobilecrunch.com [accessed: 20 July 2011].

Lichtenstein, B. 2003. Stigma as a barrier to treatment of sexually transmitted infection in the American Deep South: Issues of race, gender and poverty. *Social Science & Medicine*, 57, 2435–45. doi:10.1016/j.socscimed.2003.08.002

Lightfoot, M., Comulada, W.S. and Stover, G. 2007. Computerized HIV preventive intervention for adolescents: Indications of efficacy. *American Journal of Public Health*, 97(6), 1027–9.

Meisenbach, R.J. 2010. Stigma management communication: A theory and agenda for applied research on how individuals manage moments of stigmatized identity. *Journal of Applied Communication Research*, 38, 268–92.

Moskowitz, D.A., Melton, D. and Owczarzak, J. 2009. PowerON: The use of instant message counseling and the internet to facilitate HIV/STD education and prevention. *Patient education and Counseling*, 77, 20–26.

Murley, B. 2009, May. Is University of Missouri's iPod touch 'requirement' fair? *PBS*. Available at: http://www.pbs.org [accessed: 20 July 2011].

Noar, S.M., Black, H.G., and Pierce, L.B. 2009. Efficacy of computer technology-based HIV prevention interventions: A meta-analysis. *AIDS Care*, 23, 107–15.

Porter, S.B. 1993. Public knowledge and attitudes about AIDS among adults in Calcutta, India. *AIDS Care*, 5, 169–76.

Roberto, A.J., Zimmerman, R.S., Carlyle, K.E. and Abner, E.L. 2007. A computer-based approach to preventing pregnancy, STD, and HIV in rural adolescents. *Journal of Health Communication*, 12, 53–76.

Robinson, K.L., Price, J.H., Thompson, C.L. and Schmalzried, H.D. 1998. Rural junior high school students' risk factors for and perceptions of teen-age parenthood. *Journal of School Health*, 68(8), 334–8.

Scott, P., Castaneda, L., Quick, K. and Linney, J. 2009. Synchronous symmetrical support: A naturalistic study of live online peer-to-peer learning via software videoconferencing. *Interactive Learning Environment*, 17(2), 119–34.

Sundar, S.S. 2004. Theorizing interactivity's effects. *Information Society*, 20, 385–9.

Unger, J.B., Molina, G.B. and Teran, L. 2000. Perceived consequences of teenage childbearing among adolescent girls in an urban sample. *Journal of Adolescent Health*, 26, 205–12.

Weinstock, H., Berman, S. and Cates Jr., W. 2004. Sexually transmitted diseases among American youth: Incidence and prevalence estimates. *Perspectives on Sexual and Reproductive Health*, 36, 6–10.

Ybarra, M.L. and Bull, S.S. 2007. Current trends in internet- and cell phone-based HIV prevention and intervention programs. *Current HIV/AIDS Reports*, 4, 201–7.

6 *Beneficial Participation: Lurking vs. Posting in Online Support Groups*

GALIT NIMROD

Introduction

Using the Internet as a resource for social support in coping with health conditions is usually associated with online peer-to-peer support groups. Health-related Online Support Groups (OSGs) tend to focus on specific conditions (for example, chronic diseases, disabilities, and addictions) and operate through diverse applications such as email lists, chat rooms, or forums/bulletin boards. Compared with other immediate support alternatives (such as telephone hotlines) and face-to-face support groups, online groups have several advantages, including accessibility, anonymity, invisibility and status neutralization, greater individual control over the time and pace of interactions, opportunity for multi-conversing, and opportunity for archival search (Barak 2007, Barak, Boniel-Nissim and Suler, 2008, McKenna and Bargh 2000). These characteristics, along with availability and simplicity of use, may explain the popularity of these OSGs among Internet users (Johnson and Ambrose 2006).

Members of health-related OSGs are typically people who are diagnosed with a health condition, but they may also be undiagnosed individuals concerned about specific symptoms, as well as people caring for loved ones with the condition (Kral 2006). Previous research has demonstrated that people with stigmatized illnesses such as HIV/AIDS or mental illnesses use the Internet for health information and social support significantly more than those with non-stigmatized conditions (Berger, Wagner and Baker 2005, Davison, Pennebaker and Dickerson 2000). Apparently, "having an illness that is embarrassing, socially stigmatizing, or disfiguring leads people to seek the support of others with similar conditions" (Davidson et al. 2000: 213), and online groups enable them to receive support while remaining anonymous and invisible.

The invisibility offered by the OSGs allows for another option that is unique to these groups – "lurking." Members of online groups may be generally divided into "posters" and "lurkers." Posters are members who post messages to other members of the OSG and/or respond to their posts. Lurkers are those who do not interact with other members and simply read others' posts (White and Dorman 2001). Although the prevalence of lurking may vary considerably depending on the health condition and the nature of the specific group, it was estimated that lurkers comprise 46 percent of the membership of health-related OSGs (Nonnecke and Preece 2000). Therefore, lurkers should definitely be taken into consideration when examining the benefits of such groups.

This chapter aims to explore the association between the type of participation in health-related OSGs (that is, posting vs. lurking) and psychological well-being. The chapter is based on a recently completed research project that examined OSGs for people with depression and explored members' participation patterns, interests, and benefits gained from participation. The chapter demonstrates how being *actively* involved in communication can improve the health and well-being of individuals, and provides both theoretical and practical implications regarding Internet-based communicative practices in health contexts.

Literature Review

According to Preece, Nonnecke and Andrews (2004), the main reasons lurkers gave for not actively participating in the OSGs were:

1. lack of need to post and considering reading as sufficient;
2. thinking that posting is not helpful either because they felt they had nothing to offer or because others had already said what they wanted to say;
3. poor usability (that is, technical difficulties with the software);
4. not liking the group dynamics or perceiving it as not matching their needs; and
5. needing to find out more about the group, its norms, and communication style.

The last reason characterizes people who are moderately shy (Finfgeld 2000), and members who are relatively new to the group (White and Dorman 2001). These justifications for lurking suggest that lurkers may become posters with time, and indeed, familiarity with the group and persistent involvement contributes to eventual 'de-lurking' and active participation in the online group life (Rafaeli, Ravid and Soroka 2004).

Nevertheless, there is evidence demonstrating that posters' and lurkers' motivations for joining OSGs are somewhat different. In a study of 375 online MSN groups, Nonnecke, Andrews and Preece (2006) demonstrated that, although both lurkers and posters ranked getting a "general understanding" highly, posters reported higher expectations of the OSG from the start and exhibited higher interest in group interactions. Far more posters reported, for example, that they were interested in participating in conversations, making friends, getting empathic support, and offering their expertise. Similarly, Ridings, Gefen and Arinze (2006) found that lurkers differed significantly from posters in their willingness to give information and exchange social support. They also found that lurkers had less trust than posters in the abilities of other members to answer their questions or give advice, and had more misgivings about the benevolence and integrity of others. This lower level of trust may deter lurkers from active participation in the online groups.

As a result of the different motivations of lurkers and posters and their different views of the OSG, their experience of the group and the benefits they gain may vary as well. There is a growing body of knowledge about the potential benefits of health-related OSGs. These benefits include, among others, information exchange, social support, affect toward the discussion board, opportunity for social comparison, optimism regarding the health condition, increased skill or ability to cope with the condition, improved mood, decreased psychological distress, and strategies to manage stress (for example, Rodgers and Chen 2005, van Uden-Kraan et al. 2009, Wald, Dube and Anthony 2007). While most studies agree that online groups are beneficial to some extent, there is an ongoing debate on whether the outcomes of participation should be examined by clinical measures.

A review of studies that examined OSGs' impacts on health issues (Eysenbach et al. 2004) revealed only limited support for their effect on depression and social support. However, most of these studies combined additional interventions, hence not necessarily allowing for an accurate evaluation of the benefits of the OSGs alone. Barak and colleagues (Barak, Grohol and Pector 2004, Barak et al., 2008) argued against the application of particular therapeutic measurements in studies evaluating the effects of OSGs. They claimed that it is both unrealistic and faulty to separate the groups' impact from other interventions, since these groups do not substitute treatment. They suggested viewing OSGs as complementary to professional care, because this means of emotional support can provide empowerment, stress relief, and improved general well-being.

To date, most of the studies that examined the benefits of participation in health-related OSGs have focused on posters. Several studies (for example, Barak and Dolev-Cohen 2006, Houston, Cooper and Ford 2002) have stressed the posters' degree of activity and involvement as a major factor in determining the level of personal relief they could expect from participating in the group. These studies indicated that the more active posters were, the more they benefited from OSGs. However, relatively little is known about the benefits that lurkers gain from OSGs as compared with those who are active posters.

The aforementioned study by Nonnecke et al. (2006) demonstrated that posters' expectations were better met than lurkers' expectations. More lurkers than posters reported that they received less than the expected benefit, and far fewer lurkers than posters perceived a greater than expected benefit. While these findings imply that posting is more beneficial than lurking, the nature of the perceived benefits gained is unclear. In addition, that study did not focus on health-related OSGs, but rather examined a broad variety of different types of online groups.

Two recent studies provided an initial understanding of the differences between posters and lurkers regarding the benefits they gain from health-related OSGs. Van Uden-Kraan et al. (2008) examined members of OSGs for patients with breast cancer, fibromyalgia, and arthritis. Their study indicated that lurkers were significantly less satisfied with the OSG compared to posters, and scored significantly lower than posters with regard to empowering processes. However, they scored similar to the posters in most empowering *outcomes* (with the exception of "enhanced social well-being"). Similarly, Mo and Coulson (2010) examined members of OSGs dedicated to individuals living with HIV/AIDS. Their study, too, indicated that lurkers were less satisfied with the OSGs than posters. This lower level of satisfaction was reflected in variables related to relationships (for example, "relationships with members" and "responses from members"), but not in variables related to information (for example, content and amount of information). Hence, lurkers were less satisfied compared to posters, as "they did not enjoy the same opportunity to develop a relationship with other members of the group" (1191). They also scored lower than posters in measures of empowering processes. However, there were no significant differences between posters and lurkers in self-care self-efficacy, loneliness, depression, or optimism.

These two studies yielded similar conclusions. Based on the lack of differences in the *outcomes* of participation, these studies suggested that lurking in the OSGs may be just as beneficial as active participation. These conclusions are consistent with Nonnecke and Preece's (1999) notion that a strong sense of community can be developed even without posting. It is important to note, however, that the two studies differed significantly in their approach. The first (van Uden-Kraan et al. 2008) examined subjective non-clinical outcomes, whereas the latter (Mo and Coulson 2010) examined objective clinical outcomes. This literature review found no study that combined clinical and non-clinical measures in examining the differences between posters and lurkers in health-related OSGs. This combination may be of value, as it could highlight the associations between specific benefits of participation and the overall well-being of group members.

The Present Study

The study presented in this chapter aimed to provide some of the missing information in the current body of knowledge. The main goal of the study was to explore the association between the type of participation in OSGs (that is, posting vs. lurking) and psychological well-being. For that purpose, the study combined subjective measures, namely, perceived benefits gained from participation, with objective clinical measurement. In addition, the study explored the associations between these different measures.

The study examined posters and lurkers in online peer-to-peer support groups targeting people with depression. These groups may be regarded as representative of health-related OSGs because people with stigmatized illnesses use the Internet for information and social support significantly more than those with non-stigmatized conditions (Berger et al. 2005, Davison et al. 2000), and because among those with stigmatized conditions, people with depression use the Internet the most (Millard and Fintak 2002). In the past decade, OSGs that are dedicated to the discussion of depression have grown into a mass social phenomenon estimated at dozens of such groups worldwide, with hundreds of thousands of members. Concurrent with their increased prevalence, a growing body of research has tried to explore the online groups' potential role in the management of depressive disorders (for reviews see Griffiths, Calear and Banfield 2009a, Griffiths et al. 2009b). However, so far no study explored the differences between posters and lurkers in these groups.

This study was designed to answer the following questions:

1. What is the incidence of posters and lurkers in online depression support groups, and can these segments be differentiated using background characteristics?
2. Are there differences between posters and lurkers in the interests they have in the issues discussed in the OSGs (which may explain their motivations for being active or inactive), and do they differ in participation patterns other than posting behavior?
3. Are there differences between posters and lurkers with regard to perceived benefits gained from participation and level of depression, and if so, what explains the differences in the level of depression?

By addressing these questions, the relationships between members' behavior and well-being were explored, and some general suggestions regarding the impact of participation in OSGs were drawn.

Method

DATA COLLECTION AND SAMPLE

The study was based on an online survey of 558 members of 16 peer-to-peer OSGs for people with depression. To recruit participants, the Principal Investigator (PI) contacted the administrators of 30 active OSGs and asked for their permission to post a call for volunteers on their websites. All the groups were English-based and explicitly targeted people with depression (according to their names, home-pages, and welcome posts). Eleven administrators approved and even posted the call on her behalf, two said that they would examine the request but never answered, and one refused. Others did not respond even after three requests. In these cases, the PI independently posted messages in the OSGs. Of the 16 unauthorized messages posted, only five survived. Others were deleted by group administrators after a short period (between several hours and a couple of days) and the PI was banned. Yet, it is assumed that some respondents were recruited by the short-lived posts in the other 11 online groups.

The call for volunteers included a short description of the research aims, and a link to the survey website (a Survey Monkey application). The first page of the website included a longer description of the study, a consent form, and the PI's contact information. Volunteers were asked to read the instructions and confirm their consent to participate. Then, they were asked to fill-in an online survey. They were invited to contact the PI with regard to any question they may have, but none did. There were no sampling criteria and participation was anonymous. Therefore, the study was exempted from human subjects review. Data collection lasted two months and ended when the questionnaire was filled by 1,000 people. After screening out those who did not sign the consent form and questionnaires with less than 80 percent of the questions answered, the sample size was 793. For the purpose of the current investigation, only repeat visitors were examined. Newcomers to the OSG from which they were referred to the survey were screened out. The final sub-sample size was 558.

MEASUREMENT

The questionnaire included mostly closed and some open-ended questions regarding the following areas:

Participation patterns   The interview began with several general questions that examined how users learned about the OSG, and when they visited it for the first time. Additional questions looked at current usage patterns, including frequency of visits, posting behavior, and visiting other OSGs for people with depression. Respondents were also asked to report if there were factors constraining their participation in the OSG, and if so, what those were.

Interest in issues discussed in the OSGs   Respondents were presented with a list of the nine most-discussed topics in the OSGs for people with depression (Nimrod 2012), which included "symptoms," "relationships," "coping," "life," "formal care," "medications," "causes," "suicide," and "work." They were asked to rate their interest in these topics using a four-point scale ranging from "have no interest" to "very interested."

Benefits of participation   Respondents were presented with a list of 13 statements, which describe various benefits from participation in OSGs for people with depression. This list was based on the previous research on OSGs for people with depression (especially Alexander, Peterson and Hollingshead 2003, Barak 2007, Houston et al. 2002, Powell, McCarthy and Eysenbach 2003). Respondents were asked to rate the extent to which each of the statements described the benefits they gained from participation, using a five-point scale ranging from "totally disagree" to "totally agree."

Depression severity   Depressive symptoms were measured by the Iowa short form (Kohout et al. 1993) of the Center for Epidemiological Studies Depression scale (CES-D; Radloff 1977), asking 11 of the original 20 questions with three rather than four response categories. This measure is a self-report instrument that asks respondents to describe their mood over the past week, on a three-point frequency scale. Sample questions include items such as "In the past week I felt depressed" and "In the past week I felt lonely."

Background questionnaire   The last part of the interview included a background questionnaire with demographic and socio demographic questions. The variables examined were: age, gender, perceived health, marital status, education, economic status, country of residence, having been diagnosed with depression (and if so, what the diagnosis was).

DATA ANALYSIS

Sample participants were split into posters and lurkers based on the data concerning active participation. Lurkers in this study were defined as people who never posted messages when visiting the OSG from which they were referred to the survey. OSG members who reported being active (that is, posting messages) at least to some extent were defined as posters. To examine differences between posters and lurkers in their background characteristics, participation patterns, interests, and reported benefits, cross tabulations and Chi-square tests as well as t-tests were employed. The next step included calculating the depression scores for each respondent, and then the average for each group of users. Differences between the groups were examined by t-test procedures. To understand the association between active participation and depression, all variables that correlated with active participation were included as independent variables in a linear regression model, with the level of depression as the dependent variable. A confidence interval of 95 percent was used in all tests, and only statistically significant findings are presented in this chapter.

Results

SAMPLE CHARACTERISTICS AND PARTICIPATION PATTERNS

Most of the respondents were 20–50 years old, and the mean age was 36.1 years. Seventy percent were female. Nearly half (48 percent) were single, 36 percent were married, and most of the rest were divorced. The average number of years of education was 14.8. Fifty percent of the respondents reported having average income and 35 percent reported income lower than average. Fifty-nine percent were from the US, 21 percent were from the British islands, 7 percent from Canada, and 6 percent from Australia. Relatively few (7 percent) resided in non-English speaking countries.

Regarding health, 53 percent perceived their health as good or excellent, and only 13 percent perceived their health as poor. Most respondents (76 percent) were diagnosed with depression. Sixteen percent reported being depressed but not diagnosed, and 6 percent reported caring for someone with depression. The most frequent diagnosis was major depression (68 percent), followed by bipolar disorder (14 percent) and dysthymia (4 percent). Depression scores ranged between 11 (least depressed) and 33 (most depressed), with a mean score of 23.69 (higher than 21 – the cutoff for depression).

Twenty percent were relatively new members in the OSG from which they were referred to the survey (less than a month) and about 40 percent were "veterans" (more than a year). Sixty-one percent reported having constraints on participation, and the most common constraints were depression itself (53 percent) and lack of time (23 percent). Most respondents found the OSG either after intentional searching for OSG for people with depression (52 percent) or coincidentally (39 percent). Only 1 percent learned about the online groups from their therapists.

DIFFERENCES BETWEEN POSTERS AND LURKERS IN BACKGROUND CHARACTERISTICS, INTERESTS, AND PARTICIPATION PATTERNS

The prevalence of lurkers in the sample was rather small. Most interviewees (82 percent) reported being active (that is, posting messages) at least to some extent, and the rest were lurkers. No differences were found among the two groups in their socio-demographic characteristics, including age, gender, economic status, education, family status, health perception, and state of residence. There were also no significant differences among the groups with regard to their level of interest in most topics discussed in the OSGs. The one exception was their interest in "relationships," as the lurkers were significantly more interested in this topic than the posters ($p < 0.001$). Fifty-seven percent of the lurkers reported being very interested in relationships compared with 42 percent of the posters.

No differences were found between the two groups of users with regard to the way they found the OSG, having constraints on participation, and the type of constraints. Cross tab and chi-square test showed that the posters visited the OSGs significantly more often than the lurkers ($p < 0.001$). Fifty-nine percent of the posters reported visiting the OSGs three to seven times a week (vs. 32 percent of the lurkers), and 39 percent reported visiting them on a daily basis (vs. 15 percent). Posters also had a significantly longer membership duration ($\alpha < 0.001$). Forty-three percent of them have been members in the OSG for more than a year compared with 23 percent of the lurkers.

DIFFERENCES AMONG THE GROUPS IN PERCEIVED BENEFITS AND LEVEL OF DEPRESSION

Contrary to the findings with regard to interests, many significant differences between the groups were found in the level of agreement with statements describing benefits from participation (see Table 6.1). These differences were indicated with regard to immediate benefits of participation (for example, feeling connected, feeling understood), as well as in benefits that permeated into members' offline reality (for example, better coping,

Table 6.1   Differences between Posters and Lurkers in Perceived Benefits

Benefit	Segment	(n)	Level of agreement (%)				
			Totally disagree	Quite agree	Neither agree nor disagree	Quite agree	Totally agree
I'm getting better	Posters	(448)	6.5	12.3	36.4	27.9	17.0
	Lurkers	(98)	9.2	18.4	43.9	20.4	8.2
I cope with the depression better	Posters	(445)	2.0	7.0	30.3	39.1	21.6
	Lurkers	(98)	8.2	8.2	42.9	29.6	11.2
I have more hope	Posters	(448)	3.1	8.3	29.5	37.9	21.2
	Lurkers	(98)	8.2	8.2	35.7	35.7	12.2
I get inspiration for fighting depression	Posters	(451)	2.4	4.4	17.1	44.6	31.5
	Lurkers	(98)	6.1	3.1	34.7	42.9	13.3
I can be of help to others	Posters	(447)	2.5	4.0	17.2	41.6	34.7
	Lurkers	(98)	14.3	6.1	37.8	33.7	8.2
I feel understood	Posters	(451)	2.9	4.0	10.6	35.3	47.2
	Lurkers	(98)	6.1	4.1	25.5	36.7	27.6
I can share my difficulties with other participants	Posters	(451)	1.1	1.8	7.5	41.7	47.9
	Lurkers	(99)	5.1	10.1	26.3	34.3	24.2
I feel connected with others	Posters	(449)	2.0	4.2	15.4	38.1	40.3
	Lurkers	(98)	7.1	7.1	22.4	37.8	25.5

Note: Pearson Chi-square < 0.05 in all Cross-tabs presented.

Table 6.2   Active Participation and Associated Variables as Predictors of Level of Depression: Summary of linear Regression Analysis

Variable	Un-standardized Coefficient		Standardized Coefficient β
	B	SE B	
(constant)	24.839	3.900	
Seniority	-.302	.127	-.095*
Frequency of visits	-.358	.148	-.103*
Benefit – share difficulties	-.343	.296	.062
Benefit – feel connected	-.008	.292	-.002
Benefit – cope better	-.045	.319	-.009
Benefit – more hope	-.546	.318	-.110
Benefit – getting better	-1.958	.259	-.424***
Benefit – help others	-.705	.268	-.148**
Benefit – inspiration	.461	.306	.089
Benefit – feel understood	.555	.295	.112
Interest in "relationships"	.353	.218	.064
Active participation	.874	.558	.067

Note: R square = 0.239, F score = 13.579.

Dummy codes. Active participation: 1 = poster, 0 = lurker

*** $p < 0.001$, ** $p < 0.01$, * $p < 0.05$

feeling better). In all cases, posters agreed more than lurkers that participation provided them with these benefits. No significant differences were found in benefits associated with knowledge (better understanding and knowledge), daily functioning (dealing with daily tasks and having more control), and relationships with people outside the OSG. Hence, while lurkers were more interested in relationships than posters, they reported the same level of offline social benefits as the posters.

After calculating the average depression score for each group, and conducting a T-test, results also indicated a significant difference between the groups with regard to the level of depression ($p = 0.003$). Posters were significantly less depressed than lurkers (Mean = 23.37 vs. 25.01). No differences were found with regard to self-defined condition (that is, diagnosed, depressed but undiagnosed, caring for someone with depression) or type of diagnosis among those who have been diagnosed.

In order to understand the association between active participation and depression, all variables that correlated with active participation were included as independent variables in a linear regression, with the level of depression as the dependent variable (see Table 6.2). The overall regression model accounted for only 23.9 percent of the variance. Hence, other variables, not examined in the model, may better predict depression. Still, the findings suggest that it is not the active participation *per se*, but rather two of the benefits associated with it ("getting better" and "helping others"), as well as posters' seniority and frequency of visits, that may explain the differences in the level of depression between posters and lurkers.

Implications for Academics

Considering the sample size in this study, as well as the fact that sample characteristics were quite similar to those found in previous research (Griffiths et al. 2009b), this study seems to be quite representative of members of OSGs for people with depression. This study is the first to segment members of OSGs for people with depression based on their posting behavior, and the first to combine non-clinical and clinical measures in examining differences between posters and lurkers. This combination provided some of the missing information in the current body of knowledge, produced a detailed understanding regarding OSG members, and may serve as a basis for several arguments regarding the contribution of active participation in OSGs to members' well-being.

The frequency of lurkers in the survey was rather small, 18 percent only. Several factors may explain this low rate, the first being the high level of activity in the surveyed OSGs (Nimrod 2012). Previous research suggested that online groups with the highest traffic levels generally have the lowest lurking levels (Nonnecke and Preece 2000). Apparently, once message rates reach beyond a comfortable level, following the contents posted in an online group takes more effort and only members with a relatively high level of involvement and strong sense of community adhere to the group. Other reasons may be the tendency of lurkers to avoid responding to surveys (Nonnecke et al. 2006) and their higher level of depression. Hence, it is possible that the level of lurking in the surveyed online groups was actually higher than that represented in the sample.

The fact that lurkers and posters in this study did not differ in their background characteristics, nor in having constraints on participation and the type of constraints, suggests that taking active part in the OSGs was not a result of having fewer constraints, but rather a matter of personal choice. The single difference found with regard to posters and lurkers' interest in issues discussed in the online groups may explain that choice. As lurkers were more interested in "relationships! than posters, but chose to avoid affiliations with other members, it is possible that lurkers in this study were people who found managing relationships while being depressed challenging. It is also possible that in addition to being depressed they were socially fearful or shy (Finfgeld 2000). However, a more reasonable explanation is that they were simply less familiar with the group. The findings indicated that the posters visited the OSGs significantly more often than the lurkers, and that they also had a significantly longer membership duration. This indication suggests that those who were more familiarized with the group, either as a result of seniority or as a result of being heavy users, felt more comfortable taking part in it. This pattern is consistent with previous research that demonstrated that lurkers are relatively new to the group and feel that they need to find out more about it, its norms and communication style before taking active part in it (Preece et al. 2004, Rafaeli et al. 2004, White and Dorman 2001).

Previous studies that examined the differences between posters and lurkers regarding the benefits they gain from health-related OSGs (Mo and Coulson 2010, van Uden-Kraan et al. 2008), suggested that lurkers are less satisfied with the OSG compared to posters. However, they demonstrated that lurking in the OSGs may be just as beneficial as active participation. In contrast, the present study proposes that lurking in OSGs is *less* beneficial than active participation. The findings indicated that posters experienced more online support (for example, feeling connected, feeling understood) as well as more benefits that permeated into their offline reality and general feeling of improvement in their condition (for example, better coping, feeling better) than lurkers. In addition, they had lower levels of depression. Hence, based on both non-clinical and clinical measures, this study suggests better psychological well-being outcomes both in the *personal sphere* and in the *social sphere* for group members who publicly interact with other members of their OSG. In the social sphere, posters experience understanding and emotional support. In the personal sphere, they experience improved general well-being. The social benefits occur while participating; the personal benefits result from participation but are reflected in the individuals' daily lives.

The reason for the difference between the findings of the current investigation and the previous two pioneering studies is unclear. One explanation may be the different measures used in each of the three studies; another explanation may be the different types of groups examined. The previous studies explored OSGs for patients with breast cancer, fibromyalgia, and arthritis (van Uden-Kraan et al. 2008) and online groups for people with HIV/AIDS (Mo and Coulson 2010), whereas the current study investigated OSGs for people with depression. It is possible that the benefits gained from participation, as well as the gaps between posters and lurkers, vary between various health conditions. Similar to HIV/AIDS, depression is a stigmatized condition. However, as it is a mental condition characterized, among others, by feeling lonely and misunderstood, the active communication with other OSG members may have greater impact on the posters. Nevertheless, even previous studies (for example, Nonnecke et al. 2006) revealed a lower level of satisfaction among lurkers in general, and particularly with regard to variables related to social issues such as satisfaction with other group members (Mo and Coulson 2010) and enhanced social well-being (van Uden-Kraan et al. 2008).

Lastly, the current study was the first to combine clinical and non-clinical measures in examining the differences between posters and lurkers in health-related OSGs. This combination enabled the differences in the level of depression between posters and lurkers to be examined. The findings indicated that the better psychological well-being of the posters may be explained by two of the benefits associated with active participation ("getting better" and "helping others"), as well as by their higher frequency of visits and longer duration of membership. Hence, the posters were less depressed not just as a result of their involvement in the group, but also thanks to the empowering effect of helping others in the group (Barak et al. 2004, 2008). In addition, they were in a better condition simply because of the time that passed since they joined the group. As many of them were group members for more than a year, and most of them were diagnosed and treated, they benefited from combining the formal care and the OSG, which complemented treatment. Therefore, they were in better condition than their newer and more depressed peers, and thus could offer them help and support in the same way that others have supported them in the past.

Implications for Health Practitioners

Similar to previous studies (for example, Mo and Coulson 2010, van Uden-Kraan et al. 2008), the study described in this chapter suggests that participating in health-related OSGs may be beneficial even when participants do not take active part in the communication process. The level of agreement with statements describing benefits from participation among lurkers was rather high, and many of them reported benefits such as gaining knowledge, feeling connected, and getting inspiration for coping with depression. Hence, practitioners should recognize the value of health-related OSGs regardless of participation patterns, and encourage patients to use them. Nevertheless, the findings also indicate that active participation in OSGs is more beneficial than lurking. These findings imply that the faster non-active newcomers in OSGs de-lurk, namely, switch from lurking to active participation, the quicker they would benefit from the groups.

Previous research (for example, Bernstein-Wax 2007, Schultz and Beach 2004) suggested de-lurking strategies and improvements that OSGs may adopt in order to enhance the lurker's experience. These strategies include having a visible and active moderator, having a prominently displayed statement of purpose and code of conduct, providing technology induction, creating a special welcome area in the OSG as a safe place for lurkers to visit in order to become familiar with the group, paying special attention to acknowledging and responding to new members promptly, using ice-breakers (suggesting topics for discussion that will not threaten newcomers), promoting diversity of viewpoint, offering mentoring partnerships, and even holding offline events to strengthen online relationships.

These strategies emphasize the significance of having attentive and qualified group moderators. A study by Wise, Hamman and Thorson (2006) even provided empirical support for the importance of moderators. That study explored how moderation, response rate, and message interactivity (that is, the extent to which messages relate to one another) affect people's intent to participate in an online group. The findings demonstrated that participants who viewed a moderated online group reported a significantly higher intent to participate than participants who viewed an un-moderated group. In addition, participants reported a significantly greater intent to participate in an online group featuring interactive messages, but only when response rate was slow. These results suggest that "both structural and content features of online communities affect individuals' intent to participate in the community" (35). Moderators of health-related OSGs who wish to enhance lurkers' involvement should try to optimise both types of features.

Conclusion

This chapter provided readers with an exemplar of current research in health communication, and demonstrated health communication in a group context. The chapter enhanced the understanding of how health-related OSGs are used, what explains the different types of usages, and which usage is more effective in improving individuals' health. In so doing, it yielded both theoretical and practical implications. From the theoretical perspective, the study presented in this chapter is significant in at least three ways. First, it shows evidence demonstrating that being actively involved in OSGs is more beneficial than lurking. Second, it provides an explanation for the better psychological well-being of posters as compared to lurkers. The findings indicate that the posters may have been less depressed as a result of their frequent visits, longer membership duration, and the empowering effect of helping others. Third, the study demonstrates that lurking results from a personal choice, and thus may change. This is where the practical implications become relevant. This chapter suggests that professionals should encourage patients to use OSGs, and that group moderators should use de-lurking strategies to enhance the lurkers' experience. These practices may make the health-related OSGs even more effective in improving individuals' health.

LIMITATIONS AND FUTURE RESEARCH

Notwithstanding the strengths of the study presented in this chapter, it has limitations that should be acknowledged. First of all, there is an inherent bias in this sample – of those who use the Internet and, more specifically, those who are willing to engage with others. This group might be less depressed than those who truly avoid any contact with others, and therefore not be representative of people with acute depression. Second, despite a multi-national composition, most respondents lived in English-speaking Western countries. In addition, the present study was cross-sectional, hence only associations were examined and not causalities.

Future research, then, should investigate health-related OSGs using longitudinal methods and examine non-English OSGs to explore cultural variations. As it is possible that the benefits gained from participation as well as the gaps between posters and lurkers vary among different health conditions, additional types of groups should be examined as well. As lurkers tend to avoid responding to surveys (Nonnecke et al. 2006), studies should also explore online groups with low traffic levels, which generally have higher lurking levels (Nonnecke and Preece 2000). Additionally, as lurking is a tendency common to new group members, it may be valuable to interview members with long membership duration about their experiences, and how they turned from lurkers to posters. Because of the many benefits OSGs offer, further studies should also look for ways to promote membership among people who do not visit OSGs. With only 1 percent of OSG users referred to OSGs by their therapists, additional research should also examine professionals' awareness and attitudes, and explore educational activities.

Acknowledgment

The study was supported by a grant from NARSAD, The Mental Health Research Association. The Author wishes to thank the research assistant Shirley Dorchin for help in preparing this chapter. In addition, the author thanks the administrators of the following online support groups for their collaboration: *Beyond Blue, Depression Forums, Depression Haven, Depression Tribe, Depression Fallout, Psychlinks, Psych Forums, Talk Depression, UKDF, Walkers in Darkness,* and *Wing of Madness.*

References

Alexander, S.C., Peterson, J.L. and Hollingshead, A.B. 2003. Help is at your keyboard: Support groups on the Internet, in *Group Communication in Context: Studies of Bona Fide Groups*, 2nd edition, edited by L.R. Frey. London, UK: Lawrence Erlbaum Associates, 309–34.

Barak, A. 2007. Emotional support and suicide prevention through the Internet: A field project report. *Computers in Human Behavior*, 23, 971–84.

Barak, A., Boniel-Nissim, M. and Suler, J. 2008. Fostering empowerment in online support groups. *Computers in Human Behavior*, 24, 1867–83.

Barak, A. and Dolev-Cohen, M. 2006. Does activity level in online support groups for distressed adolescents determine emotional relief? *Counseling and Psychotherapy Research*, 6(3), 186–90.

Barak, A., Grohol, J.M. and Pector, E. 2004. Methodology, validity, and applicability: A critique on Eysenbach et al. *British Medical Journal*, 328, 1166.

Berger, M., Wagner, T.H. and Baker, L.C. 2005. Internet use and stigmatized illness. *Social Science & Medicine*, 61, 1821–7.

Bernstein-Wax, J. 2007. *What motivates participation in online communities?* [Online]. Available at: http://www.mediamanagementcenter.org/social/whitepapers/BernsteinWax.pdf [accessed: 10 July 2011].

Davison, K.P, Pennebaker, J.W. and Dickerson, S.S. 2000. Who talks? The social psychology of illness support groups. *American Psychologist*, 55, 205–17.

Eysenbach, G., Powell, J., Englesakis, M., Rizo, C. and Stern, A. 2004. Health related virtual communities and electronic support groups: Systematic review of the effects of online peer to peer interactions. *British Medical Journal*, 328, 1166–70.

Finfgeld, D.L. 2000. Therapeutic groups online: The good, the bad, and the unknown. *Issues in Mental Health Nursing*, 21, 241–55.

Griffiths, K.M., Calear, A.L. and Banfield, M. 2009a. Systematic review on Internet Support Groups (ISGs) and depression (1): Do ISGs reduce depressive symptoms? *Journal of Medical Internet Research*, 11(3), e40. Available at: http://www.jmir.org/2009/3/e40/ [accessed: 10 July 2011].

Griffiths, K.M., Calear, A.L., Banfield, M., and Tam, A. 2009b. Systematic review on Internet Support Groups (ISGs) and depression: What is known about depression ISGs? *Journal of Medical Internet Research*, 11(3), e41. Available at: http://www.jmir.org/2009/3/e41/ [accessed: 10 July 2011].

Houston, T.K., Cooper, L.A. and Ford, D.E. 2002. Internet support groups for Depression: A 1-Year prospective cohort study. *American Journal of Psychiatry*, 159, 2062–66.

Johnson, G.J. and Ambrose, P.J. 2006. Neo-tribes: The power and potential of online communities in health care. *Communication of the ACM*, 49(1), 107–13.

Kohout, F.J., Berkman, L.F., Evans, D.A. and Cornoni-Huntley, J.C. 1993. Two shorter forms of the CES-D depressive symptoms index. *Journal of Aging and Health*, 5, 179–92.

Kral, G. 2006. Online communities for mutual help: Fears, fiction, and facts, in *The Internet and Health Care: Theory, Research, and Practice*, edited by M. Murero and R.E. Rice. Mahwah, NJ: Lawrence Erlbaum, 215–232.

McKenna, K.Y.A. and Bargh, J.A. 2000. Plan 9 from cyberspace: The implications of the Internet for personality and social psychology. *Personality & Social Psychology Review*, 4, 57–75.

Millard, R.W. and Fintak, P.A. 2002. Use of the Internet by patients with chronic illness. *Disease Management & Health Outcomes*, 10, 187–94.

Mo, P.K.H. and Coulson, N.S. 2010. Empowering processes in online support groups among people living with HIV/AIDS: A comparative analysis of 'lurkers' and 'posters'. *Computers in Human Behavior*, 26, 1183–93.

Nimrod, G. 2012. From knowledge to hope: Depression online communities. *Journal of Disability and Human Development*, 11(1).

Nonnecke, B. and Preece, J. 1999. Shedding light on lurkers in online communities, in *Ethnographic Studies in Real and Virtual Environments Inhabited Information Spaces and Connected Communities*, edited by K. Buckner. Edinburgh, UK: Citeseer, 123–128.

Nonnecke, B. and Preece, J. 2000. *Lurker Demographics: Counting the Silent*. Paper to the ACM CHI 2000 Conference on Human Factors in Computing Systems, The Hague, Netherlands. 1–6 April 2000.

Nonnecke, B., Andrews, D. and Preece, J. 2006. Non-public and public online community participation: Needs, attitudes and behavior. *Electronic Commerce Research*, 6, 7–20.

Powell, J., McCarthy, N. and Eysenbach, G. 2003. Cross-sectional survey of users of Internet depression communities. *BMC Psychiatry*, 3(19). Available at: http://www.biomedcentral.com/1471-244X/3/19 [accessed: 1 May 2006].

Preece, J., Nonnecke, B. and Andrews, D. 2004. The top five reasons for lurking: Improving community experiences for everyone. *Computers in Human Behavior*, 20(2), 201–23.

Radloff, L.S. 1977. The CES-D scale: A self-report depression scale for research in general population. *Applied Psychological Measurement*, 1, 385–401.

Rafaeli, S., Ravid, G. and Soroka, V. 2004. De-lurking in virtual communities: A social communication network approach to measuring the effects of social and cultural capital, in *Proceedings of the 37th Annual Hawaii International Conference on System Sciences*. Available at: http://csdl2.computer.org/comp/proceedings/hicss/2004/2056/07/205670203.pdf [accessed: 6 July 2011].

Ridings, C., Gefen, D. and Arinze, B. 2006. Psychological barriers: Lurker and poster motivation and behavior in online communities. *Communications of the Association for Information Systems*, 18, 329–54.

Schultz, N. and Beach, B. 2004. *From Lurkers to Posters* [Online]. Available at: http://flexiblelearning.net.au/resources/lurkerstoposters.pdf [accessed: 10 July 2011].

Rodgers, S. and Chen, Q. 2005. Internet community group participation: Psychosocial benefits for women with breast cancer. *Journal of Computer-Mediated Communication*, 10(4), 5. Available at: http://jcmc.indiana.edu/vol10/issue4/rodgers.html [accessed: 10 July 2011].

van Uden-Kraan, C.F., Drossaert, C.H.C., Taal, E., Seydel, E.R. and van de Laar, M.A.F.J. 2008. Self-reported differences in empowerment between lurkers and posters in online patient support groups. *Journal of Medical Internet Research*, 10(2), e18. Available at: http://www.jmir.org/2008/2/e18/ [accessed: 10 July 2011].

van Uden-Kraan, C.F., Drossaert, C.H.C., Taal, E., Seydel, E.R. and van de Laar, M.A.F.J. 2009. Participation in online patient support groups endorses patients' empowerment. *Patient Education and Counseling*, 74(1), 61–9.

Wald, H.S., Dube, C.E. and Anthony, D.C. 2007. Untangling the web: The impact of Internet use on health care and the physician-patient relationship. *Patient Education and Counseling*, 68(3), 218–24.

White, M. and Dorman, S.M. 2001. Receiving social support online: Implications for health education. *Health Education Research*, 16(6), 693–707.

Wise, K., Hamman, B. and Thorson, K. 2006. Moderation, response rate, and message interactivity: Features of online communities and their effects on intent to participate. *Journal of Computer-Mediated Communication*, 12, 24–41.

PART 3

Health Communication and Mobile Media

7 *Effectively Promoting Healthy Living and Behaviors through Mobile Phones*

BREE HOLTZ AND LORRAINE BUIS

Introduction

The prevalence of chronic disease (for example, diabetes, asthma, and heart disease) is increasing worldwide (G. Anderson 2010, CDC 2009, Wagner, Austin, Hindmarsh, Schaefer and Bonomi 2001, Wu and Green 2000). As the number of people living with one or more chronic diseases climbs, the healthcare system is forced to re-conceptualize the ways in which healthcare and health education are delivered to patients. Because the number of mobile phones in use is increasing they may offer a potential solution for helping people manage these chronic illnesses and provide opportunities to promote healthy living. The use of mobile phones and other mobile computing devices for health service delivery is known as mHealth (Mechael et al. 2010).

This chapter discusses mobile phones as a practical intervention delivery modality within the field of health communication. A literature review of previous uses of mobile phones within the context of health promotion interventions is provided. We also highlight the theories that have been utilized in developing and evaluating mHealth applications. The chapter demonstrates the practical implications and uses of mobile phones used in healthcare settings, followed by a case study focused on the development of a SMS intervention for asthma management.

Literature Review

The International Telecommunications Union (ITU) has estimated that there are more than 5.9 billion mobile phone subscriptions worldwide (ITU 2011). Moreover, using text messaging to communicate is increasing in popularity; more than 200,000 text messages are sent every second (ITU 2010). Within the United States, mobile phone adoption is near ubiquitous, with high rates of penetration across all education and income-levels, rural and urban locations, as well as racial and ethnic groups (Fox 2010, Lenhart 2010). According to the Pew Institute, 83 percent of the American adult population owns a mobile phone (Smith 2011). Although mobile phone adoption is higher among younger groups, over half (58 percent) of the population aged 65 and over own a mobile phone (Fox 2010). Additionally, 28 percent of people ages 18–29, and 15 percent of all adults 18 years and older, have sought out health information using their mobile phones (Fox 2010). As mobile phones become increasingly integrated into daily life, these numbers are expected to rise.

A small, but growing number of studies within the literature have used mobile phones to help improve patient health outcomes. Previous uses include mobile phone approaches to lifestyle behavior change and health promotion including managing diabetes and asthma, smoking cessation, increasing physical activity, and providing prenatal care and sexual health information. Mobile phones have also been used for administrative purposes, for example sending appointment reminders or test results to patients. While not a systematic literature review, Table 7.1 provides a handful of good examples of peer reviewed literature that has been conducted in this context. Generally, these studies have been relatively small, but have demonstrated positive trends in helping support short-

Table 7.1 Examples of mHealth Interventions

Mobile Phone Interventions	Reference
Diabetes	(R. Anderson, Funnell, Gitzgerald, and Marrero 2000; Arsand, et al. 2008; Benhamou, et al. 2007; Carroll, et al. 2007; Curran, et al. 2010; Faridi, et al. 2008; Farmer, et al. 2005; Ferrer-Roca, Cardenas, Diaz-Carama, and Pulido 2007; Franklin, et al. 2008; Franklin, Waller, Pagliari, and Greene 2006; Gammon, et al. 2005; Hanauer, et al. 2009; Istepanian, et al. 2009; Katz and Nordwall 2008; Kollman, Riedl, Kastner, Schreider, and Ludvik 2007; Krishna, et al. 2009; Quinn, et al. 2008; Rami, et al. 2006; Rossi, et al. 2009; Tasker, et al. 2007; Turner, et al. 2009; Vahatalo, Virtamo, Viikari, and Ronnemaa 2004; Wangberg, et al. 2006)
Asthma	(K. Anderson, Qiu, Whittaker, and Lucas 2001; Anhøj and Møldrup 2004; Cleland, Caldow, and Ryan 2007; Holtz and Whitten 2009; Lee, Jun, Kwon, and Hong 2005; Neville, Greene, McLeod, Tracy, and Surie 2002; Pinnock, Slack, Pagliari, Price, and Sheikh 2007; Ryan, Cobern, Wheeler, Price, and Tarassenko 2005)
Smoking Cessation	(Obermayer, Riley, and Jean-Mary 2004; Rodgers, et al. 2005; Whittaker, et al. 2009; Free, et al. 2011)
Physical Activity	(Fukuoka, Vittinghoff, Jong, and Haskell; Hurling, et al. 2007; Joo and Kim 2007)
Prenatal Care	(Johnson 2010)
Sexual Health Information	(Dhar, Leggat, and Bonas 2006; Levine, et al. 2008; Lim, Hocking, Hellard, and Aitken 2008)
Appointment Reminders	(Chen, Fang, Chen, and Dai 2008; Downer, Meara, and Da Costa 2005; Geraghty, Glynn, Amin, and Kinsella 2008; Koshy, Car, and Majeed 2008; Leong, et al. 2006)
Test Results/Treatment Times	(Cheng, et al. 2008; Menon-Johansson, McNaught, Mandalia, and Sullivan 2006)

term behavior change in individuals (Fjeldsoe, Marshall and Miller 2009b, Krishna and Balas 2009). People who have used their mobile phones for health related activity have reported that they are, in general, satisfied with using their mobile phone in these types of interventions (see Table 7.1). However, many of the studies perform only short-term follow-ups, making it difficult to determine if the influence of and engagement with these interventions are ongoing. Since the focus of the majority of these interventions is clinical outcomes, the use of theory in intervention design and implementation is often lacking. However, mobile phones provide a new medium to extend the reach of health campaigns and may assist in promoting healthy behavior. Furthermore, this approach also allows for a dynamic method for tailoring messages and engaging patients through interactive messaging.

When theoretical frameworks have been used in the design and dissemination of mobile phone based interventions, they have been able to demonstrate positive behavior changes (Fjeldsoe, Marshall and Miller 2009a). This is especially true when examining self-regulation and self-monitoring focused theories (Lorig, et al. 1999). Other theories that have been used include the theory of planned behavior (Ajzen 1991), transtheoretical model/stages of change (Prochaske and Velicer 1997), theory of reasoned action (Fishbein 1979), health belief model (Becker 1974), and social cognitive theory (Bandura 1989). By rooting text message health-behavior change interventions in a theoretical framework, we may be better able to utilize the underlying mechanisms that contribute to efficacious interventions. Despite the benefits of utilizing a theoretical approach when developing text message-based behavior change interventions, many do not. In a recent systematic review of 14 text message-based behavior change interventions, only four reported using theory as part of the intervention development (Fjeldsoe et al. 2009).

Practical Applications and Uses

There are many practical benefits to using mobile phones in health promotion interventions. Mobile phones allow tailored messages to easily reach a target population and allow for real-time interaction. Many mobile phone based interventions have focused on health promotion and education, reminders, scheduling, and notifications, which are good examples of how the use of theory can better promote positive behavior change.

HEALTH PROMOTION AND EDUCATION

Health education and promotion are the cornerstones of many public health campaigns and using mobile phones in these campaigns have successfully reached large groups of individuals over a distance in a dynamic way. These devices offer an engaging way to connect a campaign or intervention with the selected audience through text messages, game applications, and videos.

Highlights There are several examples of mobile phones being utilized both for very large and diverse populations and for narrowly-targeted interventions. The Centers for Disease Control and Prevention (CDC) have been pioneers in using mobile phones to develop public health campaigns that are tailored for individuals based on their location, gender, and age. The text messages sent provide general health advice, as well as tips and information during public health emergencies (CDC 2011). Another illustration of a large-scale health promotion campaign is Text4Baby, a program that provides expectant and new mothers with prenatal and infant information. This program sends free text messages to the expectant or new mother, tailored to her week of pregnancy, or age of infant, that continue until the baby is one year old (NHMHBC 2011). The campaign has been widely disseminated, reaching more than 216,000 unique users. Evaluations of nationwide text message programs such as the CDC and Text4Baby programs are ongoing and not yet published in the literature (see Holtz and Buis, this volume). These campaigns however, have already provided valuable insights into developing text-based campaigns. For instance, using rigorous methods in developing messages with evidence-based recommendations, community feedback, continuous testing and revision of messages, and extensive collaborations with both public and private organizations are key factors to success.

Another initiative developed a program for smoking cessation called Tx2Quit, based on social cognitive theory. This campaign was developed and tested in New Zealand and targeted young adults who smoked. Tx2Quit utilized text messages to help individuals set goals, provide support, and provide distraction from smoking (Rodgers et al. 2005). Over 1,000 messages were developed by a team comprised of young adults, health researchers, and experts in adolescent smoking cessation, behavior change, and health. The group also developed an algorithm to tailor the messages to the participant based upon self-reported characteristics and habits. Txt2Quit was able to demonstrate significantly higher quit rates in a randomized trial than the control group, which received text messages unrelated to smoking cessation (Free et al. 2011). Later, the some of the researchers from the Txt2Quit project demonstrated the feasibility of using video messages instead of traditional text based messages (Whittaker et al. 2011). This video message pilot study, like many others, was unable to recruit a large enough sample to provide statistical significance, however the data trends suggest this is a feasible channel and may provide the needed assistance to help young adults to quit smoking.

Moving forward   The future for these types of health promotion and education campaigns via mobile phones is becoming more popular. While the efficacy of these campaigns is not entirely known, the evaluations that have been conducted indicate the possibility of positive outcomes. Future interventions should be developed using theory as a foundation, which may help to understand the underlying mechanisms explaining how these interventions function. Additionally, interventions need to use rigorous evaluation methods and publish the results so the interventions and results can be duplicated by other organizations.

REMINDERS

The use of text messaging for health-related reminders for medication adherence and self-monitoring has been previously documented in academic literature and may serve as a convenient way to remind individuals to engage in specific health-related behaviors. Because cell phones are widely incorporated into daily life, they may be more convenient for reminders or alerts than alarm systems, emails, or other notification devices.

Highlights Documented reports of the use of text messages to improve medication adherence through medication reminders are now emerging within the medical literature. Despite the presence of several randomized controlled trials of text message reminders to improve medication adherence, the efficacy of these reminders remains unclear. Recent work by Pop-Eleches et al. (2011) found that in a randomized controlled trial of text message reminders to promote adherence to antiretroviral treatment in sub-Saharan Africa, 53percent of the participants who received the weekly text message reminders achieved acceptable levels of medication adherence, compared to 40 percent of control group participants ($p = .03$). Moreover, Strandbygaard et al. (2009) demonstrated that asthmatic participants, randomized to receive text message medication reminders, had a 17.8 percent greater mean adherence rate to anti-asthmatic medications as compared to a control group at the end of the trial ($p = .019$). Counter to these positive trials, several studies have reported encouraging, but mixed or inconclusive results. For example, Cocosila et al. (2009) conducted a one-month randomized controlled trial in which participants receiving text message reminders to take daily vitamin C tablets were found to improve their self-reported medication adherence from 1.3 pills a week to 4.5 pills a week at the end of the trial. The control participants also improved their self-reported adherence from 1.6 pills a week to 3.7 pills a week at the end of the trial, with significant differences in the increases in adherence ($p = .001$). Despite this finding, the difference between the two groups in the number of missed pills in the last week of the trial was not significant. Similarly, work by Hou et al. (2010) found no differences in the number of missed pills for new oral contraceptive users randomized to receive daily medication reminders compared to control group participants. Likewise, Ollivier et al. (2009) found no differences in adherence to malaria chemoprophylaxis in French soldiers returning from Côte d'Ivoire randomized to receive a text message reminder intervention when compared to a control group.

Moving forward Despite the inconclusive reports of the efficacy of text message reminders to improve medication adherence, it is expected that the number of people using this technology to remember to take medications will increase. Consumer demand is constantly driving the availability of text message based programs and a simple Internet search for "text message medication reminders" yields several for-profit consumer-facing programs that individuals can sign up to use. Furthermore, with the proliferation of other consumer-oriented health information technologies such as personal health records and patient portals sponsored by health plans and healthcare provider practices, text message driven reminder systems are easily incorporated and offer providers with marketable tools to recommend to patients.

SCHEDULING/NOTIFICATIONS

Notification of appointment reminders and test results is another use of text messaging that is gaining traction, and has implications on health-related behaviors. Although much of the research documenting the use of text messaging for these purposes has been conducted outside of the United States, the implications are far reaching.

Highlights Text message reminders regarding upcoming outpatient appointments have been successful at reducing failure-to-attend rates in a variety of clinical settings in Ireland (Geraghty et al. 2008), Australia (Downer et al. 2006), Malaysia (Leong et al. 2006), the UK (Koshy et al. 2008), and Brazil (Da Costa, Salomao, Martha, Pisa and Sigulem 2009). Typically sent 24–48 hours prior to a scheduled appointment, these quick notifications of upcoming appointments usually provide recipients with a mechanism to cancel appointments via text message or phone in the event that the patient foresees their inability to keep their appointment, which has considerable implications for patient scheduling, streamlining office management, and cost-savings. Furthermore, text messaging has been recently documented as a method for notifying patients that they need to schedule routine provider visits for prevention activities such as vaccinations (Kharbanda et al. 2011) and mammograms (Lakkis, Atfeh, El-Zein and Mahmassani 2011). These simple, brief communications are perfectly suited toward a text message delivery modality.

Although the use of text messaging for administrative information tasks such as routine notifications and scheduling reminders has been established, the use of text messages to deliver test results is markedly more controversial and evidence to support this usage is sparse. Despite this lack of evidence, there exists some support in the research literature to indicate that test results delivered via text messaging may be beneficial for certain types of results. For example, Cheng et al. (2008) demonstrated that pregnant Taiwanese women who screen negative for Downs syndrome face a shorter period of anxiety while waiting for the results of their screening test when the results are delivered via text message. Furthermore, Menon-Johannson et al. (2006) showed that the use of text messaging to deliver test results to patients receiving services from a sexual health clinic in London significantly shortened times to diagnosis (7.9 days±3.6 days v. 11.2 days±4.7 days, $p < .001$) and median time to treatment (8.5 days, range 4–27 days v. 15.0 days, range 7–35 SG, $p = .005$) for chlamydia.

Moving forward   With the increasing integration of health information technology systems into general practice, the potential for sending automated scheduling and notification text messages is rapidly increasing. As many electronic medical records systems have built-in functionality that would allow providers to send notices via text message, the capability for increased use of text messaging for these purposes already exists. As these automated text message notifications have the potential to streamline work-flow processes, the potential to be a cost-effective method for improving efficiencies within the healthcare system is great. However, convincing providers to utilize this functionality remains a barrier to utilizations. Provider concerns abound regarding the privacy and security of personal health information due to national policies and regulations (for example, Health Insurance Portability and Accountability Act of 1996) continue to be an impediment for implementation. Moreover, even in the absence of privacy and security concerns, the delivery of test results via text-messaging may not always be appropriate. It could mean there are fewer opportunities for patient education and counseling, which could lead to continuation of negative health-behaviors, anxiety due to lack of information, the adoption of medically unadvised behaviors and treatments, or other negative health outcomes.

Now that the context of several mobile phone applications that can benefit from using a theoretical foundation have been demonstrated, a small case study will be presented as a basic model that can be followed when planning a theoretically informed mHealth intervention.

Case Study

The following presents a pilot study that was conducted to test the design and feasibility of using mobile phones in asthma management. This case study is presented as an example of using theory in the development of a mobile phone SMS intervention (Holtz and Whitten 2009).

BACKGROUND

Asthma is a chronic disease and a growing health problem worldwide. While there is currently no cure for asthma, adequate management of the disease leading to asthma control can allow people to live normal and independent lives. Mobile phones can serve as a potential platform to facilitate the management of asthma. The objective of this study was to employ principles from social cognitive theory (SCT) to test the feasibility of tracking asthma symptoms through a mobile phone application.

SOCIAL COGNITIVE THEORY (SCT)

SCT subscribes to a model of emergent interactive agency, stating that persons are neither "autonomous agents nor simply mechanical conveyers of animating environmental influences. Rather, they make causal contributions to their own motivation and action within a system of triadic reciprocal causation" (Bandura 1989: 1175). The overarching theme (triadic reciprocal causation) studies the interactions between a person, their environment, and their behavior. According to this understanding of reciprocal determinism, a change in any part of the system will affect other elements in the system (Bandura 1977). This theory could then explain why employing mobile technology in management of asthma will change the environmental, personal, and behavioral factors related to asthma self-management, which could lead to patients managing their condition in a different ways. However, SCT can further explain this phenomenon through examination of its constructs, such as observational learning, behavioral capability, outcome expectancy, and self-efficacy (Vankatesh et al. 2003, Miller 2005).

Self-efficacy and outcome expectancy have been suggested as being important factors in health promotion and management in chronic diseases (Grus, Lopez-Herandez, Delamater, Appelgate and Wanner 2001, Zabracki and Drotar 2004). The concept of self-efficacy is defined as the perception of one's own abilities to accomplish a particular job or task (Vankatesh et al. 2003. Bandura (1989) states self-efficacy is a key feature of an individual's belief regarding their potential to demonstrate control over events, such as asthma attacks, that affect their lives. The concept of self-efficacy is central to understanding an individual's capability to carry out a healthcare plan for chronic diseases (Grus et al. 2001).

Outcome expectancy refers to the anticipatory outcomes of behaviors. It suggests that, "people develop expectations about a situation and expectations for outcomes of their behavior before they actually encounter the situation" (Baranowski 1997: 72). Compeau and Higgins (1995) suggest that outcome expectations deal with the individual's expectations of their sense of accomplishment if successful in an undertaking. Bandura (1989) states that self-efficacy has some effect over an individual's outcome expectancy but it can also be parsed out "when outcomes are not completely controlled by quality of performance" (1180).

Self-efficacy and outcome expectancy have been studied in the context of asthma. As individuals perceive greater self-efficacy and outcome expectancy, they experience better control of their asthma, which leads to overall improved health, less missed school or work, and fewer visits to the emergency department (Zebracki and Drotar 2004). However, these factors have not been studied in conjunction with a mobile phone asthma management application. This research sought to test these two factors of SCT by demonstrating that managing asthma via a mobile phone will improve participants' self-efficacy and outcome expectancy in regards to their asthma management.

METHODOLOGY

Participants This project used a convenience sample which included four participants, with a diagnosis of asthma, to participate in a one month long (per each individual) feasibility test of a mobile phone based asthma management program. A general practitioner from a small, rural family practice selected the participants; she judged them to have mild to moderate asthma (not including exercise induced asthma) that was controlled. Participants were between the ages of 18 and 35. Participants took their peak flow reading each day and used mobile phone text messaging to send it to a web server. If they did not send a text message by 11am, they received a reminder via an automated text to their phone.

Data Collection Self-efficacy and outcome expectations were measured by using a validated questionnaire, pre- and post-intervention (Grus et al. 2001). The scale was slightly modified to reflect a self-administered questionnaire regarding the individuals' own asthma. Response items were based on a five-point Likert style rating scale, 1 indicating strong disagreement and 5 indicating strong agreement. Data from the server regarding text message usage was also collected and analyzed. At the end of the study period, participants participated in a telephone interview, at which time they answered open-ended questions regarding the mobile phone application.

RESULTS

The results suggest a trend of improved positive self-efficacy (pretest M = 3.77, SD = .66; posttest M = 4.18, SD = .72). However, the results indicate from the pre-test to the post-test there was no difference in outcome expectancy (pretest M = 4.25, SD = .28; posttest M = 4.25, SD = .13). Participants agreed the mobile SMS asthma management application was useful in monitoring their asthma (M = 4.56, SD = .52) and were satisfied using a mobile phone in this way (M = 4.13, SD = .32). During the open-ended interviews, participants stated they felt more knowledgeable about their disease and liked the reminder feature as it helped them remember to take their asthma medications.

Other interesting results that emerged include the perceived ease of use of the application (M = 4.47, SD = .52). One participant noted, "It was easy to understand, simple and easy to use." Another stated, "It was very easy to use and the results came so quickly." Participants also reported they felt they had a better way to communicate with their physician. A participant stated, "The doctor will have the same information I have, it would be easy to really talk about my asthma because we would be on the same page." A different participant said, "It gives the doctor the day to day condition of my asthma, she would have accurate information and be able to help me more."

DISCUSSION

This research indicates monitoring asthma via a mobile phone application was a feasible method for asthma management, and has the promise of improving self-efficacy of asthma sufferers. As with most studies there are some limitations that should be noted including using a convenience sample selected by the study's referring physician. Another limitation also related to the sample was its size; however, many studies of this nature tend to have a low sample size to demonstrate feasibility, a full study using randomize control groups with a larger sample should be conducted in the future to further demonstrate results and health outcomes. This study was also unable to determine if compliance would drop over an extended period. However, there were some positive trends that can be used to further this type of intervention.

Self-efficacy improved because the participants were actively managing and monitoring their asthma symptoms. This application made the participants more aware of their disease through the feedback mechanisms, which in turn increased their perceptions of self-efficacy. Improved self-efficacy in managing one's own asthma through utilization of this text message application demonstrates that the application enhanced the individual's capability to carry out their health plan. It also denotes a reduction of any perceived barriers of carrying out their asthma plan, by improving their asthma awareness and increasing positive perceptions of doctor-patient communication. Low self-efficacy has been associated with increased asthma related morbidity and is considered to be a key feature of self-management behaviors that are key to successful control of asthma (Grus, Lopez-Hernandez, Delamater, Appelgate, Brito, Wurm and Wanner 2001). This study adds to the current knowledge by advancing our understanding of how social cognitive theory can predict how patients with asthma who use their mobile phone for asthma management will have increased self-efficacy, which has the potential to improve health outcomes.

However, outcome expectancy remained the same in this population. Outcome expectancy was relatively high with these participants at the outset, implying these participants expect the actions they take regarding their asthma will have a beneficial effect. Zebracki and Drotar (2004) have also demonstrated that younger people tend to have high expectations and believe they will have good health in the future. Additional studies with larger sample sizes should be conducted to further test constructs from SCT.

Implications for Academics

There are several implications for academic professionals that should be taken from this chapter. The first is that theory can help better explain behavior change phenomenon and improve the ability to replicate studies. Additionally, longer study periods are necessary to fully understand the influence that mobile phone interventions have on individuals and their health. In order to successfully implement a mobile phone intervention it is important to work with a multidisciplinary group. This is not only because it is inherently a multidisciplinary field, but also to improve the translational impact. A multidisciplinary group should include members of the target audience, subject-area, technology, communications, and public health experts.

Implications for Practitioners

For practitioners seeking to implement a mobile phone intervention, it is important to incorporate professionals from many disciplines developing long-term interventions. Also key is to develop interventions that are evidence-based and have been found to improve health outcomes in the past. While it may not seem important in a practical context, using theory is important when developing a health intervention. Theory can be used as a foundation for the intervention and it can also help explain the behavior change that it presents. Once the interventions have been developed and completed it is important for the results to be published for others to be able to learn and replicate the outcomes.

Conclusion

Using mobile phones for health interventions and promotion is a dynamic method to connect with target populations. However, this is a rapidly changing environment and new ways to use mobile phones are being discovered. Future studies and interventions should look toward smart-phone based approaches that include games to engage people (Read and Shortell 2011). Furthermore, to understand the full impact of mobile phone and health "apps," more theoretically based interventions must be designed and tested. Moreover, it is essential that mHealth applications move beyond pilot studies with short follow-up periods to larger scale evaluations with longer-term follow-up. mHealth is currently an emerging field and the majority of the studies have been demonstration projects while beginning to build an evidence-base; as the field moves forward, longitudinal and more rigorous studies can and will need to be conducted that will be able to demonstrate health outcomes. As chronic diseases may be lifelong, it is important to understand if these interventions have a long-term benefit.

References

Ajzen, I. 1991. Theory of planned behavior. *Organizational Behavior and Human Decision Processes*, 50(2), 179–211.

Anderson, G. 2010. *Chronic Care: Making the Case for Ongoing Care*. Robert Wood Johnson Foundation.

Anderson, K., Qiu, Y., Whittaker, A. and Lucas, M. 2001. Breath sounds, asthma, and the mobile phone. *The Lancet*, 385, 1343–4.

Anderson, R., Funnell, M., Gitzgerald, J. and Marrero, D. 2000. Diabetes empowerment scale: A measure of pscyo-social self-efficacy. *Diabetes Care*, 23, 739–43.

Anhøj, J. and Møldrup, C. 2004. Feasibility of collecting diary data from asthma patients through mobile phones and SMS (Short Message Service): Response rate analysis and focus group evaluation from a pilot study. *Journal of Medical Internet Research*, 6(4), e42.

Arsand, E., Tufano, J., Ralston, J. and Hjortdahl, P. 2008. Designing mobile dietary management support technologies for people with diabetes. *Journal of Telemedicine and Telecare*, 14, 329–32.

Bandura, A. 1977. Self-efficacy: Toward a unifying theory of behavioral change. *Psychological Review*, 84, 191–215.

Bandura, A. 1989. Human agency in social cognitive theory. *American Psychologist*, 44(9), 1175–84.

Becker, M. 1974. The health belief model and personal health behavior. *Health Education Monographs*, 2, 324–508.

Benhamou, P., Melki, V., Boizel, R., Perreal, F., Quesada, J., Bessieres-Lacombe, S. et al. 2007. One-year efficacy and safety of web-based follow-up using cellular phone in type 1 diabetic patients under insulin pump therapy: The PumpNet study. *Diabetes & Metabolism*, 33, 220–26.

Carroll, A., Marrero, D. and Downs, S. 2007. The HealthPia GlucoPack (TM) Diabetes Phone: A usability study. *Diabetes Technology & Therapeutics*, 9(2), 158–64.

CDC, 12/17/2009. Chronic diseases: The power to prevent, the call to control: At a glance 2009. *National Center for Chronic Disease Prevention and Health Promotion*. Available at: http://www.cdc.gov/chronicdisease/resources/publications/AAG/chronic.htm#links [accessed: 1 April 2011].

CDC 2011. *Mobile at CDC*. Available at: http://www.cdc.gov/mobile/ [accessed: 31 August 2011].

Chen, Z., Fang, L., Chen, L. and Dai, H. 2008. Comparison of an SMS text messaging and phone reminder to improve attendance at a health promotion center: A randomized controlled trial. *Journal of Zhejiang University – Science B*, 9(1), 34–38.

Cheng, P.J., Wu, T.L., Shaw, S.W., Chueh, H.Y., Lin, C.T., Hsu, J.J. et al. 2008. Anxiety levels in women undergoing prenatal maternal serum screening for Down syndrome: The effect of a fast reporting system by mobile phone short-message service. *Prenatal Diagnosis*, 28(5), 417–21.

Cleland, J., Caldow, J. and Ryan, D. 2007. A qualitative study of the attitudes of patients and staff to the use of mobile phone technology for recording and gathering asthma data. *Journal of Telemedicine and Telecare*, 13(2), 85–9.

Curran, K., Nichols, E., Xie, E. and Harper, R. 2010. An intensive insulinotherapy mobile phone application built on artifical intelligence techniques. *Journal of Diabetes Science and Technology*, 4(1), 1–12.

Da Costa, T., Salomao, P., Martha, A., Pisa, I. and Sigulem, D. 2009. The impact of short message service text messages sent as appointment reminders to patients' cell phones at outpatient clinics in Sao Paulo, Brazil. *International Journal of Medical Informatics*, 79(1), 65–70.

Dhar, J., Leggat, C. and Bonas, S. 2006. Texting – a revolution in sexual health communication. *International Journal of STD and AIDS*, 17(6), 375–7.

Downer, S., Meara, J. and Da Costa, A. 2005. Use of SMS text messaging to improve outpatient attendance. *Medical Journal of Australia*, 183, 366–8.

Faridi, Z., Liberti, L., Shuval, K., Northrup, V., Ali, A. and Katz, D. 2008. Evaluating the impact of mobile telephone technology on type 2 diabetic patients' self-management: The NICHE pilot study. *Journal of Evaluation in Clinical Practice*, 14(465–9).

Farmer, A., Gibson, O., Hayton, P., Bryden, K., Dudley, C., Neil, A. et al. 2005. A real-time, mobile phone-based telemedicine system to support young adults with type 1 diabetes. *Informatics in Primary Care*, 13, 171–7.

Ferrer-Roca, O., Cardenas, A., Diaz-Carama, A. and Pulido, P. 2007. Mobile phone text messaging in the management of diabetes. *Journal of Telemedicine and Telecare*, 10(5), 282–6.

Fishbein, M. 1979. A theory of reasoned action: Some application and implications. *Nebraska Symposium on Motivation*, 27, 65–116.

Fjeldsoe, B., Marshall, A. and Miller, Y. 2009a. Behavior change interventions delivered by mobile telephone short-message service. *American Journal of Preventive Medicine*, 36(2), 165–73.

Fjeldsoe, B., Marshall, A. and Miller, Y. 2009b. Behavior change interventions delivered by mobile telephone short-message service. *American Journal of Preventive Medicine*, 36(2), 165–73.

Fox, S. 2010. *Mobile Health 2010*. Washington, DC: Pew Research Center's Internet & American Life Project.

Franklin, V., Greene, G., Waller, A. and Pagliari, C. 2008. Patients' engagement with "Sweet Talk" – A text messaging support system for young people with diabetes. *Journal of Medical Internet Research*, 10(2), e20.

Franklin, V., Waller, A., Pagliari, C. and Greene, S. 2006. A randomized controlled trial of Sweet Talk, a text-messaging system to support young people with diabetes. *Diabetic Medicine*, 23(12), 1332–8.

Free, C., Knight, R., Robertson, S., Whittaker, R., Edwards, P., Zhou, W., Rodgers, A., Cairns, J., Kenward, M. and Roberts, I. 2011. Smoking cessation support delivered via mobile phone text messaging (txt2stop): A single blind, randomised trial. *The Lancet*, 378(9785), 49–55.

Fukuoka, Y., Vittinghoff, E., Jong, S. S. and Haskell, W. 2010. Innovation to motivation-pilot study of a mobile phone intervention to increase physical activity among sedentary women. *Preventive Medicine*, 51(3–4), 287–9.

Gammon, D.A., Walseth, O., Andersson, N., Jenssen, M. and Taylor, T. 2005. Parent-child interaction using a mobile and wireless system for blood glucose monitoring. *Journal of Medical Internet Research*, 7(5), e57.

Geraghty, M., Glynn, F., Amin, M. and Kinsella, J. 2008. Patient mobile telephone 'text' reminder: A novel way to reduce non-attendance at the ENT out-patient clinic. *Journal of Laryngology and Otology*, 122(3), 296–8.

Grus, C.L., Lopez-Herandex, C., Delamater, A., Applegate, B., Brito, A., Wurn, G. et al. 2001. Parental self-efficacy and morbidity in pediatric asthma. *Journal of Asthma*, 38(1), 99–106.

Hanauer, D., Wentzell, K., Laffel, N. and Laffel, L. 2009. Computerized automated reminder diabetes system (CARDS): E-mail and SMS cell phone text messaging reminder to support diabetes management. *Diabetes Technology & Therapeutics*, 11(2), 99–106.

Holtz, B. and Whitten, P. 2009. Managing asthma with mobile phones: A feasibility study. *Telemedicine and e-Health*, 15, 907–9.

Hou, M., Hurwitz, S., Kavanagh, E., Fortin, J. and Goldberger, A. 2010. Using daily text-message reminders to improve adherence with oral contraceptives: A randomized controlled trial. *Obstetrics and Gynecology*, 116(3), 633–40.

Hurling, R., Catt, M., De Boni, M., Fairley, B., Hurst, T., Murray, P. et al. 2007 Using Internet and mobile phone technology to deliver an automated physical activity program: Randomized control trial. *Journal of Medical Internet Research*, 9(2), e7.

Istepanian, R., Zitouni, K., Harry, D., Moutosammy, N., Sungoor, A., Tang, B. and Earle, K.A. 2009. Evaluation of a mobile phone telemonitoring system for glycaemic control in patients with diabetes. *Journal of Telemedicine and Telecare*, 15(3), 125–8.

ITU. 2010. *The World in 2010: ICT Facts and Figures*. Geneva, Switzerland: International Telecommunications Union.

Johnson, T. 2010. Text4Baby: Educating new moms via text messaging. *The Nation's Health*, 40(3), 7.

Joo, N.-S. and Kim, B.-T. 2007. Mobile phone short message service messaging for behaviour modification in a community-based weight control programme in Korea. *Journal of Telemedicine and Telecare*, 13(8), 416–20.

Katz, D. and Nordwall, B. 2008. Novel interactive cell-phone technology for health enhancement. *Journal of Diabetes Science and Technology*, 2(1), 147–53.

Kharbanda, E.O., Stockwell, M.S., Fox, H.W., Andres, R., Lara, M. and VI, R. 2011. Text message reminders to promote human papillomavirus vaccination. *Vaccine*, 29(14), 2537–41.

Kollmann, A., Riedl, M., Kastner, P., Schreier, G. and Ludvik, B. 2007. Feasibility of a mobile phone-based data service for functional insulin treatment of type 1 diabetes mellitus patients. *Journal of Medical Internet Research*, 9(5), e36.

Koshy, E., Car, J. and Majeed, A. 2008. Effectiveness of mobile-phone short message service (SMS) reminders for opthalmology outpatient appointments: Observational study. *BMC Opthalmology*, 8(1), 9.

Krishna, S., Boren, S.A. and Balas, E.A. 2009. Healthcare via cell phones: A systematic review. *Telemedicine and e-Health*, 15(3), 231–40.

Lakkis N.A., Atfeh, A.M, El-Zein, Y.R., Mahmassani, D.M. and GN, H. 2011. The effect of two types of SMS-texts on the uptake of screening mammogram: A randomized controlled trial. *Preventive Medicine*, August 16 (Epub ahead of print).

Lee, H., Jun, S., Kwon, N. and Hong, C. 2005. A web-based mobile asthma management system. *Journal of Telemedicine and Telecare*, 11(S1), 56–9.

Lenhart, A. 2010. Cell phones and American adults [Online]. Available at: http://www.pewinternet. org/~/media//Files/Reports/2010/PIP_Adults_Cellphones_Report_2010.pdf [accessed: 17 December 2010].

Leong, K.C., Chen, W.S., Leong, K.W., Mastura, I., Mimi, O., Sheikh, M.A. et al. 2006. The use of text messaging to improve attendance in primary care: a randomized controlled trial. *Family Practice*, 23(6), 699–705.

Levine, D. 2011. Using technology, new media, and mobile for sexual and reproductive health. *Sex Research and Social Policy*, 8, 18–26.

Levine, D., McCright, J., Dobkin, L., Woodruff, A. J. and Klausner, J.D. 2008. SEXINFO: A sexual health text messaging service for San Francisco youth. *American Journal of Public Health*, 98(3), 393–5.

Lim, M., Hocking, J., Hellard, M. and Aitken, C. 2008. SMS STI: A review of the uses of mobile phones text messaging in sexual health. *International Journal of STD & AIDS*, 19(5), 287–90.

Lorig, K., Sobel, D., Stewart, A., Brown, B.W., Bandura, A., Ritter, P., Gonzalez, V.M., Laurent, D.D. and Holman, H.R. 1999. Evidence suggesting that a chronic disease self-management program can improve health status while reducing hospitalization: A randomized trial. *Medical Care*, 37(1), 5–14.

Mechael, P., Batavia, H., Kaonga, N., Searle, S., Kwan, A., Goldberger, A. et al. 2010. *Barriers and Gaps Affecting mhealth in Low and Middle Income Countries: Policy White Paper*. Center for Global Health and Economic Development, Earth Institute, Columbia University.

Menon-Johansson, A.S., McNaught, F., Mandalia, S. and Sullivan, A.K. 2006. Texting decreases the time to treatment for genital Chlamydia trachomatis infection. *Sexually Transmitted Infections*, 82(1), 49–51.

Miller, K. 2005. *Communication Theories: Perspectives, Processes and Context*, 2nd Edition. New York: McGraw-Hill.

Neville, R., Greene, A., McLeod, J., Tracy, A. and Surie, J. 2002. Mobile phone text messaging can help young people manage asthma. (Letters). *British Medical Journal*, 325(7364), 600–601.

NHMHBC 2011. Text4Baby [Online]. Available at: www.text4baby.org [accessed: 21 August 2011].

Obermayer, J.L., Riley, W.T. and Jean-Mary, J. 2004. College smoking-cessation using cell phone text messaging. *Journal of American College Health*, 53(2), 71–8.

Ollivier, L., Romand, O., Marimoutou, C., Michel, R., Tognant, C., Todesco, A. et al. 2009. Use of short message service (SMS) to improve malaria chemoprophylaxis compliance after returning from a malaria endemic area. *Malaria Journal*, 23(8), 236.

Pinnock, H., Slack, R., Pagliari, C., Price, D. and Sheikh, A. 2007. Understanding the potential role of mobile phone-based monitoring on asthma self-management: qualitative study. *Clinical & Experimental Allergy*, 37(5), 794–802.

Pop-Eleches, C., Thirumurthy, H., Habyarimana, J., Zivin, J., Goldstein, M., de Walque, D. et al. 2011. Mobile phone technologies improve adherence to antiretroviral treatment in a resource-limited setting: A randomized controlled trial of text message reminders. *AIDS*, 27(6), 825–34.

Prochaske, J. and Velicer, W. 1997. The transtheoretical model of health behavior change. *American Journal of Health Promotion*, 12(1), 38–48.

Quinn, C., Sysko-Clough, S., Minor, J., Lender, D., Okafor, M. and Gruber-Baldini, A. 2008. WellDoc(TM) mobile diabetes management randomized controlled trial: Change in clinical and behavioral outcomes and physician satisfaction. *Diabetes Technology & Therapeutics*, 10(3), 160–68.

Rami, B., Popow, C., Horn, W., Waldhoer, T. and Schober, E. 2006. Telemedical support to improve glycemic control in adolescents with type 1 diabetes mellitus. *European Journal of Pediatrics*, 165, 701–5.

Read, J.L. and Shortell, S.M. 2011. Interactive games to promote behavior change in prevention and treatment. *JAMA: The Journal of the American Medical Association*.

Rodgers, A., Corbett, T., Bramley, D., Riddell, T., Wills, M., Lin, R.-B. et al. 2005. Do u smoke after txt? Results of a randomised trial of smoking cessation using mobile phone text messaging. *Tobacco Control*, 14(4), 255–61.

Rossi, J., Nicolucci, A., Pellegrini, F., Bruttomesso, D., Bartolo, P., Marelli, G. et al. 2009. Interactive diary for diabetes: A useful and easy-to-use new telemedicine system to support the decision-making process in type 1 diabetes. *Diabetes Technology & Therapeutics*, 11, 19–24.

Ryan, D., Cobern, W., Wheeler, J., Price, D. and Tarassenko, L. 2005. Mobile phone technology in the management of asthma. *Journal of Telemedicine and Telecare*, 11(suppl_1), 43–6.

Strandbygaard, U., Thomsen, S. and Backer, V. 2009. A daily SMS reminder increases adherence to asthma treatment: A three-month follow-up study. *Respiratory Medicine*, 104(2), 166–71.

Tasker, A., Gibson, L., Franklin, V., Gregor, P. and Greene, S. 2007. What is the frequency of symptomatic mild hypoglycemia in type 1 diabetes in the young?: assessment by mobile phone technology and computer based interviewing. *Pediatric Diabetes*, 8, 15–20.

The Nielsen Company 2010. Smartphones to overtake features phones in U.S. by 2011. [Online]. Available at: http://blog.nielsen.com/nielsenwire/consumer/smartphones-to-overtake-feature-phones-in-u-s-by-2011/ [accessed: 4 February 2011].

The Nielsen Company (2011a). Apple leads smartphone race, while Android attracts most recent customers [Online]. Available at: http://blog.nielsen.com/nielsenwire/online_mobile/apple-leads-smartphone-race-while-android-attracts-most-recent-customers/ [accessed: 4 February 2011].

The Nielsen Company. 2011b. Factsheet: The U.S. Media Universe. [Online]. Available at: http://blog.nielsen.com/nielsenwire/online_mobile/factsheet-the-u-s-media-universe/ [accessed: 3 February 2011].

Turner, J., Larsen, M., Tarassenko, L., Neil, A. and Farmer, A. 2009. Implementation of telehealth support for patients with type 2 diabetes using insulin treatment: an exploratory study. *Informatics in Primary Care*, 17, 47–53.

Vahatalo, M., Virtamo, H., Viikari, J.E. and Ronnemaa, T. 2004. Cellular phone transferred self blood glucose monitoring: prerequisites for positivie outcomes. *Practical Diabetes International*, 21(5), 192–4.

Venkatesh, V., Morris, M., Davis, G. and Davis, F. 2003. User acceptance of information technology: toward a unified view. *MIS Quarterly*, *27*(3), 425–78.

Wagner, E., Austin, B.D., C, Hindmarsh, M., Schaefer, J. and Bonomi, A. 2001. Improving chronic illness care: Translating evidence into action. *Health Affairs*, 20(6), 64–78.

Wangberg, S., Arsand, E. and Andersson, N. 2006. Diabetes education via mobile text messaging. *Journal of Telemedicine and Telecare*, 12(Suppl. 1), 55–6.

Whittaker, R., Borland, R., Bullen, C., Lin, R., McRobbie, H. and Rodgers, A. 2009. Mobile phone-based interventions for smoking cessation. *Cochrane Database of Systematic Reviews*, 4(CD006611).

Whittaker, R., Dorey, E., Bramley, D., Bullen, C., Elley, C., Maddison, R. et al. 2011. A theory-based video messaging mobile phone intervention for smoking cessation: Randomized control trial. *Journal of Medical Internet Research*, 13(1), e10.

Wu, S. and Green, A. 2000. *Projection of Chronic Illness Prevalence and Cost Inflation*. Santa Monica, CA: RAND Health.

Zebracki, K. and Drotar, D. 2004. Outcome expectancy and self-efficacy in adolescent asthma self-management. *Children's Health Care*, 33(2), 133–49.

8

Targeting Young Adult Texters for Public Health Emergency Messages: A Q-study of Uses and Gratifications

HILARY N. KARASZ, MEREDITH LI-VOLLMER, SHARON
BOGAN AND WHITNEY OFFENBECHER

Introduction

Public health departments have a responsibility to be responsive to their public's communication needs, delivering information in ways that are easily accessible and fit the ways that individuals prefer to communicate. The best forms of health communication do not require people to step outside of their usual information-seeking behavior. Instead, information is better when it is provided seamlessly in the flow of the daily contexts of people's lives. From our perspective as both public health practitioners and researchers, text messaging – otherwise known as Short Message Service (SMS) – offers a potentially powerful means of outreach that meets people where they are. People use texting in ways that make it distinctive from other types of communication. By identifying how and why people use text messaging, and developing health communication strategies within the context of people's expected attitudes, uses and motivations, health communicators will be more successful in using text messaging to address fundamental communication gaps and provide wider access to health information, particularly during public health emergencies.

This chapter aims to shed insight on how and why young adults use texting – informed by a uses and gratifications theoretical approach – to help health practitioners understand what will make their text messaging programs more resonant and appealing to this audience. In addition, for communication researchers and others engaged in audience research, it demonstrates the value of Q-methodology to investigate the uses and gratifications of communications technologies.

Background

TEXT MESSAGING'S POTENTIAL

SMS text messaging's specific characteristics make it a potentially powerful channel for many forms of health communication for three reasons. First, texting is pervasive. In

2011, 73 percent of adults with cell phones reported using texting, up from 65 percent in 2009. Unlike the digital divide among users of online technologies, texting has been more quickly adopted by people across a wide range of language, ethnic, and income groups. Some ethnic minorities have even higher rates of texting use, with 76 percent of African American and 83 percent of Hispanic adult cell phone owners reporting they text, compared to 70 percent of whites (Smith 2011). Second, texting is mobile. People have their cell phones with them much of their waking hours. They even sleep with them: a 2010 survey by the Pew Research Center's Internet & American Life Project found that two-thirds of adults reported keeping their cell phone on or near them when sleeping (Lenhart 2010). Finally, texting is reliable. Text messages are more likely to get through than a phone call, especially in emergencies. Phone calls require a direct one-to-one line of connection, but text messages move through the network using multiple pathways to get to their end destination (Coyle 2005).

The accessibility, immediacy and mobility of texting offer potential for the delivery of health information as part of everyday public health practice. Its ability to reach people with urgent information, even when other communications systems are non-functional, suggests that texting could be a true lifeline in emergency contexts as well as for everyday health.

NEED FOR AUDIENCE RESEARCH ABOUT TEXT MESSAGING

Setting up a texting program at a health department that reaches a large number of people in a short time is not as simple as composing a text on one phone and sending it out to another. It requires a considerable investment in funds and resources to work with a text messaging vendor, develop and promote a texting program, develop protocols, and train staff. Before making this investment, health departments should understand their audience's needs in order to optimize texting with their residents.

For any text messaging program to be successful, it must have subscribers. If no one opts-in to a texting program, the texts will reach no one, even if the rest of the program is well conceived. Marketing of the texting program is therefore critical to its success; an understanding of what will make it appealing to target audiences is required. Equally important is an understanding of what kinds of texts target audiences want to receive. Text messages can be tailored to a specific individual's interests. Content that is more relevant is more likely to be understood, remembered and acted upon (Bull 2011). Public health communicators likely have a strong notion of what information people should get, but if we do not know what the target audience finds relevant or of value, we risk losing a subscriber base.

USES AND GRATIFICATIONS

To better understand what people want from texting, we employed a uses and gratifications approach as our theoretical foundation. The uses and gratifications approach assumes that individual differences among media users propel each person to seek out and use different media technology and content in different ways (Bryant and Thompson 2002). The gratification-seeking and audience-activity model within this tradition addresses how viewers' attention to the content of messages is influenced by the particular kinds of gratifications they seek, as well as their attitudes. Effects on the viewer's thoughts, emotions, or behavior depend on involvement with the message and behavioral intentions of the viewer (Rubin and Perse 1987).

Motivations for mobile phone use include instrumental (task-oriented) ones, such as using the phone for work or for emergencies (Roos 1993) or for the immediate accessibility it provides (Leung and Wei 2000); affective, such as the desire for security (Ling 2000) or for feeling closer to family members (Leung and Wei 2000); and social, such as the extensive use of mobile phones by teens for social networking (Ling 2000) and the display of a cell phone to indicate status or fashion (Leung and Wei 2000).

With respect specifically to text messaging on the mobile phone, prior uses and gratifications research has shown that social motives outweigh instrumental motives among young people, the earliest adopters of the technology. In a Dutch study of 12–25-year-olds, researchers found that immediate access and social interaction were primary motives for text messaging use (Peters et al. 2003). Similarly, Grant and O'Donohue (2007) found that social stimulation and entertainment were primary motivations for older adolescents. Younger texters used texting much less for informational purposes, and widely disliked the use of texting for advertising. The researchers concluded that although social gratifications drive texting use for young people, they do not want social interaction with outside entities; to reach young audiences, marketers and others outside young people's social networks should instead develop texting content that supports young people in maintaining their relationships. Manhatanankoon (2007) found that personality traits – like personal innovativeness and playfulness – predicted text messaging usage patterns.

As demonstrated by these studies, texting programs must take into account what target audiences want and support them in their desired uses of texting if they are to successfully engage people. An analysis of the uses and gratifications of different consumer segments can delineate the types of people, or "personas" that use texting, how they use it, and why. In technology industries, personas are constructed characters used to document the goals, behaviors, needs, and limitations of a group of technology users. Technology developers use personas to help understand the end user and guide decisions about product development based on users' characteristics, needs, and desires (Snyder et al. 2011). Public health communicators can borrow this technique to guide development of text messaging programs.

To help public health communicators construct personas for text messaging users that can aid in the development of relevant text messages and marketing of text messaging programs, we sought answers to the following research questions: RQ 1: What are the uses and gratifications that young, urban adults seek or obtain from SMS text messaging? RQ 2: What are the different types of text message users among young adults and what attitudes do they hold towards text messaging?

Method

Q METHOD FOR USES AND GRATIFICATIONS AND ATTITUDINAL AUDIENCE RESEARCH

To better understand why and how people use texting, we wanted to segment the audience by their uses and gratifications, rather than major demographic groups, like ethnicity, age and gender. Q methodology is a useful tool in this endeavor because it elicits groupings or "types" of people based on their own subjective viewpoints about a topic – in this case, what they think about text messaging (Brown 1980, 1991). Q methodology allows researchers to uncover how types of like-minded individuals think about an issue in similar ways and in ways that are different from others. Q is powerful in part because of its internal validity and authenticity; it allows participants to model their beliefs independent of constructs or categories predetermined by researchers. Additionally, using Q methodology to construct texter types or "personas" can assist with the creation and marketing of public health text messaging programs and optimizes the chances that audiences will find it useful and relevant.

DEVELOPMENT OF STATEMENT SET

Q method involves the rank ordering of opinion statements about the topic by research participants. To develop the set of opinion statements, we reviewed the grey and academic literature and conducted interviews with people who use text messaging to determine what they liked and did not like about texting until we reached a saturation of opinions; this process resulted in an initial list of 100 opinion statements about texting. An advisory group winnowed the list down to a more manageable list of 46 statements that reflect attitudes, uses and gratifications identified by previous studies (see the Appendix for a complete list of statements).

RECRUITMENT OF PARTICIPANTS

We chose to study young adults because they are heavy users of text messaging (Smith 2011) and because they may be harder to reach with traditional media. Following Q method, which typically includes a number of participants that is significantly smaller than the statement set (Brown 1991), we recruited a convenience sample of 31 young adults between the ages of 18 and 29 from across King County, Washington. Interviewees were recruited at community colleges and other educational facilities, county employees, and community based organizations. Each participant received a $20 gift card upon completion of the interview. Participants were interviewed alone, and interviews were audio recorded and transcribed verbatim. Each participant "sorted" the opinion statements across a continuum of negative six, representing "least agree" to positive six, representing "most agree." As shown in Table 8.1, the number in parentheses is the number of statements sorted under each ranking of agreement in a forced distribution format.

Researchers documented the order in which participants ranked the statements. Using the software program, PQ Method 2.11, we ran a factor analysis on the individual

Table 8.1   Q-Sort Statement Distribution

Least Agree						Neutral					Most Agree	
-6	-5	-4	-3	-2	-1	0	1	2	3	4	5	6
(1)	(2)	(2)	(3)	(3)	(4)	(16)	(4)	(3)	(3)	(2)	(2)	(1)

rankings of statements – or "sorts" – to extract different groupings from the data set. PQ Method first created a correlation matrix, in which each individual sort is compared to every other sort. Factors were then extracted using the principal components method. Varimax rotation helped distinguish the differing perspectives between factors.

This process produced eight factors that we examined to see which factors to include in the final rotation. Following the principal of parsimony (Brown 1980) we looked for the number of factors that loaded as many of the sorts as possible, while still presenting a factor picture that was illuminating.

To assist with qualitative analysis of the transcribed interviews, all interview data was assigned codes connected to uses and gratifications identified in previous studies. Three research assistants conducted the coding, reaching intercoder reliability at Krippendorff's α of .67 or greater for each coefficient.

Results

Of our 31 participants, 25 loaded significantly on one of four factors.

Table 8.2   Participant Factor Loadings

	Factor 1	Factor 2	Factor 3	Factor 4	Did not load
Number of participants significantly loading on each factor	10	8	3	4	6

This study revealed four types of texters among the people in the sample. Each texter type represents a distinct way of thinking about the technology, how it is used, and what benefits texting brings to the individual. We have named the four types:

1. the On-the-Go texter;
2. the Strategic texter;
3. the Personal texter; and
4. the Security texter.

A discussion of these types follows.

PERSONA 1: THE ON-THE-GO TEXTER

Uses and gratifications   On-The-Go texters are characterized by their busy lifestyles. Texting to them is the tool with which they organize and manage all the facets of their lives. Texting is a useful and necessary tool for planning events, connecting quickly with friends and family, and taking care of errands. In essence, texting allows them to more efficiently multitask. Texting does not strengthen or deepen relationships; it is a necessary tool for communicating. There is no question in their minds that texting is here to stay.

On-the-Go texters most strongly agreed with the following statements:

- "Texting has become part of the social protocol. It's just the way we communicate now" (rank 6; factor loading: 2.16).
- "I like texting because it's efficient, short, and to the point" (rank 5; factor loading 1.89).
- "There are often times during the day when it is inconvenient to talk on the phone but where sending a text is much easier" (rank 5; factor loading 1.84).
- "I text because it's an easy way to let someone know you're thinking of them" (rank 4; factor loading 1.61).
- "I text to verify social plans" (rank 4; factor loading 1.47).

Key attitudes held by on-the-go texters

Texting is the communications norm   Significant at p <.01, a key statement for On-the-Go texters that distinguished them from the other texters was "Texting has become part of the social protocol. It's just the way we communicate now" (factor loading 2.16. This underscores the On-the-Go texter's belief that texting is fundamental to communication. These texters believe that texting is a communications technology that is here to stay, that "it's the communications norm." Their friends and co-workers use text, and they "can't see it not being a tool in phones, like any time in the near future…it's pretty simple and pretty timeless."

Texting is always appropriate   On-the-Go texters always have their phones with them and texting is so quick and easy. There are few situations where their impulse is not to text first. For example, when privacy is an issue, "a lot of times it's more appropriate to text than have … a conversation that's audible throughout the room." On-the-Go texters even confess to "sneakily text[ing]" during movies.

Text me only useful information, not spam   This texter type uses text to get information, for example, "where I need to be, what time, [I get] updates from my friends as the plan is changing." They do not particularly use text to get news, however, and those that reported signing up for news-type messaging services have found it disappointing because of the spam that followed:

> There have been a couple of things [I've signed up for] and I ended up getting the like "go to this thing and buy this ringtone" and some span stuff and I have to cancel … That gets obnoxious in my opinion.

With respect to emergency text messages, one On-the-Go texter said:

> I'd definitely sign up for something like that. Anything important is good to have. [a bus arrival text] wasn't that important to have, but if it was like an earthquake … [that would be valuable].

PERSONA 2: THE STRATEGIC TEXTER

Uses and gratifications   Strategic texters are characterized by their use of texting exclusively as a tool for quick, targeted communication. They use texting to avoid long conversations.

They are suspicious of texting's influences on society and therefore tend to resist texting too often. They prefer to use other forms of communication to deepen their relationships. To them texting is convenient and efficient in situations where small amounts of information need to be communicated. Texting has its place, but that place is limited.

Statements with which Strategic texters most strongly agree:

- "There are often times during the day when it is inconvenient to talk on the phone but where sending a text is much easier" (rank 6; factor loading 2.17).
- "I hate it when I'm hanging out with people and instead of socializing, they text with other friends" (rank 5; factor loading 1.64).
- "I text when I don't want to talk or get into a lengthy conversation" (rank 5; factor loading 1.27).
- "I text only when I can't call, email or meet in person" (rank 4; factor loading 1.23).
- "Texting is too expensive" (rank 4; factor loading 1.20).

Key attitudes held by strategic texters

Texting is useful to control social interactions   Making a phone call is a preferred form of communication, but the Strategic texter finds texting useful when making a call would be problematic. Strategic texters strongly agree that there are times when talking is inconvenient and texting is a good option. For example, when you want to avoid a lengthy conversation:

> *you just feel awkward calling somebody and somehow it's just easier to text them. Then you don't have to hear their voice or have to interrupt them.*

Texting meets the needs of others as well   Strategic texters note the advantages of texting, such as when people like to contact others who live in another time zone, and they've already gone to bed: you "aren't going to wake them up with the phone ringing. They can check it when they're awake." Similarly, sometimes it is more appropriate to text rather than call: "we have to respect their time … maybe they were doing something else or sleeping."

Texting is most helpful with coordination and planning   Common uses included setting up plans, with texts such as "You need to be here at this time," and coordinating location, "I'm sitting in this seat at the concert." According to Strategic texters, texting is good for planning because it does not require sitting down at a computer, and rather than risk getting into a lengthy or unwelcome phone call, text is easier. "I send specific targeted messages generally if I'm coordinating and even with friends because it's less intrusive, for example, if someone's driving," noted one Strategic texter.

Texting doesn't strengthen relationships   The Strategic texter uses texting under certain circumstances, but does not use text as a means to foster social relationships. The ranking of statements that were distinguishing for this type include "I text to deepen my relationships" (-1.98), underscoring this type's strong disagreement with the notion that text messaging can be used in cementing relationships. In addition, the Strategic texter strongly and uniquely disagreed with the statement that "If I'm not constantly connected to my social network of friends via texting I feel left out" (-.208), demonstrating that texting is simply a tool in the Strategic texter's repertoire, not an essential means to connect to others.

One Strategic texter explained:

I don't think text messaging ... impacts my relationships other than coordinating in person meetings ... I never explained my thoughts to anyone over a text message or anything.

In fact, texting helps maintain superficial relationships:

I just don't think it's very emotionally deep. With acquaintances I'd probably just text message so I could avoid calling them, so I use it for the opposite [of maintaining deep relationships].

The cost of texting is another reason texting does not help with relationships, and this group strongly agreed that cost was a barrier. In fact, strategic texters considered cost of texts more than other types of texters:

I actually hope people don't text me back because then it's just a waste of money ... I'll text you, assume you got it and unless there's a question in it you don't need to text me back.

PERSONA 3: THE INTIMATE TEXTER

Uses and gratifications Intimate texters are characterized by their use of texting as a way to maintain relationships with close friends and family members. These relationships tend to be the major focus of their texting. Although they do use it for some practical reasons, they think of it as being a tool to use with a tight knit circle of close people. Because they do invest themselves personally into these communications, it is also important to them that people be considerate about their texting and therefore think it is impolite to text in a group. They are not interested in the technology for the flashy features, constant access or social status.

Statements with which Intimate texters most strongly agree:

- "I hate it when I'm hanging out with people and instead of socializing, they text with other friends" (rank 6; factor loading 2.38).
- "I text because it's an easy way to let someone know you're thinking of them" (rank 5; factor loading 2.03).
- "I text to deepen my relationships" (rank 5; factor loading 1.98).
- "There are often times during the day when it is inconvenient to talk on the phone, but where sending a text message is much easier" (rank 4; factor loading 1.26).
- "I like texting because it's efficient, it's short and to the point" (rank 4; factor loading 1.12).

Key attitudes held by intimate texters

Texting can be rude The Intimate texter perceives that texting can play a strong role in social connections, for better or worse. They use text messaging to strengthen relationships, but note that texting also can get in the way. The Intimate texter most strongly agreed with the notion that it is annoying when people text in front of him:

If you're telling a story to someone … they get on their phone and then you have to repeat it … I just get annoyed so much when they're not paying attention.

Getting a quick response to text messages is also important, even if the other person is busy, as one Intimate texter explained:

It is disrespectful … and a sign of weakness on the part of the person who has kept quiet.

Texting is for connection   A defining statement for Intimate texters was "I text to deepen my relationships" (1.98). However, texting is reserved for only a few people close to the Intimate texter. In particular, family is important to this type of texter:

I am family oriented and I'm becoming more as I get older and so I just want to keep those relationships that I have and make sure we are communicating and on the right path.

Texting is a quick way to keep the connection to family and close relationships simmering:

If you're tired after a long day, but you're thinking about that person, you just want to say 'how was your day' and they'll respond, hopefully.

Another Intimate texter uses it as a means to stay connected when no other option is available:

When I'm home alone or during the night, or when my [girlfriend] can't talk to me, that's all I'll do. I prefer calling, but she told me not to so I can't help [but text].

Texting is not a good way to get information   Unlike the other types of texters, the Intimate texter does not use texting to get information. They disagreed with the statements, "I like texting because I can text to get directions/ names of restaurants directly to my phone" (-1.91) and, "I like texting because I can text to get news and information" (-1.70). Even though it is easy to text, the Intimate texter prefers to call and ask for directions, or use the Internet for news and information. Possible exceptions to receiving texts for information would be if the texts were emergency oriented:

I have this bad habit of not watching television or reading the newspaper, and most of the time I don't know what's happening. So if I were to get a text … telling me about a plane that is hijacked and crashed in Puget Sound like 15 minutes ago … that would be helpful so I can take a precaution.

PERSONA 4: THE SECURITY TEXTER

Uses and gratifications   Unlike other texter types, this group strongly valued the privacy and security aspects of text messaging. To them, texting is a security blanket that provides peace of mind. It works as a tool not only to save important information that could come in handy in times of need, but it also works as a way of keeping important personal information private. Texting is also a tool used for physical protection in cases of emergencies and when they feel personally threatened. These are the people who think about unsafe situations that might happen and who feel better that their phone is with them at all times just in case. Texting is a dependable tool for communicating with friends and family who live far away.

Statements with which Security texters most strongly agree:

- "I like texting because texting is private. I can text without my kids/friends/parents knowing the subject matter" (rank 6; factor loading 2.19).
- "I like texting because I can store a message and look up a message later" (rank 5; factor loading 1.80).
- "I like texting because I can avoid interrupting someone" (rank 5; factor loading 1.77).
- "I feel safer knowing I can text someone if I were in a dangerous situation" (rank 4; factor loading 1.58).
- "I like texting because I can get/send messages while I'm doing something else" (rank 4; factor loading 1.33).

Key attitudes held by security texters

Texting is private   While The Security texter and the On-the-Go texter share many of the same opinions about the utility of texting, there were significant differences. A distinguishing statement for the Security texter was "I like texting because texting is private. I can text without my kids/friends/parents knowing the subject matter" (2.19) The Security texter likes being able to communicate without anyone hearing the conversation, unlike a voice call:

> *I think when you're calling someone, other people will listen in and would ... infer something from your conversation.*

Another Security texter values texting because:

> *I like knowing it's really safe and I'm having a one to one conversation.*

Whether the topic is school, or romantic partners, or just avoiding an awkward situation, Security texters note the freedom in being able to express oneself via text in private:

> *If us two friends [want to] hang out, and I didn't ask my roommate and he listens to me, that would be a little bit rude so it's better to text.*

Another benefit of texting is that messages can be stored securely. One Security texter commented:

> *I have siblings that check my phone sometimes, but that's why there's a lock thing. So you can lock it and that's good. It is pretty private.*

Texting provides a sense of security. Another distinguishing statement for this group was "I feel safer knowing I can text someone if I were in a dangerous situation" (1.58). For example, a Security texter described a situation where there is a person who is volatile, and you want to call for help discreetly:

> It's really quiet and no one can really notice. Especially since I have a phone that you can just touch it, without the buttons clicking. It's easy.

Another Security texter described a more dire use:

> ... if like I am kidnapped by someone and it's really not appropriate to call, maybe, I mean, in that case text messaging is definitely the best choice.

Texting allows a person to stay in touch with a particular friend for help:

> My friend, my best friend, we always text, so if I cannot do anything I know I can text her and then she can get me help. That safety, you just know it's there.

IMPLICATIONS FOR ACADEMICS: WHY Q METHOD IS EFFECTIVE FOR AUDIENCE RESEARCH ABOUT TEXT MESSAGING AND USES AND GRATIFICATIONS

Unlike methods that highlight respondent differences based on demographics, Q method provides a window into the nuanced viewpoints within a group. Studies in the uses and gratifications tradition have typically used survey methods, where respondents are forced to choose among a few pre-identified answer choices. In contrast, Q explores the subjective perspectives of respondents and allows for deeper reflection of the topic by the respondent. It is also a mixed method approach that employs the process of rank ordering statements to engage the respondent in thinking through the complex attitudes behind a topic, and allows responses to be quantified. Q method is particularly effective for exploring text messaging viewpoints because it can capture the nuances of the varied and flexible ways people text. Using Q, researchers can directly analyze differences between people's texting experiences according to their uses and gratifications rather than their demographic categories.

IMPLICATIONS FOR HEALTH PRACTITIONERS: MARKETING AND TEXT MESSAGE DESIGN STRATEGY FOR IDENTIFIED PERSONAS

The four different texting personas that emerged from this analysis can be used to aid health departments and providers in the development of more successful texting programs. Health communicators can target efforts to fit the distinct uses of texting, gratifications sought from texting experiences, and attitudes about the technology found in these personas. By focusing on the characteristics of the personas, practitioners can craft more enticing marketing campaigns to increase opt-in as well as inform the development of text messages that resonate with the audience. Using the public health emergency preparedness as an example, we developed the following suggestions for shaping materials around the four personas.

The On-the-Go texter has fully embraced text messaging as a part of his or her life and communication style. Marketing materials that use phrases like "fits into your busy lifestyle," "texting is the best way to receive this information," and "easy to get updated information," will be attractive to this group. Emphasizing that the information will be highly useful and can be read at the On-the-Go texters' convenience will be an important caveat. Health programs that craft messages with the On-the-Go texter in mind may use multi-tasking as a hook. For example, an emergency preparedness texting program could focus on helping this group manage their busy lives with a text like "Stopping by the pharmacy? Don't forget to get a flu shot too. It will help you stay protected against a flu outbreak."

The Strategic texter is far more selective about texting. Since the Strategic texter appreciates texting for its quick and controlled interaction, emphasizing the briefness and limited number of the messages may be a good approach. For example, marketing materials may say something like: "Texts will be short and to the point, allowing you to follow up only on the information that interests you." Texting programs will also be more inviting to Strategic texters if you emphasize that the information provided by text will allow them to coordinate and plan. Marketing the business-like quick communication style of text messaging will appeal to the Strategic texter, who values the targeted nature of texted communications. For the Strategic texter, an emergency preparedness program might include messages that emphasize tips for coordinating post-emergency meet-up with family, or identifying an out-of-state contact if local land lines are down. These messages focus on the Strategic texter's positive attitude about using text to coordinate.

The Intimate texter does not use texting much for news and information, but rather to deepen relationships. The best approach to encourage the Intimate texter to sign up for texting program may be to emphasize how the information provided may be of use to family and friends. For example, appropriate appeals could include "receive important emergency health information you can forward to your close friends and family," or "make sure you have the information your close friends and family need in the event of an emergency." Similarly, text messages would highlight the importance of taking steps to become more prepared to ensure close friends and family are safe. The text messages may also emphasize sharing the texts with their close network such as "forward this message to a close friend to make sure they are safe too."

The Security texter clearly is an excellent target for an emergency text messaging program. Phrases like "information to stay safe in an emergency" will appeal to this type of texter. "Have information at your fingertips in case of a dangerous situation," and "receive texts with critical information for your safety to store right in your phone" are likely types of marketing appeals that will be effective with this type. Clearly, the Security texter may respond well to a range of emergency preparedness texts, particularly ones that emphasize ways to increase their readiness and increased safety. Texts like "Have a supply of water for 3 days? In an emergency, this can be a lifeline" should be appealing.

When health departments or providers are recruiting broadly for a text messaging program, marketing materials and individual texts should include a mix of appeals designed to reach each of the personas. In addition, this study found one key "consensus" statement, which each texter type tended to place in the same location on the least agree to most agree continuum. Identification of a consensus statement may be used by public health to develop messages that will resonate with all texter types. In this case, all four texter types disagreed with the statement:

I wouldn't rely on texting in an emergency because power and signal availability is unreliable.

An effective marketing appeal might be:

You know that texting can be the most reliable way to get info during an emergency. Sign up today to receive important messages to help you during a public health emergency.

Conclusion

Provision of health information is a core mission for health departments in the promotion and protection of community health. In this time of limited resources, health departments need to use all the tools available to them to assist in this critical mission. In light of texting's wide and increasing adoption, to ignore texting is not merely a missed opportunity but also a refusal to engage the public using a highly accessible, common, and frequently preferred means of communication.

At the same time, we recognize that strained resources make it challenging for health departments and other providers to keep up with technology. It is our hope that this study will encourage practitioners to consider how texting might fill communications gaps and will assist health departments in maximizing any investment they make in texting programs. A clearer understanding of the contexts within which people use texting, their reasons for using it, how they use it, and how types of texters cluster together can help ensure that members of the public will sign up for health texts and find them relevant to their needs and expectations.

This study also points to the practical benefits of integrating communication theory and diverse research methods to meet everyday needs of health communicators. As members of a public health department communications team, we embarked on this research to improve our communications practice. In the process, we found that application of uses and gratifications theory offered insights about how people in our community use and think about communications technology that would have been missed through a less rigorous focus group or survey study. The use of Q method allowed the subjective perspectives on texting to emerge from the community we serve, rather than from our own assumptions, and made it possible to organize their perspectives into personas that we can employ on a practical level. The study also demonstrated the value of applying an innovative method to the long-standing communications tradition of uses and gratifications. We, therefore, recommend and encourage more collaborative research teams between health communication professionals and researchers, which can result in fruitful outcomes for both parties.

Future Research

Text messaging is still a relatively new technology. As the use of text messaging continues to grow, the social norms and practices will also evolve. With the expansion of other technologies such as Smartphones and social media sites, the ways people use SMS text messaging are likely to shift. Future research will need to continue to capture this evolution to ensure that organizations align their health communication strategies with the ways their audiences use the technologies.

This research sheds light on the ways people use text messaging, their gratifications and attitudes about the technology. There is still much to be learned about how health departments can be most effective in promoting and protecting health using this communication channel. Given the different types of texters in the community, what types of messages will be most effective in leading to behavior change? How can health organizations customize messages more effectively to take advantage of the personal nature of text messaging? What are the most effective ways to market texting programs to ensure we are closing the gap in access to information, not expanding it? Further research is needed to address these issues.

Acknowledgment

This work was supported by the Centers for Disease Control and Prevention, Grant no. 5PO1TP000297. Its contents are solely the responsibility of the authors and do not necessarily represent the official views of the Centers for Disease Control and Prevention.

References

Brown, S.R. 1980. *Political Subjectivity: Applications of Q Methodology in Political Science*. New Haven, CT: Yale University Press.

Brown, S.R. 1991. A primer on Q methodology. Operant Subjectivity [Online], 16, 91–138. Available at: http://facstaff.uww.edu/cottlec/QArchive/Primer1.html [accessed: 22 September 2011].

Bryant, J. and Thompson, S. 2002. *Fundamentals of Media Effects*. New York: McGraw-Hill.

Bull, S. and McFarlane, M. 2011. *Technology-based Health Promotion*. Los Angeles, CA: Sage Publications.

Coyle, D. 2005. *The Role of Mobiles in Disasters and Emergencies* [Online: Enlightenment Economics]. Available at: www.dinkom.no/FILES/gsm_disaster_relief_report.pdf [accessed: 22 September 2011].

Grant, I. and O'Donohue, S. 2007. Why young consumers are not open to mobile marketing communication. *International Journal of Advertising*, 26(2), 223–46.

Lenhart, A. 2010. *Cellphones and American Adults* [Online: Pew Internet and American Life Project]. Available at: http://www.pewinternet.org/Reports/2010/Cell-Phones-and-American-Adults.aspx [accessed: 18 August 2011].

Leung, L. and Wei, R. 2000. More than just talk on the move: A uses and gratification study of the cellular phone. Journalism and Mass Communication Quarterly, 77(2), 308–320.

Ling, R. 2000. "We will be reached:" The use of mobile telephony among Norwegian youth. *Information Technology and People*, 13(2), 102–20.

Mahatanankoon, P. 2007. The effects of personality traits and optimum stimulation level on text-messaging activities and m-commerce intention. *International Journal of Electronic Commerce*, 12(1), 7–30.

Peters, O., Almekinders, J., Van Buren, R.S. and Wessels, J. 2003. *Motives for SMS Use*. Paper to the International Communication Association: 2003 Annual Meeting, San Diego, CA.

Roos, J.P. 1993. Sociology of the cellular telephone: The Nordic model (300,000 yuppies? Mobile phone in Finland). *Telecommunications Policy*, 17(6), 446–57.

Rubin, A.M. and Perse, E.M. 1987. Audience activity and television news gratifications. *Communication Research*, 14, 58–84.

Smith, A. 2011. *Americans and Their Cell Phones* [Online: Pew Internet and American Life Project]. Available at: http://www.pewinternet.org/Reports/2011/Cell-Phones.aspx [accessed: 17 August 2011].

Snyder, M., Sampanes, A., White, B. and Rampoldi-Hnilo, L. 2011. Personas on the move: Making personas for today's mobile workforce, in *Design, User Experience, and Usability, Pt. II*, edited by A. Marcus. Berlin: Springer-Verlag, 313–20.

Appendix 8.1

Final Statement Set

FASHION/STATUS/ SELF PRESENTATION

1. If I'm not constantly connected to my social network of friends via texting I feel left out.
2. Having a nice phone is less embarrassing for texting in front of friends.
3. I think other people text because they think it's cool. It makes people feel popular and in demand.
4. I text because I think other people get a better impression of me.

AFFECTION/SOCIABILITY

5. I text because it's simple for just checking in.
6. I text because it's an easy way to let someone know you're thinking of them.
7. Texting has become part of the social protocol. It's just the way we communicate now.
8. I typically text all day long to lots of different people.
9. I text to always be available to my family.
10. Texting makes me feel involved with what's going on with other people.

INTIMACY

11. I text to feel closer to family members.
12. I text to deepen my relationships.

RELAXATION/ ESCAPISM

13. Texting is a fun addiction!
14. I text to gossip or chat.
15. Texting helps me pass the time while I'm waiting.
16. I text to put off something I should be doing.

IMMEDIATE ACCESS

17. What I like about texting is that I'm always available at any time.
18. One of the best things about texting is that people always have their cell phones with them.
19. There are often times during the day when it is inconvenient to talk on the phone, but where sending a text message is much easier.

INSTRUMENTALITY

20. I like texting because I can store a message and look up a message later.
21. I like texting because I can text for work-related reasons.
22. I like texting because I can text to get directions/ names of restaurants directly to my phone.
23. I like texting because I can text to get news and information.
24. I text to verify social plans.
25. I text because it is too early or too late in the day to call.

REASSURANCE

26. I text to let people know I'm running late.
27. I feel safer knowing I can text someone if I were in a dangerous situation.
28. I wouldn't rely on texting in an emergency because power and signal availability is unreliable.

LAST RESORT

29. I text only when I can't call, email or meet in person.

BARRIERS/NEGATIVES

30. I think that people text because they have nothing better to do with their lives.
31. Texting is too expensive.
32. Texting is a fad.
33. Texting people is quite stupid because you can call that person quicker than typing.
34. One problem with texting is receiving spam texts/junk mail and/or marketing texts.
35. I hate it when I'm hanging out with people and instead of socializing, they text with other friends.
36. In many situations it's rude to text when in a group.
37. Texting is hard because the buttons are too small for my fingers.
38. I don't like having to press the buttons so many times to get the letter I need.

MISCELLANEOUS

39. I like texting because it's efficient, it's short and to the point.
40. I like texting because I can get/send messages while I'm doing something else.
41. I text when I don't want to talk or get into a lengthy conversation.

42. I like texting because I can avoid interrupting someone.
43. I like texting because texting is private. I can text without my kids/friends/parents knowing the subject matter.
44. I like using short hand or abbreviations.
45. I think people text so that they can avoid conversations.
46. It's rude if I text someone and they don't text me back.

9

Reaching the Unreachable: How eHealth and Mobile Health Technologies Impact At-Risk Populations

ROWENA L. BRIONES AND BETH SUNDSTROM

Introduction

According to the Pew Internet and American Life Project, 80 percent of American users (or about 113 million adults) search the Internet for at least one specific health topic, and about eight million of those users turn to the Web for health information on just a typical day (Fox 2006). In addition, the online health-information environment is increasingly turning mobile, with 17 percent of cell phone users using their phones to look up health or medical information and 9 percent of users utilizing software or "apps" to help manage their health (Fox 2010). Among these users are communities of color, with the proportion of Internet users who are black or Latino nearly doubling between 2000 and 2010 (Smith 2010). For many of these populations, the Web and mobile technologies are one way that they can access health information quickly and efficiently.

Because the Internet and mobile technologies have become such pervasive tools for health consumers, it is imperative to learn exactly *how* these groups use the Web and mobile technology for health purposes and *why* they prefer to use these channels. The contributions of extant research on eHealth and mobile health technologies are influential because they not only enhance the theoretical frameworks surrounding this phenomenon, but they also greatly impact the practice of medicine and health communication. Therefore, the purpose of this chapter is to explore these questions through four different sections.

First, an extensive review of literature on the Internet, mobile technology, and health will be explicated. Special attention will be given to aspects of mobile health and its relationship with at-risk populations (Smith 2010). The second section will be a case example of the Text4Baby campaign. This campaign was chosen due to its broad reach and success; it was the first grand-scale, national mobile health initiative in the United States with more than 3.5 million messages sent and more than 300 outreach partners joining the initiative (Text4Baby 2011). The theories and evaluation underlying the campaign will be presented, along with original qualitative research to explore pregnant women's perceptions of the campaign and to understand how the Internet and mobile technology impact understandings of risk and health among women on the margins. The third section includes the challenges and opportunities for using Web technologies in health contexts. Finally, the chapter will conclude with implications and future directions for health communication research and practice.

eHealth and Mobile Technology from the Provider's Perspective

One emerging phenomenon in clinical practice is patients attempting to incorporate information from the Internet into the medical consultation (Ahmad et al. 2006). A study by Sommerhalder and colleagues (2009) found that adding health-related Internet information (HRII) to consultations was appreciated by physicians; however, it oftentimes led to misleading interpretations. Another study by Ahmad et al. (2006) found that physicians felt that integrating Internet information into consultations caused misinformation on the part of the patient, leading to confusion, distress, and inaccurate self-diagnoses and self-treatment.

However, there have been instances in which physicians thought positively about the use of Web technologies in their practice. Houston and colleagues (2003) found that physicians who were satisfied with the use of email in their consultations thought the practice was not only time saving but also helped them deliver better care. Nordqvist and colleagues (2009) found that the development of a diabetes education portal led to a sense of community, saved time, and offered practical and social support to patients. Yet, they also found that the use of this technology could not replace face-to-face communication, but might complement it. In addition, physicians felt that the use of technologies in their patient interactions can also pose some medicolegal risks within the patient-provider relationship (Houston et al. 2003).

The use of the Internet for health information may also increase a patient's frequency of contact with a health professional for health information and for ailment treatment (Lee 2008a), as patients feel more equipped with what they have gathered. Imes and colleagues (2008) found that many patients believed the quality of information found on the Internet is worth sharing in a medical consultation, despite feeling uncomfortable with their providers.

When discussing health-related Internet information with providers, patients' satisfaction with the overall medical experience increased, as was found in Bylund et al.'s (2007) study on cancer patients. Though few of these patients were directly assertive with their oncologists, Bylund and colleagues found that those patients were comfortable making it explicit that they received their information from the Web. Additionally, Lee (2008a) argued that patients sought information on the Internet in the first place because they were overall more sensitive to health conditions and wanted to start a discussion with their doctors. By being equipped with this information, patients felt more legitimated by their providers, leading to a decreased concern about the health problem (Sabee et al. 2005).

Wald and colleagues' (2007) review of the literature found a few key points in regards to the various outcomes that result from the use of eHealth technologies. First, they found that the emergence of eHealth now leads to the triangulation of information, from patient to the Web to the physician. This triangulation not only helps augment the information provided by the physician, but it also shifts the conventional notions of the patient-provider relationship by straying from the "traditional" idea of medical authority. However, this shift does lead to more positive outcomes, increasing shared decision-making, collaboration and teamwork between the two parties and creating a more efficient use of clinical time.

eHealth and Technology from the Patient's Perspective

The Pew Internet and American Life Project conducted a series of telephone interviews to determine the motivations behind seeking health information on the Internet. Among the main reasons, individuals turn to the Web because:

a) someone they know has been diagnosed with a health condition and they are looking on behalf of someone else;
b) they themselves are diagnosed with a new health problem and are conducting their own research;
c) they are searching from home to answer a specific question;
d) they are being prescribed a new medication or course of treatment; and/or
e) they have unanswered questions after a doctor's visit (Fox and Rainie 2002).

In addition, a number of studies have been conducted to explore what factors predict whether or not a person will conduct information searches on the Internet. Rains (2007) discovered that trust plays a large role in this regard; in particular, having trust in the Web as a credible information source leads to more information seeking on the Internet, while simultaneously increasing distrust in the more traditional sources of information such as medical providers and entertainment-oriented media. Furthermore, Rains found that individuals prefer using the Web for health information because it offers them more control over an overabundance of sources, as opposed to more traditional media such as magazines and newspapers that are more limited in their reach and scope.

Control was also a factor that was shown to be important in Lieberman and colleagues' (2003) study. They found that users preferred an interactive system that offered not only a high level of control but also shared tailored information. When websites or interventions personalized their feedback to users, their perceptions of the quality of content, as well as the informativeness of the content, increased. And, finally, in Lee's (2008b) analysis of what constituted repeated search behavior on the Web, he found that participants were more likely to conduct searches if it satisfied their utilitarian needs (that is, treatment for a health condition), was relevant and credible, and increased their satisfaction.

Warner and Procaccino's (2007) review of the literature found that frequent Web users had greater success of finding health information, found online information to be more useful, and had many of their health questions answered through the Internet. In addition, the decisions about health treatments made by Web users were more influenced by the health information that was found via online. Tian and Robinson (2009) discovered similar findings in their study on incidental Internet searching; those who inadvertently found health information online had positive overall Internet usage, more active health information seeking, and more frequent use of other media channels such as television, newspapers, and magazines for supplemental information. Other outcomes included more frequent visits to the physician's office and higher levels of health knowledge, though Web users claim that finding health information was not any easier for them as compared to non-Web users (Warner and Procaccino 2007). Another way that users could find health information is through their mobile devices from campaigns such as Text4Baby, which is detailed as a case example below.

Text4Baby Case Example: The First National Mobile Health Campaign in the U.S.

The infant mortality rate in the United States is over 6 per 1,000 live births. This places the United States 30th worldwide, behind developing countries such as Hungary and Cuba (Central Intelligence Agency 2010). Hispanic and African American women are about 2.5 times more likely than white women to delay prenatal care until the third trimester or to forego prenatal care (Rochman 2010). Text4Baby seeks to promote healthy birth outcomes among underserved populations. This campaign is the first grand-scale, national mobile health initiative in the United States, aiming to change prenatal and postpartum health behaviors.

MOBILE HEALTH AND UNDERSERVED POPULATIONS

Mobile health (mHealth) has been used successfully in developing countries to spread health messages. In the United States, 87 percent of African Americans and Latinos own cell phones. Furthermore, African American and Latino cell phone owners are more likely than whites to use a range of cell phone features including the Internet and text messaging (Smith 2010). Formative research for the Text4Baby campaign mirrored these results, finding that African-American and Hispanic moms are "avid" users of text messages. In this way, cell phones can provide broad reach to underserved populations.

The target audience for the Text4Baby campaign includes pregnant women, new mothers, and underserved populations. This audience has been operationalized as Medicaid-eligible women and Spanish-speaking women. The U.S. Department of Health and Human Services plans to evaluate whether Text4Baby subscribers have better outcomes than nonsubscribers. The evaluation seeks to answer whether the access to advice prompts the desired behavior changes of increased doctor's visits, reduced smoking rates, and other health behaviors. The ultimate goal is the decline of incidence of low birth weight and prematurity among the targeted audience populations.

The cornerstone of the Text4Baby campaign is the text messaging service offered completely free to women. Cell phone companies waive the text message fee for women receiving the service. Women sign up for the service by texting BABY (or BEBE for Spanish messages) to 511411. This nationwide campaign was launched in February 2010. In November 2010, Text4Baby campaign planners announced a new goal of 1 million users by the end of 2012 (Remick 2010).

During registration, women provide their due date or their baby's date of birth to receive messages tailored with timely advice. Women receive a standard series of start-up health messages, such as advice to visit a doctor, followed by three messages per week during pregnancy and the first 12 months of their baby's life. The messages are written by the National Healthy Mothers, Healthy Babies Coalition (HMHB) and evaluated by doctors, nurses, health care practitioners, and public health professionals. The messages cover diverse topics ranging from health care access, influenza, nutrition, prenatal care, mental health, labor and delivery to car seat safety. For example, a safe sleeping message reminds women, "babies go on their backs, not their bellies."

The goals of Text4Baby are:

1. to promote positive self-efficacy for pre-natal care;
2. to encourage pre-natal and post-partum health care behaviors;
3. to demonstrate the potential of mobile health technology to address maternal and child health; and
4. to demonstrate the potential of mobile health technology to reach underserved populations with critical health information.

The campaign will also develop a base of evidence on the efficacy of mobile health interventions and catalyze new models for public-private partnerships in the area of mobile health.

PUBLIC-PRIVATE PARTNERSHIP

The founding organization of the Text4Baby campaign is the National Healthy Mothers, Healthy Babies Coalition (HMHB). The organization is a recognized leader and resource in maternal and child health, reaching an estimated 10 million healthcare professionals, parents, and policymakers through its membership of over 100 local, state and national organizations. HMHB's mission is to improve the health and safety of mothers, babies and families through educational materials and collaborative partnerships. HMHB's (2010) core values include:

1. a child's right to be born healthy and raised in a safe and nurturing environment;
2. equal access to quality health care;
3. a collective voice to facilitate change;
4. eliminating health disparities among all populations;
5. cultural competence and respect for diversity; and
6. education to encourage healthy choices.

Text4Baby is made possible through a broad, public-private partnership that includes government, corporations, academic institutions, professional associations, tribal agencies, and non-profit organizations. Forty states are creating Text4Baby coalitions. Some of the partners include the White House Office of Science and Technology Policy, the U.S. Department of Health and Human Services, CTIA Wireless Foundation, Johnson & Johnson, Voxiva, Wellpoint, and George Washington University.

The campaign involves social marketing strategies and a variety of tactics, including text messages, a website, Ning, billboards, events, education entertainment, logo, posters, and flyers. One example of education entertainment is the inclusion of Text4Baby on an episode of the reality television show "16 and Pregnant." The campaign is also being promoted by MTV, local health departments and Telemundo.

Between February and August 2010 more than 64,000 subscribers signed up for the service, more than 3.5 million messages were sent, and more than 300 outreach partners, including national, state, business, academic, non-profit, and other groups joined the initiative (Text4Baby 2011). Text4Baby also won a Health and Human Services Outstanding Innovation Award (Chen 2010). The broad reach of the campaign highlights the success of new media and the social interactivity of the campaign.

EVALUATION

The U.S. Department of Health and Human Services is leading a nationwide evaluation of Text4Baby in a randomized controlled cross-site design. Demonstration sites follow a common protocol based on comparison of text messaging plus usual healthcare compared to usual care alone. The data collection includes measurement of mother's recall and response to Text4Baby messages, pre-natal behaviors, and neo-natal outcome data. The data is collected through an Interactive Voice Response (IVR) survey over mobile phones via a 10-minute survey and will be integrated with partner data collections and health status measures. Evans (2010) described the George Washington University researchers' plans for long-term program evaluation over a three-year period. The evaluation uses a multi-theory approach to behavior change including the social cognitive theory (SCT), health belief model (HBM), and diffusion of innovations. Finally, the evaluation examines Text4Baby social marketing strategies and development of brand equity among Medicaid-eligible pregnant women and new mothers.

Local analyses of Text4Baby audiences provide supplementary data to the national evaluation. The National Latino Research Center at California State University and the University of California, San Diego, presented a preliminary assessment of Text4Baby at the American Public Health Association annual meeting in November 2011. The study included interviews with 38 Text4Baby users and a survey of 122 Text4Baby users in San Diego County. Participants rated Text4Baby as an 8.5 out of 10 overall. In brief, the study found an increase in knowledge, improved interaction with healthcare providers, increased attendance at appointments and increased uptake of immunizations and health resources by users (Chen 2011).

Perceptions of Text4Baby: The Current Study

Local, process evaluations of Text4Baby, such as the one conducted in San Diego County, are an important supplement to the comprehensive national evaluation. To provide an interim, local analysis of Text4Baby, original qualitative research was conducted to explore pregnant women's perceptions of the campaign and to understand how the Internet and mobile technology impacts women's understandings of risk and health in the mid-Atlantic region of the United States. At the time of this study, there was no published data exploring women's perceptions of Text4Baby. This study aimed to provide a local preliminary, in-depth understanding of women's perceptions of Text4Baby. This original research was part of a comprehensive audience analysis project examining pregnancy. In-depth interviews with seven pregnant women provided a rich and detailed understanding of the Text4Baby campaign in the lives of these women. Purposive and snowball sampling techniques were used to recruit participants through acquaintances, informal contacts, and word of mouth (Silverman and Marvasti 2008).

DATA COLLECTION

In-depth interviews were conducted with seven participants during the spring of 2011 at sites comfortable for participants, such as coffee shops, office locations, or the participants' homes. Interviews lasted from an hour to over one and a half hours. Participants ranged in age from 24 to 38. The women were between 15 and 37 weeks pregnant at the time of the interview. With participants' permission, all interviews were recorded and transcribed for accuracy. An open-ended question guide facilitated discussion during the interviews. Participants were prompted with questions, such as "Do you read or participate in any new media communities for pregnant women?" "Do you use any new media to find information or advice about pregnancy?" and "Do you remember seeing any new media campaign messages telling you what to do as a pregnant woman?" Probing questions further explicated the types of new media, such as websites, cell phone applications, and text messaging, among others.

DATA ANALYSIS

Data analysis was conducted using a grounded theory approach developed by Corbin and Strauss (2008). The transcripts were analyzed using axial and open coding to reduce the data and identify and relate concepts and themes across the data (Berg 2009, Corbin and Strauss 2008). Particular attention was paid to anomalies and deviant cases in the data (Silverman and Marvasti 2008). Memos and observer comments throughout the data collection and analysis process helped to maintain reflexivity and to identify emerging concepts (Rubin and Rubin 2005). The themes that emerged from these interviews are discussed in further detail below.

RESULTS

Temporality Participants were impressed that text messages were tailored based on due date. In particular, participants appreciated timely reminders to schedule doctor's appointments. One participant noted:

> you are at the doctor's office so much, and appointments get more and more frequent throughout pregnancy, so it is helpful to get a text message reminder about when you are supposed to go to the doctor this month.

Women were most comfortable receiving text messages once per week; however, they sought the opportunity to seek out additional information online. According to one participant:

> I look for information online that addresses the life of being a mom. I like to connect with other women, who can provide timely suggestions about the issues I am dealing with, today.

At the same time, these women negotiated issues of access and privacy. According to one participant, "I do like to read message boards about pregnancy and parenting, but I never post or really become part of that community." Another participant described her experience contributing to the online community: "even though I am not contributing as a blogger, I did guest blog once, and I often comment on others' posts and engage in the conversation."

Tailoring   Participants suggested that the Text4Baby campaign could provide additional tailoring of messages based on an individual's preferences. According to one participant:

> *a lot of the messages just didn't apply to me because I already have a doctor, pediatrician, day care...I wish they had a check list of what kinds of messages I am interested in.*

Participants expressed interest in a variety of topics, ranging from appropriate nutrition and exercise throughout pregnancy to coupons or product suggestions. Women also described the importance of protecting themselves from certain information. According to one participant:

> *in general, I don't go on the Internet to search [for information] related to pregnancy. I think there is too much on there to scare pregnant women ... what could happen "if" it [information] is not empowering or helpful.*

These women described the importance of maintaining control over the type of information they seek during pregnancy.

Interactivity   The current Text4Baby campaign offers one-way communication. An opportunity exists to provide two-way communication to create a dialogue with the audience to identify frequently asked questions and unknown barriers to positive health outcomes. Participants sought additional opportunities for two-way communication through the Text4Baby campaign. Specifically, participants desired an opportunity to text questions to Text4Baby and to receive personal answers to their health and pregnancy related questions. One participant shared, "I had a question about the safety of bedding for the baby's crib. I read that bumpers aren't safe for the baby. I think that is a question that probably a lot of pregnant women have." The Text4Baby campaign serves as a source of expert information for pregnant women on a variety of topics, including health and safety for themselves and their babies.

Locality   Participants appreciated that Text4Baby offers specific phone numbers for information and assistance with a variety of topics, such as day care and healthcare services. There is an opportunity to expand on this specificity by exploring additional local connections or creating local clubs or support groups that are connected through Text4Baby. One participant shared, "I am much more interested in what is going on in my community and connecting with pregnant women in real life." Another participant noted, "the city and the community is kind to pregnant women. People are warm, they will talk to you. It is really lovely." This perspective suggests the importance of capitalizing on opportunities for making local connections to improve health. Participants discussed the need for maternity clothes swaps and opportunities to share baby products, such as highchairs.

LIMITATIONS OF TEXT4BABY STUDY

There were several limitations to this particular study. First, the study sample included only pregnant women in the mid-Atlantic region of the United States. In addition, only seven women were interviewed, which do not make the findings generalizable to the entire population of pregnant women. Finally, the interviews constituted only preliminary, exploratory data designed to inform the national discussion regarding mhealth/text campaigns. However, despite these limitations, the importance of looking at Text4Baby as a case study helps offer insight into the promise of a national evaluation and the importance of theory-informed evaluation.

DISCUSSION

Text4Baby's strength lies in its mHealth universal messaging system to reach underserved populations. Text4Baby finds the audience where they live. The public-private partnership extends the campaign's reach and fosters community buy-in to the campaign. The campaign illustrates the importance of cultural competency in mobile health campaigns targeting underserved populations. Text4Baby offers Spanish language messaging with culturally sensitive advice to improve prenatal and postpartum health. As the campaign increases its participation among underserved populations, the opportunity to evaluate and refine messages to increase cultural competency should be leveraged.

Text4Baby is an innovative, effective model of an mHealth communication campaign. This effort provides an exemplar for public campaigns that wish to leverage mobile technologies in the U.S. The future success of the campaign hinges on its ability to continue to diffuse the innovation to a wide audience and to enhance two-way models of communication, which will ultimately improve individualization. Text4Baby's ability to reach targeted audiences with discrete advice and information will narrow the gap between knowledge and behavior change.

Challenges and Opportunities to Using the Web in Health Contexts

Based on the findings in terms of how both patients and providers use the Web and Text4Baby for health information dissemination and sharing, there are a series of challenges as well as opportunities in utilizing these technologies for information, education, community building, and outreach that emerge from this research.

CHALLENGES IN eHEALTH

Enhancing interactivity The use of eHealth calls for more interactive communication with audiences, which at times can be a challenge as compared to the traditional, linear one-way process of disseminating messages. Although Neuhauser and Kreps (2003a) found one-way messages to equally as effective as interactive messages, once way messages can be seen as intimidating and off-putting. The interactivity with audiences can be instantaneous, in which an individual receives immediate feedback from the online program based on their responses (Fotheringham et al. 2000), or it can include social interactivity, in which more open forums, support groups, and social networking opportunities are made available to health consumers.

Creating dynamic and engaging communication With the number of different demographic groups within the U.S. population increasing, it can be challenging to segment and target specific audiences to receive health communication messages. Not only do health educators need to keep their demographic information in mind, but they also have to take into account the various levels of health literacy within a community, causing difficulty in creating one consistent and cohesive health message or program. Therefore, online health program developers should include interesting narratives, graphics, audio and video clips that are easy to comprehend, yet still engaging for a variety of different audiences (Kreps and Neuhauser 2010). In addition, eHealth interventions should also be dynamic, in which program delivery is constantly changing to be individualized and tailored according to the characteristics of the consumer using the program, in real-time (Fotheringham et al. 2000). Creating dynamic communication, however, can also be seen as a challenge to researchers. Because it cannot be guaranteed that the experiences of two people will be exactly the same while participating in an online health program, it may be difficult for scholars to effectively determine whether the outcomes were based on features of the intervention itself (Eng 2002).

Designing proper outcome measures and metrics   Because interactive health technologies are relatively still in their early stages, there has yet to be strong evaluative research to determine the effectiveness of online programs. For many organizations, success is solely measured by number of unique users or page views. Though this metric is helpful in determining the usage of the website or web portal, it does not effectively measure the actual quality of the application. Two ultimate questions that Eng (2002: 270) asks in this regard are: "Does the application improve the user's health status?" and "What is the health and social impact of the application on the population level?" Health program educators need to determine how to accurately measure these items to better assess the impact of their programs. In addition, researchers need to work outside of the formative stages of eHealth programs through rigorous scientific methods to determine outcome measures that can be replicable in the future.

Privacy, confidentiality, and security   One advantage of the use of the Web for health is the openness within communication, as participants are interacting directly with computers as opposed to people, allowing for them to respond to sensitive questions willingly and openly without any fear, shame, or embarrassment (Fotheringham et al. 2000). However, as the number of online health applications increase, so does the volume and scope of health-related data on Web, which calls for program developers and professionals to assess the issues of privacy, confidentiality, and security. Health program developers and professionals need to pay special attention to this issue, to ensure that this information remains secure and confidential. In addition, health communication scholars can conduct qualitative research studies to explore consumers' concerns about online privacy, confidentiality, and security (Eng 2002).

OPPORTUNITIES FOR eHEALTH

Increasing access and usability   One of the many advantages of using the Web in a health context is the automated nature of many online programs, in which individuals can enter their data fairly seamlessly with instant results, as well as the convenience of this medium, as eHealth technologies eliminate the time restrictions to those who have access to it (Fotheringham et al. 2000). Therefore, one opportunity for health professionals is to increase the accessibility of information, which is more than just providing computer hardware and Internet access to hard-to-reach populations. Increasing access should also include working to increase the *usability* of the Web for health information, by offering tools to increase online literacy, technical assistance, and multi-media interfaces with easier to understand graphics and sound files (Eng 2002). In addition, health communication scholars should turn their focus on these special populations. Previous studies have focused on solely traditional demographic subgroups; researchers should center their work on the more subtle nuances surrounding having access to online health applications (Eng 2002).

Enhancing user's control   The trend towards health information seeking via the Web also opens up the opportunity for giving control to the consumer, allowing for them to take part in the decision-making process in regard to their health. One advantage of using this Internet is the flexibility of the channel, as audiences can seek out materials whenever they would like and how often they would like, putting the impetus in the hands of the consumer (Fotheringham et al. 2000). Consumers are readily accepting this power shift, as one study by Hesse and colleagues (2005) found that the majority of Americans would rather turn to the Internet first before going to their physician.

Customization   Kreps and Neuhauser (2010) offer some suggestions in terms of how customization can change health computer-mediated communication: health educators can use computer systems to match individual's preferences with select information from large databases; computers can send automated e-mail prompts to individuals reminding them about appointments or their personal care; and online communities can be formed through social support groups. Customizing messages leads to what Walther (1996: 5) refers to as "hyperpersonal communication" in which information is personally relevant to every individual while still maintaining its broad reach.

Increasing quality of content   Because there is no formal control over what can be posted on the Web, it can be difficult for users to know whether information posted online comes from a reputable source, or whether the information posted is false, manipulative, or otherwise problematic for the user. Therefore, another opportunity for eHealth communication is maintaining quality assurance over content. Suggestions for ensuring online sources are credible include methods such as "accreditation, certification, rating systems, public disclosure of key information about a site or product, and posting of seals and logos indicating compliance with a set of quality standards" (Eng, 2002: 268). However, the argument of free speech may inhibit this progress, and so it is ultimately up to the consumer to decide what is credible in the online space, thereby increasing the need for online literacy and numeracy education. Health researchers can take this need into account and conduct studies on how these factors of quality of content, quality assurance, online literacy, and online numeracy affect consumers' perceptions of eHealth applications.

Academic research   In terms of the scholarship that can be conducted surrounding eHealth, Eng (2002) proposes that more research needs to be done on the following topics: impact of eHealth applications on health outcomes and healthcare quality, access, and cost on the individual and population levels; individual and population-specific differences in use and impact of online health resources; cost-effectiveness of technology-based tools; data integration models; and implementation, adoption, and reimbursement models for eHealth. Though these are promising areas of study, a review of the literature by Neuhauser and Kreps (2003b) found that research on the effectiveness of eHealth interventions in particular have been promising, specifically with the use of personally tailored communication, the use of computer-controlled telephone counseling, and the proliferation of online support groups. However, future studies need to be conducted to determine whether the Web's impact on health has changed over the past several years, and discovering what the newest developments are and how the general public is being affected by the constant shifting and changing of eHealth interventions and programs. Key research questions can ask what the most frequently used online applications are among certain audiences, what behavioral motivation techniques are employed by these applications, and how theoretical frameworks play a role in the creation, dissemination, and reception of these eHealth applications.

Implications for Academics

eHealth research poses several implications for health communication scholarly research. As was found in Lustria et al.'s (2007) research, web-based interventions are more successful if they utilize a theoretical framework. This suggestion goes for all web-based applications; by using a theory as the underlying foundation for a website, web portal, or program, health professionals can more easily evaluate the true effectiveness of the campaign through the testing of different variables. Research can be conducted similar to Whitten and colleagues' (2008) study, where they tested the utilization of three major behavioral change theories by breast cancer websites. Their findings revealed that there was a lack of strategic behavior change motivators present on these websites, which in turn led to a lack of attitude and behavioral change on the part of the intended audience. Future research can work to replicate studies such as these to determine whether theoretical frameworks are being underutilized in Internet and health research.

Implications for Health Practitioners

eHealth research greatly impacts the practice of health communication as well. As was stated in the opportunities section, the use of eHealth calls for more dynamic, engaging, and interactive programs that not only reach multiple segments of the population, but also individualizes it to a more personally relevant level. With individuals inundated with health messages on a daily basis, health professionals can use web-based technologies to discover new and innovative ways to attract audiences and motivate them to undertake healthy behaviors. The Web can also help health educators increase the general public's knowledge of certain health risks, reaching populations that may be harder to target and access.

Conclusion

In the past decade alone, an increasing number of scholars are asking questions about how eHealth affects perspectives of patient-provider relationships, dissemination of health information, promotion of health education programs, online health literacy, and use of the Web for emotional and social support. The research in this chapter revealed that there are a number of advantages and disadvantages in using the Internet as a channel for communicating health. There are mixed reactions from both patients and providers as to whether using the Web is easier and more effective, with some individuals still preferring traditional routes to disseminating and seeking health information.

Though the Internet is not replacing doctor-patient interaction per se, it is undoubtedly changing it by allowing consumers to have more active conversations with their physicians in an attempt to better understand health. Studies have found that patients armed with health-related Internet information felt more satisfied with their visits and felt more comfortable talking with their doctor. Because individuals can now seek their own health-related information, they can gain more control of their health, learning more about possible treatments, therapies, prescriptions, and other medical options that may not have been adequately explained by their doctor. The use of eHealth technology has dramatically shifted from the more traditional, authority/ expert model to a more consumer controlled, collaborative process. People can now take their health into their own hands, which several decades ago would not have even been possible.

FUTURE RESEARCH

The current state of research on the Internet and health brings insight to future research that needs to be conducted. Researchers should aim to explore whether perceptions have changed for both patients and providers in terms of whether eHealth helps enhance their relationship. With more and more individuals using the Internet, it would be interesting to discover whether eHealth literacy continues to be an issue and whether misinterpretations and misunderstandings still ensue. In addition, more research needs to be conducted testing the relative advantage of web-based technologies – why should individuals use it, and what additional information or benefits does it offer as compared to other media such as television or magazines. And finally, more theoretical approaches need to be discovered that will optimize eHealth for patients, providers, educators and professionals. Scholars should work to discover what health communication theories can be best applied to eHealth contexts, and whether these theories can be shaped to better explain why individuals use the Internet for health information.

The use of the Internet and mobile technologies to gain perspectives on health is quickly becoming an area that will surely continue to grow and shape the way individuals practice health communication. This chapter has shown the rich and diverse literature on this topic, particularly on how eHealth affects medical providers, health educators, consumers, patients, and vulnerable populations. However, this chapter also demonstrates how rapidly technology is changing and evolving, which calls for much more to be done in order to fully understand and determine the effects of these channels on health issues. With the ever-changing media landscape, the study of eHealth and mobile health will continue to be an ongoing learning process, affecting personal relationships, organizations, and society for many more years to come.

References

Ahmad, F., Hudak, P.L., Levinson, W., Bercovitz, K. and Hollenberg, E. 2006. Are physicians ready for patients with Internet-based health information? *Journal of Medical Internet Research*, 8, 6.

Bylund, C.L., Sabee, C.M., Imes, R.S. and Sanford, A.A. 2007. Exploration of the construct of reliance among patients who talk with their providers about Internet information. *Journal of Health Communication*, 12, 17–28.

Central Intelligence Agency. 2010. *World Factbook* [Online]. Available at: https://www.cia.gov/ [accessed: 10 March 2011].

Chen, H. 2010. Text4Baby wins outstanding innovation award. Office of Science and Technology Policy [Online, 4 August]. Available at: http://www.whitehouse.gov/administration/eop/ostp/blog [accessed: 12 March 2011].

Chen, H. 2011. Text4Baby shows promising results for moms. *Office of Science and Technology Policy Blog* [Online, 2 November]. Available at: http://www.whitehouse.gov/blog/2011/11/02/text4baby-shows-promising-results-moms [accessed: 9 January 2012].

Eng, T.R. 2002. eHealth research and evaluation: Challenges and opportunities. *Journal of Health Communication*, 7, 267–72.

Evans, W.D. 2010. *Evaluation of the Text4Baby Mobile Health Program*. American Public Health Association Annual Meeting, Denver, Colorado.

Fotheringham, M.J., Owies, D., Leslie, E. and Owen, N. 2000. Interactive health communication in preventive medicine: Internet-based strategies in teaching and research. *American Journal of Preventive Medicine*, 19, 113–20.

Fox, S. 2006. *Online Health Search 2006*. Washington, DC: Pew Internet and American Life Project [Online]. Available at: http://www.pewinternet.org [accessed: 9 March 2011].

Fox, S. 2010. *Mobile Health 2010*. Washington, DC: Pew Internet and American Life Project [Online]. Available at: http://www.pewinternet.org [accessed: 9 November 2011].

Fox, S. and Rainie, L. 2002. *Vital Decisions*. Washington, DC: Pew Internet and American Life Project [Online]. Available from http://www.pewinternet.org [accessed: 9 March 2011].

HMHB. 2010. *National Healthy Mothers Healthy Babies Coalition* [Online]. Available at: http://www.hmhb.org [accessed: 3 March 2011].

Hesse, B.W., Nelson, D.E., Kreps, G.L., Croyle, R.T., Arora, N.K. and Rimer, B.K. 2005. Trust and sources of health information: The impact of the Internet and its implications for health care providers: Findings from the first health information national trends survey. *Archives of Internal Medicine*, 165, 2618–24.

Houston, T.K., Sands, D.Z., Nash, B.R. and Ford, D.E. 2003. Experiences of physicians who frequently use e-mail with patients. *Health Communication*, 15, 515.

Imes, R.S., Bylund, C.L., Sabee, C.M., Routsong, T.R. and Sanford, A.A. 2008. Patients' reasons for refraining from discussing Internet health information with their healthcare providers. *Health Communication*, 23, 538–47.

Kreps, G.L. and Neuhauser, L. 2010. New directions in eHealth communication: Opportunities and challenges. *Patient Education and Counseling*, 78, 329–36.

Lee, C. 2008a. *Internet Engagement and SES-based Health Knowledge Gap*. International Communication Association annual conference, Montreal, Canada.

Lee, C. 2008b. Does the Internet displace health professionals? *Journal of Health Communication*, 13, 450–64.

Lieberman, D., Lingsweiler, R., Yao, M. and Chesler, Z. 2003. *Effects of User Control and Perceived Message Tailoring on Responses to a Health Web Site*. International Communication Association annual conference, San Diego, CA.

Lustria, M., Brown, L. and Davis, R. 2007. *10 Years of Consumer Health Informatics: What Have We Learned About How to Design Successful Web-based Interventions?* National Communication Association annual conference, Chicago, IL.

Neuhauser, L. and Kreps, G.L. 2003a. The advent of e-health: How interactive media are transforming health communication. *Medie and Kommunickations-Wissenchaft*, 51, 541–56.

Neuhauser, L. and Kreps, G.L. 2003b. Rethinking communication in the e-health era. *Journal of Health Psychology*, 8, 7–22.

Nordqvist, C., Hanberger, L., Timpka, T. and Nordfeldt, S. 2009. Health professionals' attitudes towards using a web 2.0 portal for child and adolescent diabetes care: Qualitative study. *Journal of Medical Internet Research*, 11, 1.

Rains, S.A. 2007. Perceptions of traditional information sources and use of the world wide web to seek health information: Findings from the health information national trends survey. *Journal of Health Communication*, 12, 667–80.

Remick, A. 2010. Text4Baby announces plans to reach one million moms [Online 9 November]. Available at: http://www.hmhb.org/onemillion.html [accessed: 20 March 2011].

Rochman, B. 2010. Take two texts and call me in the morning. *Time* [Online 3 May]. Available at: http://www.time.com/ [accessed: 25 March 2011].

Sabee, C., Aldridge, A., Imes, R. and Bylund, C. 2005. *Clinician-patient Dialogue about Internet Health Information: Legitimating Patients through Communication*. International Communication Association annual conference, New York City, NY.

Smith, A. 2010. *Mobile Access 2010*. Washington, DC: Pew Internet and American Life Project [Online]. Available at http://www.pewinternet.org/ [accessed: 10 March 2011]

Sommerhalder, K., Abraham, A., Zufferey, M.C., Barth, J. and Abel, T. 2009. Internet information and medical consultations: Experiences from patients' and physicians' perspectives. *Patient Education and Counseling*, 77, 266–71.

Text4Baby. 2011. Text4Baby website [Online]. Available at: http://www.text4baby.org [accessed: 15 March 2011].

Tian, Y. and Robinson, J.D. 2009. Incidental health information use on the Internet. *Health Communication*, 24, 41–9.

Wald, H.S., Dube, C.E. and Anthony, D.C. 2007. Untangling the web – The impact of Internet use on health care and the physician–patient relationship. *Patient Education and Counseling*, 68, 218–24.

Walther, J.B. 1996. Computer-mediated communication: Impersonal, interpersonal and hyperpersonal interaction. *Communication Research*, 23, 3–43.

Warner, D. and Procaccino, J.D. 2007. Women seeking health information: Distinguishing the web user. *Journal of Health Communication*, 12, 787–814.

Whitten, P., Smith, S., Munday, S. and LaPlante, C. 2008. Communication assessment of the most frequented breast cancer websites: Evaluation of design and theoretical criteria. *Journal of Computer-Mediated Communication*, 13, 880–911.

Health Communication and Communication Systems

10 Coming Full Circle in Rural Trauma: Chronicling the Development and Testing of Communication Systems in Rural Trauma Networks

THEODORE A. AVTGIS AND E. PHILLIPS POLACK

Introduction

The importance of efficient triage and treatment of trauma patients has been evident since the Napoleonic Wars when Larrey developed the *ambulance volantes* (flying ambulance) as a means of reducing the interval time from injury to treatment (Trunkey 1983). The *golden hour* for treatment of trauma patients was first conceptualized by Cowley (1975) using French data obtained from the treatment of soldiers during World War I (Santy 1918). These data suggested that patients treated within the first hour of injury have a mortality rate of 10 percent, versus a mortality rate of 75 percent if treatment occurred within eight hours. Therefore, the reduction in time to definitive treatment is one of the most significant teaching points in surgical education.

In assessing the magnitude of trauma and the financial and human costs to society, the impact is quite alarming. Trauma is a significant and major killer of Americans under 45 years of age claiming 150,000 lives annually. Globally, this mortality number jumps to three million lives annually (Adams 2009). To put this statistic into perspective, more people die from trauma than from the combined total of deaths from cancer, heart disease, HIV or lung related illness. Death by trauma is also an equal opportunity killer in that it claims lives regardless of racial, ethnic, socio-economic or cultural factors (Adams 2009). In light of these data coupled with the paucity of communication scholarship and research in this specific field of medicine, this chapter traces an ongoing intervention of message transmission within a rural trauma network, we identify promising results from the use of competent communication and appropriate computer mediated communication, and generalize those results to global rural trauma network communication practices.

Waller, Curran, and Noyes (1964) reported that when treated within the *golden hour*, 44 percent of rural trauma deaths were salvageable compared with 36 percent of urban trauma deaths. Yet, they determined that a greater number of rural fatalities resulted from less severe injuries than those observed in urban settings. That is, rural injuries tend to be the result of blunt trauma (for example, caused by auto accidents and falls) as opposed to urban trauma which is more representative of penetrating trauma such as gunshot wounds and stab wounds. In fact, according to Mitchell and Medzon (2005), 80 percent of all deaths by penetrating trauma are caused by gunshot wounds. Although these data may seem counter-intuitive in terms of rural and urban trauma death percentages, delays in accident reporting as well as extended transport times were identified as contributing to preventable mortality of rural trauma patients. Given the increased mortality rates associated with rural trauma patients, researchers need to investigate all factors contributing to time delay in any efforts to work toward more efficient treatment and transport of rural trauma patients. Such factors include both process and procedure of medical triage as well as the level of coordination and collaboration among the trauma treatment team and members throughout the entire trauma care network. In terms of the communicative and psychological aspects of coordination and collaboration in trauma, communication researchers have begun research efforts (see, for example, Avtgis and Polack 2010, Avtgis et al. 2010, Kappel, Rossi, Polack, Avtgis and Martin 2011) but there is an abundance of research and education efforts that still need to be developed.

DIFFERENTIATING RURAL TRAUMA

The United States Bureau of the Census defines rural as an area with an urban population of 50,000 or less and a population density not exceeding 1000 people per square mile (Rogers, Shackford, Osler, Vane and Davis 1999). The American College of Surgeons, Committee on Trauma defines rural as an area where geography, population density, weather, distance or availability of professional or institutional resources combine to isolate the trauma victim in an environment where access to definitive care is limited. (Rogers et.al.1999). While approximately one-third of the American population resides in a rural area, only 9 percent of the U.S. physicians reside in these areas (American College of Surgeons 2006, Rogers, Osler, Turner, Camp and Lesage 1999). Therefore, this gap in doctor to patient ratio makes competent and efficient communication that much more important in order to maximize and effectively manage resources.

In the state of West Virginia, there are 55 counties covering 24,232 square miles. The medical facilities available within the state include two Level 1 trauma centers (that is, a referral hospital that is capable of handling any injury regardless of severity) which are located in the northern and southern parts of the state. There are four Level II (that is, slightly less comprehensive but have the ability to handle the majority of traumatic injuries) trauma centers [in reality two (2) because the facilities alternate trauma call and are in the same city (2) in Wheeling and (2) in Huntington]. The remaining 27 trauma facilities, Level III–IV (capable of stabilizing and transferring to a higher level facility), are located throughout the state. Figure 10.1 indicates the trauma facility resources throughout the entire state.

As can be seen from Figure 10.1, the importance of appropriate triage in order to reduce morbidity and mortality in light of the challenges of weather, terrain, and distance is sometimes a Herculean task. In order to most efficiently triage patients, reduce costs, increase safety, and reduce trauma physician burnout, concise appropriate and effective message exchanges are vital. In an effort to overcome such challenges, the state of West Virginia has five strategically located medical command centers that are staffed by

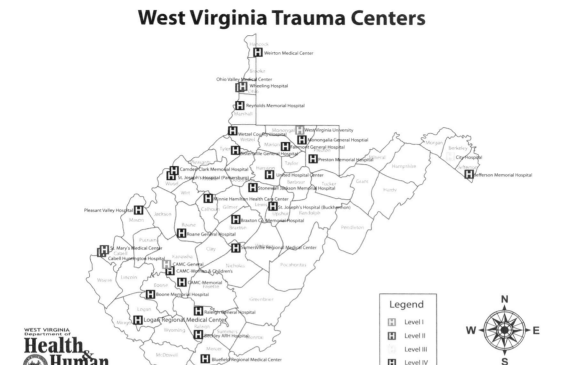

Figure 10.1 The State of West Virginia Trauma Facility Location Map

Emergency Medical Technician/Paramedics who are available 24 hours a day, 7 days a week via a microwave tower communication system. The medical command personnel provide field direction, utilizing state approved protocols to move through particular decision making schemes (for example, a victim is trapped for prolonged periods of time prior to discovery and/or extrication that is found over a mountain or down a creek bank).

COMMUNICATION AND EFFECTIVE TRIAGE

As demonstrated in the data presented earlier in this chapter, trauma is a significant health issue for all people and as such, researchers are constantly looking for best-practice solutions that lead to effective systems for the expeditious triage and management of trauma. Such processes come at great expense for the healthcare system. The need for accurate and effective triage is vital for several reasons. First, Kouzminova, Shatney, Palm, McCullough and Sherck, (2009) studied 20,332 trauma team activation processes. Of these, 5881 were activations for major trauma and 14,451 were activations for minor trauma. To distinguish between major (Priority I) and minor (Priority II) trauma, Kouzminova et al. (2009) used the American College of Surgeons – Committee on Trauma, Trauma Center Triage Criteria (ACS-COT). These criteria specify physiologic, anatomic, and mechanism of injury as risk factors in prioritization determination. Table 10.1 lists the factors involved in Priority designation.

Table 10.1 ACS-COT Regional Field Trauma Triage Criteria*

Physiologic criteria
- Systolic blood pressure <90 mm Hg
- Respiratory rate <10, >29
- Glasgow Coma Scale score ≤ 12

Anatomic criteria
- Flail chest
- Two or more fractures of femur/humerus
- Penetrating injury, mid-thigh to head
- Amputation above wrist or ankle
- Spinal cord injury with paralysis

Mechanism of injury
- Heavy extrication > 20 min
- Death of same car occupant
- Ejection from closed vehicle
- High energy transfer situation
- Fall > 20 feet
- Pedestrian hit 20 mph or thrown 15 feet
- Motorcycle/ATV/bicycle crash
- Vehicle rollover
- Impact or significant intrusion

Risk factor criteria
- Medical illness
- Pregnancy
- Presence of intoxicants
- Hostility of environment (heat, cold, etc.)
- Age < 5 or > 55 (some agencies use < 12 or > 55 yr)
- EMS provider judgment

Note: * Criteria are based on those included in the American College of Surgeons Committee on Trauma Field Decision Scheme and were developed and successfully implemented by the Oregon Trauma System.

The results of the study revealed that activation (for example, personnel or equipment) for major trauma is considerably more expensive than that of minor trauma. More specifically, it costs $3,726 less to respond to a minor trauma alert (that is, Priority II) rather than a major trauma alert (Priority I). Using projection calculations based on these data, Kouzminova et al. (2009) estimate that over a ten-year period, the ability to accurately determine trauma priority would save $53,000,844. Second, appropriate triage determination would result in lower levels of surgeon burnout. According to Plaisier, Meldon, Super, Jouriles, Barnoski, Fallon and Malangoni (1998), trauma systems that utilize the two tiered trauma triage designation system (Priority I and Priority II) would realize a reduction of 578 physician hours every six months. In light of these conclusions, proper information for priority determination becomes a vital factor in increasing patient safety and fiscal responsibility and as well reducing physician 'burn out' by over-utilization of scarce resources.

Given that trauma is the 6th leading cause of death (accounting for 10 percent of global mortality) and the 5th leading cause of significant disability (Soreide 2009), to be effective, there needs to be a seamless transition in all phases of care for time, as demonstrated by Cowley (1975), is life. The remainder of this chapter will trace a longitudinal effort (a multi-study collaboration) to identify problematic issues associated with communication and the practice of surgery within the rural trauma system in West Virginia. Through focusing on affirming communication [that is, a practice of communication where the communicator, while being effective, also validates the experience of the other individual while also providing a climate for continuing discussion in a less aggressive, more productive and pro-social form (Infante 1988, Rancer and Avtgis 2006)]. Using both qualitative and quantitative methodologies, the results indicate promising outcomes in terms of:

a) an actual time reduction in the trauma process;
b) a recognition (via the integration of affirming communication training) of the importance of improving communication by trauma governing bodies; and

c) the development and assessment of a standardized communication curriculum predicated on the principles developed as a result of these studies.

To further realize time reduction in the trauma patient transfer process, efforts are fully underway in the development and testing of SMART technology to determine if system-wide interface between medical personnel, via trauma transfer application protocols mediated through SMART technology, will result in more favorable outcomes for both the patient and the surgical team.

STUDY ONE: EXPLICATING PROBLEMATIC COMMUNICATION

The first study sought to investigate the problematic communication perceptions and patterns between and among trauma personnel (Rossi, Polack, Kappel, Avtgis and Martin, 2009). More particularly, we sought to investigate these patterns in relation to the specific process of trauma patient transfer and the way in which information is packaged and delivered. There is an assumption that the packaging and transferring of such critical medical information is something that has been engrained and concretized in the culture of trauma networks within which surgery is practiced. The trauma patient transfer process is considered a vital link to providing effective transfer to definitive care for trauma patients. It involves a delicate balance of coordination and logistics that are almost exclusively communicative in nature (see Polack and Avtgis 2011). Using the rural trauma centers of West Virginia as the back drop for the studies, the investigators sought to illicit feedback from individuals practicing in *Level I and Level II* facilities (that is, definitive care facilities for the sickest of patients) which are staffed by highly credentialed medical personnel utilizing some of the most technologically advanced equipment, and *Level III and Level IV* facilities which are staffed by medical personnel limited by the technology and manpower available to them. Of the 32 out of the 52 hospitals throughout the state of West Virginia, 54 people participated. Of these 52 participants, 28 were physicians, 18 were nurses, three were trauma registrars, and one was EMT (four did not identify their role in their respective facility). Participants were provided with an open ended questionnaire asking two questions.

Question One

Please indicate the most detrimental aspects of the trauma patient transfer process (both transferring in as well as transferring out of your facility). This may include issues of communication or technology between facilities and also communication or technology within your facility.

The *transferring in* process is something that is generally engaged in by Level I and Level II facilities while the *transferring out* process is something that is generally engaged in by Level III and Level IV facilities.

These data were probed for common themes among participants based on their trauma facility designation (for example, Level I). The findings of this study were most intriguing in that most frustration was centered on communication exchanges as opposed to treatment based concerns. More specifically, personnel in the Level III and IV facilities commonly identified *condescension, dismissal, defensiveness, lack of teamwork,* and *time constraints* when communicating with personnel from Level I and Level II facilities. For example, cutting people off in mid-sentence, asking "if they are sure" regarding aspects of the medical evaluation and opinion. On the other hand, personnel at Level I and Level II facilities reported a lack of competence, both medical and communication, as well as a perception that personnel at Level III and Level IV facilities provide too much extraneous information that is relatively unimportant with regard to patient care. For example, if there is a patient injured from an ATV vehicle accident, reporting the size of the ATV during the accident are less important to the more pressing vital signs and other data needed to provide the best prioritization possible.

While it is important to assess the "stylistic" and perceptual aspects of communication exchange, the content of what is exchanged also needs to be accounted for. More specifically, which information about the patient's condition is seen as vital/less vital, important/unimportant, and essential/nonessential? To answer these questions, we utilized an established information exchange protocol that has been shown effective within the ambulance service of New South Wales, Australia. This protocol is known as MIST (*M*echanism of injury, *I*njuries, *S*igns and symptoms, and *T*ransport) (Trauma Triage Tool, Major Trauma Criterion, MIST 2011).

To assess the MIST protocol, which is primarily targeted at those who receive medical information (that is, Level I and Level II personnel at definitive care facilities), the following question was asked:

Question Two

Please rank in order from 1 to 4 where 1 is the most important and 4 is the least important, your perceptions of the following information types.

—— Mechanism (details of the accident).

—— Injury (what injuries the patient has or has been observed to have).

—— Signs (what are the patient's vital signs including airway status).

—— Treatment (to the point of transfer, what treatments and/or diagnostic studies were performed with the results included).

The results of this ranking procedure indicated that there were particular categories of the MIST acronym that appeared to be more superfluous or irrelevant when generalized to other environments and systems. For example, due to factors unique to the state of West Virginia, which include unique geographic and cultural factors as well as frequency and types of injuries commonly encountered, the MIST acronym excluded important information that the respondents in this study expected/demanded for effective triage and treatment. The criteria of the MIST as well as that outlined by the American College of Surgeons Committee on Trauma (ACS-COT; see Table 10.1) only include the physiologic [vital signs] and anatomic criterion [what part of the body is injured], mechanism [how the accident happened] plus special risk factors. These are also the prioritized criteria outlined by the Centers for Disease Control (Sassu, Hunt, Sullevent, Wald, Mitchko, Jurkovich, Henry, Salomone, Wang, Galli, Cooper, Brown and Satten 2009). What is missing from these trauma criteria, as indicated by the West Virginia respondents, were the *environment* in which the accident occurred and the patient's *response* to treatment.

As such, a new acronym was developed for the West Virginia rural trauma system known as MISER (Mechanism of injury, Injury, vital Signs, Environment in which the trauma occurred, and Response to treatment) (see Kappel, Polack and Avtgis 2010). The MISER acronym was adopted as a suggested acronym for consideration and published in the 3rd edition of the American College of Surgeons RTTDC (Rural Trauma Team Development Course Manual 2010).

Such use of cognitive chunking and acronyms are being readily employed in field triage as "pattern recognition" is believed to be vital in trauma triage decision making. For example, Jensen, Croskerry and Trathers, utilizing the DELPHI technique (Goodman 1987), found that paramedics when faced with clinical decision making in emergency situations, engage in two different systems of decision making. *System one* decision making reflects the rapid formation of a hypothesis based on history learned from the dispatched information as well as visual cues encountered when the responder (for example, EMT) arrives at the scene. However, if the responder arrives at the scene and there is nothing obvious or few visual cues, then *System two* decision making is engaged. This decision making system involves the use of standardized protocol (for example, MIST, MISER, according to Table 10.1). In a test of system usage within the Portland, Oregon metropolitan area, Newgard, Nelson, Kampp, Saha, Zive, Schmitt, Daya, Jui, Wittwer, Warden, Shani, Stevens, Gorman, Koenig, Grubler, Rosteck, Lee and Hedges (2011) analyzed 9637 trauma activations and concluded that 23 percent of trauma activations were attributed to *system one* decision making. In light of so many (77 percent) cases being determined by *system two* decision making and the fact that including judgments of elements such as information about the environment in which the accident occurred are not universally acceptable or standard in information transfer protocol (Baxt, Jonesand Fortlage 1990), it would only make sense to develop a system that includes elements that are unique to a trauma system's own jurisdiction (for example, topology, geography, resources available). Therefore, the MISER acronym, based on the needed information from trauma team personnel garnered from Study One, was developed in an effort to decrease the estimated 50 percent of patients who are over-triaged as well as decrease the rate of patients who are under-triaged. Currently, the under-triaged acceptable rates range from 5 percent to 10 percent (American College of Surgeons 1993).

STUDY II ASSESSING THE MISER

The second study sought to assess the quality of the triage information being exchanged. More specifically, the focus was to evaluate the communication exchange between field personnel and medical command personnel to assess the effectiveness of the MISER acronym. To evaluate adherence to the MISER acronym in properly determining Priority I or Priority II status of the patient based on the information provided, and whether redundancy (that is, two different modes of communication containing the same information) in the communication system would result in improved prioritization. The communicating parties consisted of field personnel, whose training is primarily at the basic level of emergency medical technician (EMT-B) and trained state paramedics who are well skilled and experienced emergency medical technicians (EMT-P). The EMT-P directs the field squads as to the appropriate type of transfer based on information provided by the field personnel. It is primarily based on this information from the field that the state trained paramedic will conclude the level of triage needed. The EMT-Ps are located in five strategically located medical command centers throughout the state of West Virginia. There is an EMT-P available 24/7 via a microwave tower communication system. These operators provide direction and guidance to the field squad via state approved protocol.

The need to effectively triage, as has been discussed earlier in this chapter, results in the reduction of death rates of seriously injured patients by 15 to 20 percent (Jurkovich and Mock 1999). Given the state of West Virginia contains primarily Level III and Level IV trauma centers with only (2) Level I and (4) Level II trauma centers state-wide, appropriate triage (which also means allocation of scarce resources such as surgeons and equipment) is all the more important. In addition to having limited resources, being a mountainous region also presents challenges in terms of volatile weather, terrain, and greater distance from scene to treatment facility. Therefore, testing the MISER acronym in an environment (that is, West Virginia) for which it was developed seemed only natural, timely, and appropriate.

Transcripts and audio tapes were obtained from a 60-day period of medical command operation. In total, there were 50 P1 and 47 P2 (total $N = 97$) case transfers to the Level I trauma facility studied. Coders consisted of 13 graduate/upper level undergraduate students in communication studies and health science related majors. The coders were randomly assigned to one of three coding conditions; C1 = *transcript of the communication between field personnel and medical command* ($n = 5$ coders); C2 = *audio recording of the communication between field personnel and medical command* ($n = 4$ coders); C3 = *both transcript and audio communication between field personnel and medical command* ($n = 4$ coders). Each coder underwent three iterations of training in the MISER acronym and proper priority classification of trauma patients using audio examples of high, average, and low quality exchanges between the field personnel and medical command. The coders were further trained on what constitutes effective and appropriate information exchange in this high stress environment. The coders in all conditions were provided with a coding sheet (see Appendix 10.1). Each of the MISER elements were assessed by three questions assessing:

a) the overall quality of the information;
b) the effectiveness of the information;
c) the appropriateness of the information.

Each question was assessed via Likert-type scaling ranging from 1: *extremely poorly relayed* to 10: *extremely well relayed*. Each of the MISER elements had a total maximum score of 30 and a combined total score of 150.

The findings of the study revealed significant differences among experimental conditions in both correct priority determination as well as adherence to the elements of the MISER acronym. More specifically, the audio only condition yielded an accurate priority determination in 71 percent of the cases followed by the transcript only condition with 69 percent and both the transcript and audio condition had a 48 percent accuracy rate.

Regarding the adherence to the MISER criteria, the audio only condition was found to be superior to the other conditions with a total adherence to MISER elements mean score of 102.22 ($SD = 32.36$) or 68 percent adherence, followed by transcript only ($M = 94.00$, $SD = 33.55$) or 63 percent, adherence and both audio and transcript ($M = 68.06$, $SD = 21.91$) or 45 percent adherence to the MISER elements. Regarding specific

MISER categories, the audio condition was significantly higher than both transcript only and audio/transcript conditions on *Injury* ($M = 23.95$; $M = 22.06$; $M = 22.35$), *Environment* ($M = 9.25$; $M = 9.00$; $M = 3.84$), and *Response* ($M = 14.90$; $M = 12.80$; $M = 12.19$) respectively. No significant differences were observed with regard to *Mechanism* ($M = 21.55$; $M = 19.44$; $M = 21.19$) and (vital) *Signs* ($M = 21.43$; $M = 20.28$; $M = 21.56$). The audio only condition also rated the information exchange between field personnel and medical command as significantly more effective, appropriate, and of higher overall quality than either transcript only or both transcript and audio conditions.

The results of this study indicate that overall, audio transmission from the responding squad to medical command is more effective in almost every dimension assessed when compared to having the information provided in written transcript form or with redundancy of both audio and transcript combined. However, regardless of the fact that audio is the most effective means for relaying information. Is having communication exchange that results, on average, a 71 percent accuracy in priority designation acceptable? We believe that this rate of correct prioritization and inefficiency in adherence to the MISER criteria is unacceptable and as a result, we believe that only the integration of SMART technology in the trauma triage process will serve to improve the numerous problematic communicative features that have emerged as a result of these two studies.

Implications for Academics

We argue that most if not all of the issues and findings from the two studies reviewed in this chapter are not within a "context" such as *health*, *organizational communication*, or *computer mediated communication*. Instead, we believe that these are simultaneously "context-less" and "context-full" studies in that coordination of human beings is a general human communication phenomenon and/or issue, not one that is necessarily bound by the context within which it occurs or owned by some domain of communication research scholarship. To provide meaningful and relevant interventions, researchers from all contexts of the communication discipline and research paradigms are necessary as the problems that are being encountered are complex and require complex skill sets and approaches. Technology and its manifestation on human relationships and endeavor will forever be linked. Explication of "contextual forces" should be avoided in lieu of the analyses of the complexities as they are occurring naturally. In this case, we would be remiss to attempt to isolate any particular aspect of the trauma transfer without accounting for the dynamic interactions among all aspects of process that involve people, technology, and naturally occurring phenomenon (that is, environment).

The communication scholar has real opportunity for interdisciplinary collaboration in the implementation of technological systems in critical care networks and other "crisis" driven ventures. The continued use of technology and its role in rural trauma will require scholarly inquiry as such practices and protocols that were described in this chapter are laden with ethical implications. When focusing specifically on rural trauma, based on the disparities described earlier, implicates both distributive and procedural justice issues. Scholars also have the opportunity to assess such disparities and monitor such efforts as changes in protocol and technology are implemented.

Implications for Health Practitioners

We believe that to provide some meaningful answers for improving the processes reviewed here are not in seeking new technology (medical and otherwise), but seeking the right technology for the users, the system, and in the end, the technology and the proper use of that will result in the ultimate goal of increased patient safety and decreased mortality rates. To this end, we are currently testing the use of SMART (Self Monitoring Analysis and Reporting Technology) phones in conjunction with audio transmission in hopes of increasing proper priority determination. Such technology is currently in the development stage and is bringing together researchers from computer science, surgery, communication studies, mathematics and a variety of other relevant disciplines. A prototype of such a device is currently being built and will be tested in 2012. We believe that information transfer and coordination are aspects of human communication that will be well served with the integration of SMART to provide the rubric from which system-relevant data will be generated, transferred and interpreted.

The implementation of such systems is as crucial as the systems themselves. Healthcare practitioners, if involved in such innovation implementation need to be aware of all systemic influences that can have a negative result on the trauma transfer process. The role of technology in this process is one of added value in that technology is not the reason for the reduction in transfer time, but the healthcare practitioner's proper use and coordination of the technology is. Therefore, as new systems and protocols are being tested, we should look to them not as the cause of increased patient safety, but as a tool. One would not say that a scalpel saved someone's life and nor should we conclude the same for technology. Rural trauma is especially in need of technological intervention as it fits the unique challenges that trauma personnel face on a daily basis. Based on our data, we believe that the SMART technology holds the most significant benefit for the rural trauma team in the goals of time reduction and patient safety.

Should scholars heed our call for more attention to other complex phenomena such as the trauma patient triage process and resulting communication, great contributions are waiting to be realized as information transfer, regardless of who is doing it or what the outcome may be, is a communication phenomenon?

Conclusion

This chapter traces the evolution of an ongoing research program that seeks to improve the communication-related aspects of trauma team function, interaction, and coordination for the ultimate outcome of increased performance and patient safety. When investigating any process that involves human coordination and technological activation within high stress environments, the communicative interactions that occur in the system are the generator from which all other outcomes of the system are dependent. We believe that the trauma triage process and the trauma transfer process are not issues of *health communication*, but issues of *human communication*. The paucity of communication research in the area of trauma triage and transfer is alarming given the gravity of inefficiency and the amount of time and effort expended on the more mundane aspects of healthcare (for example, patient-provider interviewer during a wellness visit). This advocacy for increased research attention should not be at the expense of other types of research but instead draw attention to a sorely under-researched area that has profound impacts on tens of thousands of people annually.

LIMITATIONS

While rural trauma networks share many of the same characteristics such as resource scarcity, difficult terrain, and large geographical areas, there are unique features to each rural system that may not necessarily be positively affected by conclusions based on one rural system. We cannot say conclusively that what works in West Virginia will work equally as well as Oklahoma or in Alaska. Trauma systems, like all other state and federally funded things, are also a derivative political system and as such subject to influences that are not necessarily medically mandated. We believe that such nuanced influences will indeed vary the results of any technological innovation. However, with that said, we also believe that there are enough commonalities in rural trauma that at the very least, some benefit would be realized from the integration of technology and competent communication training as that which was implemented in the West Virginia Trauma System. This is evidenced by the American College of Surgeons adopting the competent communication protocol for all rural trauma (American College of Surgeons 2010).

It should also be noted, that the research program synthesized in this chapter is ongoing and that results will invariably change as the SMART system is implemented and longitudinal assessment takes place. Such efforts should not be interpreted as end points but processes that are undergoing constant assessment and improvement efforts as we move forward toward a better protocol for the treatment of the rural trauma patient.

References

Adams, C.A. 2009. Care of the trauma patient: A discipline in flux. *Medicine and Health*, 92, 164–5.

American College of Surgeons. 2006. *Resources for the Optimal Care of the Injured patient*. Chicago, IL: American College of Surgeons.

American College of Surgeons. 1993. *Resources for Optimal Care of the Injured Patient*. Chicago, IL: American College of Surgeons.

American College of Surgeons. Committee on Trauma. 2006. *Rural Trauma Training Development Course*, 2nd Edition. Chicago, IL: American College of Surgeons.

American College of Surgeons. Committee on Trauma. 2010. *Rural Trauma Development Course*, 3rd Edition. Chicago, IL: American College of Surgeons.

Avtgis, T.A. and Polack, E.P. 2010. Communication in rural trauma medicine: A practice/art unto itself. *China Media Research*, 6, 100–108.

Avtgis, T.A., Polack, E.P., Martin, M.M. and Rossi, D. 2010. Improve the communication, decrease the distance: The investigation into problematic communication and delay in inter-hospital transfer of rural trauma patient. *Communication Education*, 59, 282–93.

Baxt, W.G., Jones, G. and Fortlage, D. 1990. The trauma triage rule: A new, resource-based approach to the pre-hospital identification of major trauma victims. *Annals of Emergency Medicine*, 19, 1401–6.

Cowley, R.A. 1975. A total emergency medical system for the state of Maryland. *Maryland State Medical Journal*, 24, 37–45.

Goodman, C.M. 1987. The DELPHI technique: A critique. *Journal of Advanced Nursing*, 12, 729–34.

Infante, D.A. 1988. *Arguing Constructively.* Prospect Heights, IL: Waveland.

Jensen, J.L., Croskerry, P. and Travers, A.H. 2009. Paramedic clinical decision making during high activity emergency calls: Design and methodology of a Delphi study. *BMC Emergency Medicine*, 9, 17.

Jurkovich, G.J. and Mock, C. 1999. Systematic review of trauma system effectiveness based on registry comparison. *Journal of Trauma*, 47(3), S46–S55.

Kappel, D.A., Rossi, D.C., Polack, E.P., Avtgis, T.A. and Martin, M.M. 2011. Does the RTTDC (rural trauma team delivery course) shorten the interval from trauma patient arrival to decision to transfer. *Journal of Trauma*, 70, 315–19.

Kouzminova, N., Shatney, C., Palm, E., McCullough, M. and Sherck, J. 2009. The efficacy of a two tiered trauma activation system at a level I trauma center. *The Journal of Trauma, Injury, Infection, and Critical Care*, 67, 829–32.

Mitchell, E.J. and Medzon, R. 2005. *Introduction to Emergency Medicine.* Philadelphia, PA: Lippincott, Williams and Wilkens.

Newgard, C.D., Nelson, M.J., Kampp, M., Saha, S., Zive, D., Schmitt, T., Daya, M., Jui, J., Wittwer, L., Warden, C., Shani, R., Stevens, M., Gorman, K., Koenig, K. Grubler, D., Rosteck, P., Lee, J. and Hedges, J.R. 2011. Out-of-hospital decision making and factors influencing the regional distribution of injured patients in a trauma system. *The Journal of Trauma*, 79(6), 1345–53.

Plaisier, B.R., Meldon, S.W., Super, D.M., Jouriles, N.J., Barnoski, A.L., Fallon, W.F. and Malangoni, M.A. 1998. Effectiveness of a 2 specialty 2-tiered triage and trauma team activation protocol. *Annals of Emergency Medicine*, 32, 436–41.

Polack, E.P. and Avtgis, T.A. 2011. *Medical Communication: Defining the Discipline.* Dubuque, IA: Kendall Hunt.

Rancer, A.S. and Avtgis, T.A. 2006. *Argumentative and Aggressive Communication: Theory, research, and application.* Thousand Oaks, CA: Sage.

Rogers, F.B., Osler, T.M., Turner, M., Camp, L. and Lesage, M. 1999. Study of the outcome of patients transferred to a Level I hospital in a rural setting. *Journal of Trauma*, 46, 328–33.

Rogers, F.B., Shackford, S.R., Osler, T.M., Turner, M., Vane, D.W. and Davis, J.H. 1999. Rural trauma: Challenge for the next decade. *Journal of trauma: Injury, infection, and critical care*, 47, 802.

Rossi, D., Polack, E.P., Kappel, D., Avtgis, T.A. and Martin, M.M. 2009. It's not about being nice: It's about being a better doctor: The investigation into problematic communication and delays in trauma patient transfer. *Medical Encounter*, 23, 7–8.

Santy, P. 1918. Marquis moulinier, Da Shock Tramatique dans les blessures de Guerre, Analysis d'observations. *Bulletin de la Societe de Chirurgie de Paris* [Online], 44, 205. Available at: http://www.trauma.org/archive/history/resuscitation.html [accessed: 23 August 2007].

Sassu, S.M., Hunt, R.C., Sullevent, E.E., Wald, M.M., Mitchko, J., Jurkovich, G.J., Henry, M.C., Salomone, J.P., Wang, S.C., Galli, R.L., Cooper, A., Brown, L.H. and Sattin, R.W. 2009. Guidelines for field triage of injured patients: Recommendations of the national expert panel in field triage. *MMWR Recommendations and Reports*, 58, 1–35.

Trauma triage tool, major trauma criterion, MIST. 2001. Available at: http://nswhems.files.wordpress.com/2011/09/o-13-pre-hospital-trauma-triage.pdf

Soreide, K. 2009. Epidemiology of major trauma. *British Journal of Surgery*, 96, 297.

Trunkey, D. 1983. Trauma. *Scientific American*, 249, 28–36.

Waller, J.A., Curran, R. and Noyes, F. 1964. Traffic deaths: A preliminary study of urban and rural fatalities in California. *California Medicine*, 101, 272–6.

Appendix 10.1

Coding Sheet for Assessment of Priority and Adherence to the MISER Criteria

Medical Command Study
Coding Sheet
2011

Coder#_____   Case #_____

(Circle One)   Priority 1   Priority 2

Using the MISER criteria presented to you during the training, please answer the following questions:

A: Mechanism of Injury:
        Was the mechanism of injury relayed to medical command?

                (Circle One)   Yes   No

        Using a scale ranging from *0 = extremely poorly relayed* to *10 = extremely well relayed*, answer the following questions:

                How well was the information regarding the mechanism of injury relayed? _____
                To what degree was the information regarding the mechanism of injury relayed in an *effective way*? _____
                To what degree was the information regarding the mechanism of injury relayed in an *appropriate way*? _____

B: Injuries:
        Were the injuries relayed to medical command?

                (Circle One)   Yes   No

        Using a scale ranging from *0 = extremely poorly relayed* to *10 = extremely well relayed*, answer the following questions:

                How well was the information regarding injuries relayed? _____
                To what degree was the information regarding injuries relayed in an *effective way*? _____
                To what degree was the information regarding injuries relayed in an *appropriate way*? _____

C: Vital Signs:
         Were the vital signs relayed to medical command?

              (Circle One)   Yes   No

         Using a scale ranging from *0 = **extremely poorly relayed*** to *10 = **extremely
         well relayed***, answer the following questions:

              How well was the information regarding the vital signs relayed? _____
              To what degree was the information regarding the vital signs relayed in an
              effective way? _____
              To what degree was the information regarding vital signs relayed in an
              appropriate way? _____

D: Environment:
         Were environmental conditions relayed to medical command?

              (Circle One)   Yes   No

         Using a scale ranging from *0 = **extremely poorly relayed*** to *10 = **extremely
         well relayed***, answer the following questions:

              How well was the information regarding environmental conditions relayed?
              _____
              To what degree was the information regarding environmental conditions
              relayed in an *effective way*? _____
              To what degree was the information regarding environmental conditions
              relayed in an *appropriate way*? _____

E: Response to Treatment:

         Was the response to treatment relayed to medical command?

              (Circle One)   Yes   No

         Using a scale ranging from *0 = **extremely poorly relayed*** to *10 = **extremely
         well relayed***, answer the following questions:

              How well was the information regarding the response to treatment relayed?
              _____
              To what degree was the information regarding the response to treatment
              relayed in an *effective way*? _____
              To what degree was the information regarding the response to treatment
              relayed in an *appropriate way*? _____

11

From Patient-based Records to Patient-centered Care: Reconfiguring Health Care Systems for Interoperable Electronic Health Records

NICOLE MARDIS

Introduction

Health care is an information intensive sector – an enormous amount of clinical, logistical, and administrative information is generated and used every day in the delivery of care (Rivard-Royer, Beaulieu, and Friel 2003). Much of this information is collected and stored on paper (Hillestad et al. 2005). The persistence of paper-based record keeping in healthcare has become an issue of national attention in Canada, the United States, and many other industrialized countries (Arnold et al. 2007, Zimlichman et al. 2011). It is hoped that the deployment of interoperable Electronic Health Records (EHRs) – longitudinal health records for an individual that can be viewed and contributed to from many different points of care – will improve medical practice by improving the accessibility and usability of patient information, which is frequently fragmented across care providers and not readily available to clinical and administrative decision makers (Rivard-Royer, Beaulieu, and Friel 2003). Over the past decade governments in Canada, the United States, and the United Kingdom, have committed substantial funding to EHR initiatives with the expectation that going electronic will improve the speed and accuracy of diagnoses, reduce errors and adverse events, reduce costly duplications of effort, and produce better data for public health research and surveillance (Baron et al. 2005, Arnold et al. 2007, Hillestad et al. 2005, Office of Health and the Information Highway 1997, Protti 2007, Zimlichman et al. 2011).

Despite considerable variation in the different national EHR initiatives that are currently underway, a common theme has emerged: these systems are more complicated and time consuming to develop than many expected (de Roos 2008). Popular explanations for the difficulty experienced getting interoperable EHR systems off the ground tend to pit the investors, developers, and end users of these systems against one another. For example, governments are criticized for being overly optimistic about the benefits that can be expected from EHR implementations (Sidorov 2006), the technical experts developing these systems are criticized for failing to grasp the complexity and heterogeneity of clinical information needs, uses, and exchanges (de Roos 2008), and healthcare practitioners are criticized for resisting information technology out of fear of losing professional autonomy (Berg 1997). While some support may be found for each of these claims, they are all manifestations of a bigger issue: building an intereoperable EHR is a massive undertaking that forges new, and sometimes tense, interdepedencies between clinical, technical, and administrative practices and requirements.

The purpose of this chapter is to draw attention to an element of Computer-Mediated Communication (CMC) that is underrepresented in discussions of what information technology can do for the healthcare sector: standards. Computers require detailed specifications and instructions to function. The average modern day computer draws on over 250 standards just to operate (Biddle, White, and Woods 2010). Using computers to augment human communication is not a simple task. While computers are excellent tools for managing large volumes of information, they cannot mitigate ambiguity or interpret information as humans do. Therefore, humans must specify and configure their information collection practices and patterns in ways that are conducive to CMC. These tasks are performed through the development and adoption of common standards.

A major challenge facing EHR initiatives is the volume and complexity of the standards work needed to achieve interoperability. The typical starting point for EHR standards work is to focus on the development of health IT standards – technical specifications designed specifically for communicating health information. It is widely recognized that these standards must be informed to some extent by clinical and administrative information needs, uses, and collection practices (Hammond 2008). What is not well recognized, however, is just how heterogeneous clinical and administrative practices and requirements are (Berg 1997), and how influential this heterogeneity will be on the design and function of EHR systems. The purpose of this chapter is to demonstrate that the interoperable EHR is not a quick technical "fix" that can be "applied" to healthcare systems; healthcare systems must undergo significant transformations (that is, harmonizing and coordinating information collection needs, practices, and uses) to make the interoperable EHR possible.

CMC research offers a useful conceptual framework for studying the co-shaping of human and technical systems, as it does not treat technology as a neutral tool. Rather, as Norman (1993) explains, each technology is viewed as having "constraints, preconditions, and side effects that impose requirements and changes on the things with which it interacts, be they other technology, people, or human society at large" (243). The goal of this chapter is to make use of the CMC perspective to broaden understandings of the scope, complexity, and interdisciplinary nature of the interoperable EHR. In doing so, the interoperable EHR is reconceptualized as the embodiment of the degree of uniformity (that is, standardization) that can be negotiated between clinical, administrative, and technical domains. It is argued that a major weakness of EHR development initiatives is that they are narrowly focused on technical requirements (de Roos 2008) and disproportionately informed by technical experts. Establishing a national health infostructure is a major project that no entity or profession has the time, resources, or expertise to carry out alone. A broad collaborative effort that is informed by inter-disciplinary research and theory, as well as smaller-scale applications of CMC, is needed to support the negotiation of interoperability.

The Interoperable EHR: What it is and is Not

The interoperable EHR is one of the more recent and complex conceptualizations of how to make better use of computers and IT in the delivery of healthcare. The Healthcare Information and Management Systems Society (HIMSS 2009) provide a general description of what EHRs are expected to contain and how they might be used:

The EHR is a longitudinal electronic record of patient health information generated by one or more encounters in any care delivery setting. Included in this information are patient demographics, progress notes, problems, medications, vital signs, past medical history, immunizations, laboratory data, and radiology reports. The EHR automates and streamlines the clinician's workflow. The EHR has the ability to generate a complete record of a clinical patient encounter, as well as supporting other care-related activities directly or indirectly via interface—including evidence-based decision support, quality management, and outcomes reporting.

The system described above represents an advanced form of computer-mediated communication. In general, CMC refers to "the process by which people create, exchange, and perceive information using networked telecommunications systems (or non-networked computers) that facilitate encoding, transmitting, and decoding messages" (December 1997a). An important component of CMC is that it involves "people, situated in particular contexts, engaging in processes to shape media for particular purposes" (December 1997b). The elements of the EHR that are advanced from a CMC perspective include: the scope of transmission (for example, potentially including all care providers in a healthcare system); the range of contexts and activities to accommodate (for example, from e-prescribing to health surveillance); the various ways in which information has to be formatted for these different contexts and activities (for example, raw data is made viewable through a multitude of different interfaces and electronic documents); and, the amount of "coding" and "decoding" needed to share the information in consistent, secure, and unambiguous formats.

It is important to distinguish EHR systems from other forms of CMC in health communication, such as Electronic Medical Record (EMR) systems. An EMR is an application "used by healthcare practitioners to document, monitor, and manage health care delivery within a [care providing organization] ... that is owned by the [care provider]" (Garets and Davis 2006: 2). Adopting an EMR represents the transition from paper-based record keeping to electronic record keeping within a single point of care. While this transition from paper to electronic record keeping may represent a major internal change for care providers, doing so without establishing interoperability is not fundamentally at odds with the current structure of the health care system in which information is typically collected by care providers for their own use.

There are many EMR applications available today that can run on basic computers. The reported benefits of EMR usage include: improved document management; improved data organization and representation; improved quality of patient care and chronic disease management; improved management of prescriptions; improved performance monitoring capabilities; a reduction in costs associated with transcribing and maintaining paper records; and, a reduction in the time it takes to complete certain tasks (Chaudhry et al. 2006, Hillestad et al. 2005, Miller and Sim 2004). Several European countries achieved very high EMR adoption rates years ago in association with financial incentive programs (Schoen et al. 2006). EMR adoption rates by office-based physicians in Canada and the United States – countries that did not offer similar incentives until recently – are much lower (that is, less than 20 percent in Canada and less than 35 percent in the U.S.) (Commonwealth Fund Commission on a High Performance Health System 2008, Hing and Hsiao 2010, The National Physician Survey 2008).

Interoperable EHR systems differ from EMRs in that EHR systems are aggregators of patient information from many different care providers. This is an important distinction that is sometimes lost in the literature due to the common, yet incorrect, practice of using the terms EHR and EMR interchangeably. The main purpose of interoperable EHR systems is to enable the sharing of information across care providers. EHRs, therefore, depend upon the widespread use of point-of-service applications in clinical practice (for example, lab systems, pharmacy systems, and EMR systems) to collect information electronically, as well as the ability of these systems to exchange information in mutually useful and understandable ways (Garets and Davis 2006, Hammond 2008).

Most nations that are currently engaged in developing EHRs are still far from having systems in place that enable widespread interoperability (de Roos 2008). This limitation is not to deny the existence of any form of interoperability; there are many examples of electronic patient records being shared within small clusters of hospitals and clinics, as well as between a large number of care providers belonging to the same managed care consortium or associated with particular benefit providers (for example, the Veterans Health Administration) (Burton, Anderson, and Kues 2004, Etheredge 2007, Silvestre, Sue, and Allen 2009). For example, in 2010 an American-based insurer, Kaiser Permanente, announced that its own interoperable EHR system was up and running in 36 hospitals and 431 doctor's offices, providing approximately 8.6 million patients with electronic health records (Charette 2010).

Kaiser's EHR is one of the largest systems in existence today. It is frequently cited as a success story that national governments should try to replicate on a grander scale. Kaiser's system, however, cost over four billion US dollars to build, was 40 years in the making, and was not the insurer's first attempt at an EHR – a US$400 million EHR project with IBM failed before Kaiser started on its current system (Charette 2010). For perspective, Canada launched an ambitious national EHR initiative in 2001. Approximately C$2.6 billion was invested towards the goal providing at least 50 percent of the population (almost 16 million people) with an interoperable electronic health record by 2009 (Infoway 2005). This goal has since been pushed back and expectations about the degree of interoperability that can be achieved in the near future have changed significantly since the project's initiation (Infoway 2007).

Why is the Interoperable EHR such an Elusive Goal?

The difficulty encountered in establishing the interoperability of health information and systems is not a technical issue only, it is also an alignment issue. Take for example the requirement of establishing semantic interoperability for the communication of health information. Semantic interoperability is achieved by "coding" health information with "controlled vocabularies, lexicons, taxonomies and ontologies" to aid in its interpretation (Groen and Wine 2009: 1). This coding helps information systems receive, organize, and retrieve information appropriately. Semantic interoperability also helps care providers establish a shared understanding of the information they exchange. Establishing the technical framework to support semantic interoperability includes specifying the common data elements, terminologies, structures, and system organization needed to "share and use data from multiple institutions" (Hammond 2005: 1205).

From a technical standpoint, semantic interoperability may not be so difficult to pull off if care providers and health practitioners agreed on how to code and represent clinical information. However, this is not the case; there are competing terminologies and strategies for representing clinical information electronically. The situation becomes even more complicated when one takes into account all of the different organizational practices and legacy information systems currently in existence. For example, a single hospital may have multiple information systems in use – some built in house and some purchased from different vendors – that use different data elements and vocabularies. To achieve interoperability, these legacy systems will have to be accommodated for in EHR standards, connected via costly interface, or replaced altogether (Mardis 2009).

Semantic interoperability provides just one example of how interdependent clinical, administrative, and technical considerations are with one another in the development EHR systems. Semantic interoperability happens to be one of the more immediately apparent examples because the use of clinical terminology in clinical practice and in health information systems is well established. There are, however, other less obvious interdependencies between these domains. Of particular concern in subsequent sections of this chapter is how the nature and use of clinical information, along with variances in administrative priorities and regulations for electronic record keeping, complicate the design of EHR systems.

CLINICAL INFORMATION AND SPECIFICATIONS: A HISTORY OF VARIABILITY

The interoperable EHR represents a new, high-tech approach to solving an old "problem" in clinical practice: managing and using information more efficiently. This problem was first explored academically in the late 1970s and early 1980s in a series of studies that found significant variation in physician practice patterns, the widespread use of outdated and inappropriate procedures, and a lack of correspondence between clinical research and practice (Eddy 2005, Timmermans and Berg 2003). The main explanations provided for these variations were: humans are incapable of processing all of the information needed to make complex medical decisions; and there is a "lack of good evidence" to identify best practices (Eddy 2005: 3). Over the 1980s and 1990s, numerous agencies, associations, and collaborations arose around the world to develop and disseminate clinical findings and recommendations with the hope of reducing the noted inconsistencies in clinical practices and better informing clinical decision making (Eddy 2005, Timmermans and Berg 2003). Timmermans and Berg (2003) describe this rapid growth in the production of "evidence" and "evidence-based guidelines" as the outcome of a "cottage industry" of standards development bodies and organizations that arose without coordination (2–29). In short, the first widespread effort to better coordinate clinical practices via standards resulted in the uncoordinated production of numerous competing standards. This legacy is of major relevance to EHR initiatives, which represent a much more complicated and intense standardization movement entering clinical practice. The difficulties encountered by previous standardization attempts can provide insight into a major problem that has surfaced thus far in EHR initiatives: aligning clinical and technical requirements.

Getting to the source of non-standard practices in clinical domains Efforts to explain the ongoing variation in clinical terminologies, protocols, and diagnoses tend to link it to the nature of medical practice and/or the manner in which clinical standards (for example, protocols) are developed. Studies that point to the nature of medical practice as the source of the "variation problem" argue that the discipline is too abstract to lend itself to standardization (Berg 1997, Stinchcombe 1986) and/or that clinicians have accumulated too much professional autonomy, which translates into idiosyncratic practices (Berg 1997). Arthur Stinchcombe (1986), who approaches the subject of standardization from a theoretical standpoint, argues that both "formal rationality" ("standardized methods of calculation") and "substantive rationality" (an understanding of the "substance" of "matters") are necessary for the successful "routinization" of a profession (157). Medical practice contains some of the features necessary for achieving greater routinization (e.g. it has a supply of trained practitioners who are knowledgeable of the system of reason employed in the field). However, these practitioners often fail to arrive at "the same judgments after applying their methods of calculation to produce an authoritative judgment" suggesting that the "core" of medical practice is "irrational" (not easily reproduced) (Stinchcombe 1986: 157). According to Stinchcombe (1986), efforts to rationalize professions with an irrational core may, at best, achieve greater standardization of the more trivial or peripheral activities.

In a more empirical investigation of the debate over whether medical practice is an art or a science, Berg (1997) suggests that medical practice is more complicated than it is irrational. The practitioner is frequently confronted with far more information to take into consideration than is accommodated for in the rules, so she/he must often rely on her/his expert judgment and experience, which can lead to significant variations in practice (Berg 1997). Berg (1997) argues that outsiders (to the practice) often interpret this use of expert judgment and experience as a failure to apply medical knowledge or a blatant refusal to comply with standards. Berg (1997) does not deny that judgments can be poor, experience misleading, and clinicians' protective of professional autonomy. His goal is to highlight the complexities of medical practice and the ways in which clinicians are relied upon to manage it. To change this complexity would require a transformation of the practice, of the protocols produced (which would have to be expanded to absorb the complexity), and of the tools for enforcing adherence to them (Berg 1997). Berg (1997) concludes that the achievability and desirability of such a transformation has yet to be demonstrated.

Using technology to make better use of clinical standards While the debate over the extent to which medical practice can be routinized lingers, efforts have been placed into making better use of the standards that already exist, such as by using information systems to help increase adherence rates. These efforts have enjoyed some success, but this success has been highly variable (Chaudhry et al. 2006, Sidorov 2006). For example, in perhaps the most comprehensive review of literature on the use of EMR systems in clinical practice, Chaudhry et al. (2006) found that improvements in protocol adherence ranged from 5 percent to 60 percent and decreases in adverse events or complications ranged from 0.4 percent to 8.2 percent (based on a limited number of activities, such as increasing the rate of influenza vaccinations given, increasing fecal blood testing, decreasing adverse drug events, and decreasing deep venous thrombosis and pulmonary embolism). In a more limited review of seven different studies, Sidorov (2006) found that while EMRs may increase adherence to some "omission-type error reductions" such as "inpatient vaccination and anticoagulation reminders; diabetes, hypertension, vitamin B12 deficiency, thyroid, and anemia screening in the elderly; [and] health maintenance and counseling in a pediatric practice," these systems have been shown to have no effect on adherence to primary care guidelines for asthma or angina management; "variable" and "limited" adherence to diabetes and coronary artery disease reminders; no effect on evidence-based interventions for heart disease and heart failure; [no] change in the care of patients with depression; [and] no impact on diabetic glucose control (1080–81). Although it has not been shown why adherence to some standards and not others seems to increase with the use of computer-based decision support systems, it is worth noting that the improvements in adherence rates identified by Chaudhry et al. (2006) and Sidorov (2006) were achieved among the more routine activities, such as screening for a B12 deficiency. These findings are consistent with Berg (1997) and Stinchcombe's (1986) argument: reminders to follow the rules will not help all that much if the situation at hand does not easily fit within the rules.

The implications clinical heterogeneity for the HER   On the surface, it may be hard to see how this discussion of clinical practices and standards relates to the EHR. The argument made here is that although health IT standards are largely technical in focus, they implicate a broad range of non-technical activities in the clinical domain. For example, developing health IT standards necessitates the specification of how health information is collected, coded, exchanged, and used, which itself necessitates some specification of how a health care system is organized, what the roles and responsibilities of entities in that system are, how end-users use information, and what policies and guidelines are adhered to (Hammond 2008). This already tremendous undertaking becomes a much greater endeavor if those who are to share information cannot agree on how to collect, code, organize, present, interpret, and use it. The difficulties encountered by previous attempts to reduce variability in the way clinical information is collected, used, and interpreted suggest that much of medical practice may never give way to widespread standardization. Popular thinking regarding EHRs misses this dilemma. Computers, with their tremendous processing power and capacity for connectivity, are assumed to contain all of the order and structure that is needed to improve the accessibility, usability, and shareability of health information. This is, at best, a half truth: computers provide a context for communication that has certain constraints, capacities, and implications, but humans must go through the process of organizing, detailing, and reconciling their patterns of communication to fit within that context. Reducing the variation in medical practices, terminologies, and protocols may, therefore, be more of a prerequisite for improving the quality and flow health information than an outcome. As the following section demonstrates, the variability of administrative practices and requirements adds another layer of complexity to EHR standardization work.

THE HETEROGENEITY OF ADMINISTRATIVE RULES AND ROUTINES

There are two broad categories of administrative rules and routines that are of particular relevance to EHRs: privacy and security policies and regulations; and information collection practices. The former refers primarily to legislation that cuts across different organizations. The latter refers to a wider range of information collection practices – such as what information is collected, how, and the manner in which it is formatted and coded (if at all) – that are established at the organizational level. The nature of, and variances between, these different types of rules and routines can have serious implications for EHR systems.

The lack of specificity and consistency in provincial legislation relating to the electronic management and exchange of personal information is a major threat to the pan-Canadian EHR. As Michener (2010: 9–12) explains, if the basic principles/standards for EHR security are not established upfront, it will be left up to a rather slow and indirect approach – case law – to work out:

> *The question that may be posed is the following: Should Canada's laws reflect a pro-active leadership role in establishing basic principles for EHR security, or should we rely on general legal precepts of security to ultimately generate a set of rules, through a more circuitous process?*

Technical progress on the EHR is, therefore, heavily implicated with the modernization of privacy and security legislation to account for the exchange of personal information via CMC. Unfortunately for EHR developers, the legislative domain parallels the medical domain in many ways: it is full of complexity and ambiguity, and reliant on highly trained professionals to interpret and apply general precepts to specific situations.

Variances in organizational practices and routines regarding the collection, coding, and usage of health information also signifies a tremendous challenge for achieving interoperability. Hammond (2008: 8) explains:

> *Health care occurs in many different settings. Data requirement differ, priorities are different, and other influences such as culture and environment affect what is done … The key to interoperability is to make sure all pertinent classes of interoperability are satisfied. Any data element used at any site must come from the common meta-data registry.*

Hammond (2008) puts on a brave face in explaining the "key to interoperability," as if establishing a common meta-data registry and satisfying "all pertinent classes of interoperability" for all care providers in a healthcare system is not too daunting of a task (8). Reflecting on the earlier discussion of clinical heterogeneity, however, gives reason to expect this task to absorb a lot of time and give rise to a massive common meta-data registry.

The implications of administrative heterogeneity for the HER   Both of the examples described above illustrate an important point: EHRs rely on a higher degree of inter-organizational and inter-jurisdictional coordination than is currently present in many healthcare systems. Achieving widespread interoperability requires all relevant organizations and authorities to align their policies and data collection practices with one another, and/or to embed legal and administrative constraints and requirements into EHR systems so usable information is collected for all parties and no legislation is violated in the process of transmitting patient information across organizations and jurisdictions. The former solution (aligning legislation, priorities, and data collection practices) requires organizations, health authorities, and governments to establish common rules and routines. The challenge with this solution is that the rewards, sanctions, chains of command, and mechanisms for setting priorities and establishing rules are not as well defined between organizations and jurisdictions as they are within organizations and jurisdictions (Heckscher 2007). The latter solution of developing systems that can interface between numerous different requirements and practices greatly complicates EHR development work (de Roos 2008). Finally, both alternatives require time, resources, and collaboration, and may unearth all sorts of additional variances in practice.

REFRAMING THE EHR AS A BALANCE ACT

The interoperable EHR is still largely conceptualized as a technical fix that will generate all sorts of efficiencies and cost savings in the delivery of healthcare by revolutionizing health communication. This view is problematic in that it misspecifies the source and timing of much of the change associated with achieving interoperability. The end result is that considerable time and attention is invested in developing the technical components of the EHR without a full appreciation of the scope and heterogeneity of clinical and administrative requirements that must be factored into the equation. A more accurate conceptualization of the interoperable EHR is the embodiment of the degree of uniformity that can be negotiated between clinical, administrative, and technical domains. This shift in thinking is needed to gain a more accurate understanding of the preconditions, constraints, side effects, and transformations involved in establishing the interoperability of health information and systems. A major challenge follows this shift in thinking, however: establishing a forum to support this negotiation process and a framework to integrate relevant research, theory, and real-world CMC implementation experience. In perhaps the closest attempt yet to such a framework, the Pan-Canadian EHR initiative established the Standards Collaborative (SC), an open and participatory body designed to serve as "… a single point of domestic contact for collaboration, co-ordination, development, maintenance and on-going support …" of health IT and EHR related standards for use in Canada (Infoway 2007). While the SC brings together groups that are directly implicated in the development and use of EHR systems to work together on the content and direction of EHR related standards, this body does not view clinical and administrative standards (or the lack of them) as central to its work (Mardis 2009).

Implications for Academics

At the conceptual level, the interoperable EHR represents a cohesive "system" that can be "built" as a single project. In practice, however, it consists of many different ideas and activities that cut across different professions, organizations, and even jurisdictions. This multifaceted and fragmented nature of EHR work is not frequently picked up on in academic literatures, nor is much of the relevant research and theory on CMC used to inform EHR work. In this section it is argued that EHR work has the potential to influence academic work, and conversely, academic work has the potential to shape EHR work. Two examples from the Pan-Canadian EHR initiative are provided to illustrate this point.

In a case study on the pan-Canadian EHR, Mardis (2009) found that there is a considerable amount of academic research occurring on EMRs and local integration (achieving interoperability between a small number of hospitals and clinics) in Canada that is disconnected from the Pan-Canadian EHR initiative. Mardis (2009) linked this disconnect to the national initiative's strategy for achieving interoperability: care providers are to exchange information indirectly by viewing and contributing to a common data source (a shared repository). Peer-to-peer integration – having care providers exchange information directly with one another as many academic-based, local integration projects do – is discouraged by the national initiative (Mardis 2009). This barrier has generated some criticism of the pan-Canadian EHR as a top-down approach that is not only out of touch with clinical practice, but also with clinician-driven research on the adoption and use of health IT systems.

In the same case study, Mardis (2009) found new, mutually beneficial relationships being forged between EHR development initiatives and academic institutions. For example, the Pan-Canadian EHR initiative received considerable criticism for asking vendors to adopt a complicated messaging specification that had not been tested in the field. A technical expert who saw this as a deficit in the national approach rallied support from a collection of public and private partners to establish an EHR Reference Implementation (a mock EHR built to spec that can be used for testing). Mohawk College's Applied Centre in Health Informatics stepped in to house the Reference Implementation. Within a short period of time the center managed to integrate the Reference Implementation into its curriculum and get a mock EHR up and running. Since its establishment, the Reference Implementation Project has generated lessons learned from the implementation process, feedback on how the pan-Canadian EHR specifications perform, and recommendations for tooling and simplified message formats that may make the development and implementation of EHR projects less onerous and complicated (Mardis, 2009).

As the above examples demonstrate, EHRs, and more broadly speaking, the application of CMC in health communication, can influence academics in many ways, such as by placing new constraints on the institutions in which they work, changing priorities for research, creating new research opportunities, and providing new sites for investigation. At the same time, EHR work is so vast and complicated that it stands to benefit from the knowledge, resources, and rigor that academics and academic institutions can bring to the study and implementation of CMC in health communication.

Implications for Health Practitioners

It is difficult to scope out all of the implications EHRs will pose for health practitioners, as the design and function of these systems have yet to be settled. At present time descriptions of the role EHRs will take in clinical practice vary from automating the main information exchanges that currently occur in healthcare, such as enabling clinicians to order and receive lab results electronically, to reconfiguring clinical practices and workflows around computers and decision support systems. Despite this uncertainty, one thing is clear: for the most part health practitioners have been treated as passive end users of health information and systems, rather than important stakeholders whose active participation is needed in shaping the design and function of these systems, as well as in reconfiguring their own practices and patterns of communication in ways that are consistent with CMC. Feedback from EMR implementations suggests that even small scale implementations of CMC produce many implications for health practitioners. Take for example Baron et al.'s (2005: 223) description of the work involved in implementing a standalone EMR system in a single medical office:

> [W]e found ourselves making innumerable decisions about how we would use the system before we really understood how it worked, and our vendor did not know enough about how our office worked to help us. We were forced to rapidly adjust our workflows during implementation, which seemed akin to rebuilding an airplane in flight … Going live rendered everyone in the office incompetent to do their jobs … variations in clinical style and work flow among the physicians – which had seemed acceptable if unnoticed before – now became the subject of scrutiny.

The description above highlights not only how work-flow-altering aligning human practices with CMC can be, but also how difficult it is for anyone, from vendors to clinicians, to anticipate the challenges that will be faced and the adjustments that will have to be made, even in small-scale implementations. Pursuing widely interoperable systems dramatically increases the number of practitioners and providers who have to coordinate their practices with one another.

Conclusion

The persistence of paper-based record keeping in healthcare has received much atten over the last 15 years. Ambitious technical solutions have been designed to imp the accessibility, usability, and share-ability of health information via the establishm of nation-wide interoperable EHRs. To date no nation has been successful in getti fully functional and widely interoperable EHR system up and running. Three interre arguments have been put forward in this chapter to explain the difficulty experie establishing the interoperability of health information and systems. First, it is a that the interoperable EHR represents an advanced form of computer-me communication. Achieving the interoperability of health information and syste not simply about exchanging packets of information, it is about employing com to interpret, organize, and manage that information so it is presented to hum consistent, secure, and unambiguous formats (Hammond 2005, Hammond Giving computers this larger role in health communication comes at the cost of to structure health communication in a way that is amenable to computer-m communication. Second, it is argued that popular conceptions of the intero EHR misspecify the source and timing of much of the change associated with acmeving interoperability. The transformative potential of the EHR lies in its development, not its application. It is the settling of agreement on where and how enough uniformity can be achieved in health information uses, interpretations, and collection practices to enable interoperability that is radical, not the technical manifestation of this agreement. Third, just how transformative EHRs prove to be depends on the extent to which clinical, administrative, and technical considerations and requirements can be aligned. At present time there is a poor understanding of how heterogeneous clinical and administrative practices and requirements are, and the ultimate impact that this diversity of information needs and uses will have on the design and function of EHR systems. While some EHR initiatives, such as the Pan-Canadian initiative, have established forums to engage clinicians, administrators, and other implicated parties in EHR standardization work in the hope of speeding up progress, this work is still predominately technical in focus (Mardis 2009). Additionally, it is hard to establish a venue for negotiation that is mutually accessible and engaging for all of the relevant stakeholders. This is where academia can assist. Research that explores the multi-disciplinary nature of health communication, particularly in computer-mediated contexts, can help illuminate the coordination requirements and challenges facing EHR initiatives.

References

Arnold, S., Wagner, J., Hyatt, S., Klein, G. and The Global EHR Task Force Members. 2007. *Electronic Health Records: A Global Perspective* [Online: Healthcare Information and Management Systems Society]. Available at: http://www.himss.org/content/files/DrArnold20011207EISPresentationWhitePaper. pdf [accessed 23 October 2011].

Baron, R.J., Fabens, E.L., Schiffman, M. and Wolf, E. 2005. Electronic health records: Just around the corner? Or over the cliff? *Annals of Internal Medicine*, 143(3), 222–6.

Berg, M. 1997. *Rationalizing Medical Work: Decision-support Techniques and Medical Practices*. Cambridge, MA: MIT Press.

Berg, M. 2000. Orders and their others: On the construction of universalities in medical work. *Configurations*, 8(Winter 2000), 31–61.

Berner, E.S., Detmer, D.E. and Simborg, D. 2005. Will the wave finally break? A brief view of the adoption of electronic medical records in the United States. *Journal of the American Medical Informatics Association*, 12(1), 3–7.

Biddle, B., White, A. and Woods, S. 2010. *How Many Standards in a Laptop? (and Other Empirical Questions)*. ITU-T Kaleidoscope 2010 – Beyond the Internet? Innovations for future networks and services Conference, Pune, India, 13–15 December 2010.

Burton, L.C., Anderson, G.F. and Kues, I.W. 2004. Using electronic health records to help coordinate care. *Milbank Quarterly*, 82(3), 457–81.

Charette, R. 2010. Kaiser Permanente marks completion of its electronic health records implementation. *IEEE Spectrum* [Online]. Available at: http://spectrum.ieee.org/riskfactor/ computing/it/kaiser-permanente-marks-completion-of-its-electronic-health-records- implementation [accessed: 10 January 2012].

Chaudhry, B., Wang, J., Wu, S., Maglione, M., Mojica, W., Roth, E., Morton, S. and Shekelle, P. 2006. Systematic review: Impact of health information technology on quality, efficiency, and costs of medical care. *Annals of Internal Medicine*, 144(10), 742–52.

Commonwealth Fund Commission on a High Performance Health System. 2008. *Why not the best? Results from a national scorecard on U.S. health system performance* [Online]. Available at: http:// www.commonwealthfund.org/Publications/Fund-Reports/2008/Jul/Why-Not-the-Best--Results -from-the-National-Scorecard-on-U-S--Health-System-Performance--2008.aspx [accessed: 23 October 2011].

December, J. 1997a. *What is Computer-Mediated Communication* [Online]. Available at: http://www. december.com/john/study/cmc/what.html [accessed: 10 January 2012].

December, J. 1997b. *Notes on Defining of Computer-Mediated Communication* [Online CMC Magazine]. Available at: http://www.december.com/cmc/mag/1997/jan/december.html [accessed: 10 January 2012].

de Roos, A. 2008. Towards a realistic interoperable EHR [Online]. Available at: http://albertderoos. nl/pdf/EHRpercent20approach.pdf [accessed: 6 December 2010].

Eddy, D. 2005. Evidence-based medicine: A unified approach. *Health Affairs,* 24(4), 9–17.

Etheredge, L.M. 2007. A rapid-learning health system. *Health Affairs,* 26(2), 107–18.

Fau, J. and R. Haynes. 1998. The Cochrane Collaboration–advances and challenges in improving evidence-based decision making. *Medical Decision Making,* 18(1), 2–18.

Garets, D. and Davis, M. 2006. Electronic medical records vs. electronic health records: Yes, there is a difference, *HIMSS Analytics™ White Paper.* Chicago, Il: HIMSS Analytics™ [Online]. Available at: http://www.himssanalytics.org/docs/wp_emr_ehr.pdf [accessed: 23 September 2010].

Grace, S. 2007. Technology: Calculating an EMR's ROI. The case for EMRs in dollars and cents. *Physicians Practice,* 17(1).

Groen, P., and Wine, M. 2009. *Medical Semantics, Ontologies, Open Solutions and EHR Systems* [Online]. Available at: http://www.hoise.com/vmw/09/articles/contentsvmw200909.html [accessed: 23 September 2010].

Hammond, E. 2005. The making and adoption of health data standards. *Health Affairs,* 24(5), 1205–13.

Hammond, E. 2008. A perspective on interoperability. *Making the eHealth Connection,* July. Available at: http://www.dbmotion.com/multimedia/upl_doc/doc_221008_200153.pdf [accessed: 12 June 2010].

Healthcare Information and Management Systems Society (HIMSS). 2009. *The EHR* [Online]. Available at: http://www.himss.org/ASP/topics_ehr.asp [accessed: 26 August 2009].

Hillestad, R., Bigelow, J., Bower, A., Girosi, F., Meili, R., Scoville, R. and Taylor, R. 2005. Can electronic medical record systems transform health care? Potential health benefits, savings, and costs. *Health Affairs,* 24(5), 1103–17.

Hing, E. and Hsiao, C.J. 2010. Electronic medical record use by office-based physicians and their practices, 2007 *National Health Statistics Report* (Vol. 23). Washington, DC: U.S. Department of Health and Human Services.

Infoway. 2006. *Annual Report. 2005-2006.* Canada: Infoway.

Infoway. 2006. *The Electronic Health Record Solution Blueprint V2.* Canada: Infoway.

Infoway. 2007. *Overview of the SC.* Canada: Infoway.

Mardis, N. 2009. *The state of health information technology standards: the conflation of the technical and the political in the development of a pan-Canadian electronic health record system,* unpublished master's thesis, McGill University.

Michener, L. 2010. *Electronic Health Records – Privacy and Security Issues.* [Online: Lang Michener LLP]. Available at: http://www.langmichener.ca/index.cfm?fuseaction=content.contentDetail&ID= 10940&tID=244 [accessed: 23 September 2010]

Miller, R.H. and Sim, I. 2004. Physicians' use of electronic medical records: barriers and solutions; a survey of physician practices shows slow but steady progress in adopting this new technology. *Pursuit Of Quality,* (March/April).

Nagel, L. 2007. Informatics: emerging concepts and issues. *Nursing Leadership,* 20(1).

Norman, D.A. 1993. *Things That Make Us Smart: Defending Human Attributes in the Age of the Machine.* Reading, MA: Addison-Wesley.

Office of Health and the Information Highway. 1997. *Health Information Technologies in Canada 1997 – Survey of Initiatives in Progress.* Canada: Health Canada.

Protti, D. 2007. Comparison of information technology in general practice in 10 countries. *Healthcare Quarterly*, 5(4), 107–16.

Rivard-Royer, H., Beaulieu, M. and Friel, T. 2003. *Healthcare Ecosystem: Linking Logistical Flows and Clinical Flows*. Montreal: HEC Montreal [Online]. Available at: http://web.hec.ca/chaine/fichiers/texte_auto/CR03-04.pdf [accessed: 12 September 2010].

Sackett, D., Rosenberg, W., Gray, J., Haynes, R. and Richardson, W. 1996. Evidence based medicine: What it is and what it isn't. *British Medical Journal*, 312(July), 71–72.

Schoen, C., Osborn, R., Huynh, P.T., Doty, M., Peugh, J. and Zapert, K. 2006. On the front lines of care: Primary care doctors' office systems, experiences, and views in seven countries. *Health Affairs*, 25(6).

Sidorov, J. 2006. It ain't necessarily so: The electronic health record and the unlikely prospect of reducing health care costs. *Health Affairs*, 25(4), 1079–85.

Silvestre, A.L., Sue, V.M. and Allen, J.Y. 2009. If you build it, will they come? The Kaiser Permanente Model of online health care. *Health Affairs*, 28(2), 334–44.

Sinha, S.K., McElhaney, J. and Rockwood, K. 2009. Canada's coming of age: How demographic imperatives will force the redesign of acute care service delivery. *BCMJ*, 51(7).

Smith, P.D. 2003. Implementing an EMR system: One clinic's experience. *Family Practice Management*, 10(5), 37–42.

Stinchcombe, A. 1986. Reason and rationality. *Sociological Theory*, 4(Fall 1986), 51–66.

The National Physician Survey. (2008). *How Are we Doing? Reported IT use in the National Physician Survey* [Online: The National Physician Survey]. Available at: http://www.nationalphysiciansurvey.ca/nps/reports/PDF-e/NPS&IT.pdf [accessed: 21 October 2011].

Zaroukian, M. 2006. *EMR Cost-Benefit Analysis: Managing ROI into Reality* [Online: Healthcare Information and Management Systems Society]. Available at: http://www.himss.org/content/files/EMRCost-BenefitReality.pdf [accessed: 21 October 2011].

Zimlichman, E., Rozenblum, R., Salzberg, C.A., Jang, Y., Tamblyn, M., Tamblyn, R. and Bates, D.W. 2011. Lessons from the Canadian national health information technology plan for the United States: Opinions of key Canadian experts. *Journal of the American Medical Informatics Association*, 7(15).

12 The Role of Communication in Health Informatics Integration Success: Case Study of an Ontario Pediatric Critical Care Unit

VICTORIA ACETI AND ROCCI LUPPICINI

Introduction

Effective communication is essential to the functioning of the healthcare system, particularly in the sharing of information between healthcare providers and between providers and patients. Poor communication leads to poor quality healthcare services. Researchers have concluded that communication errors were twice as likely to cause preventable patient disability or death as inadequate medical skill (Zinn 1995). Coiera (2003) contends that "the sheer scale and complexity of these [interdisciplinary] interactions within the healthcare system puts a heavy burden on the process of communication" (232). As a way to ameliorate such problems, several organizations have recently turned to health information and communication technologies, also known as health informatics. While many of these technologies show great promise, integrating health informatics into practice is more challenging.

Health informatics is defined as a "systematic approach to the collection, organization, storage, use, and evaluation of health data, information and knowledge" (Layman and Watzlaf 2009: 6). Health informatics integration is often met with resistance, technical issues and insecurities, and resource shortages; the coordinated efforts of providers and researchers are needed to effectively develop strategies for easier integration.

Integrating a new technology is a difficult process in which mistakes can disrupt clinical workflows and patient care. Berg, Aarts, and van der Lei (2003) suggest that, "as information systems require interaction with people and thereby inevitably affect them, understanding information systems requires a focus on the interrelation between technology and its social environment" (297, see also Aarts, Peel and Wright 1998, Coiera 2003). Effective integration of health informatics into an organization is only a technical issue, but a socially negotiated one between users, middle management, strategic leaders;

indeed, "it is the outcome of all these interactions that in the end settles the system's fate" (Berg 2001:144, Kaplan 2001). This interaction between social and technological systems within an organization can be explored through sociotechnology theory.

SOCIOTECHNOLOGY THEORY

Sociotechnology theory is concerned with the influence that social contexts and technology have on each other. The main concept behind sociotechnology is that social contexts and technology are not separate, but occur in the same environment and thus influence each other in varying ways. Under sociotechnical theory, it is necessary to understand the interaction of social and technological contexts to ensure the successful use of health informatics within an organization.

In this chapter, we use a sociotechnology lens to present a case study of the integration of mHealth technologies within an Ontario pediatric critical care unit and the processes by which these technologies were integrated. MHealth (or mobile health) is the "development, dissemination and application of mobile information and wireless telecommunication technologies in the area of healthcare" (Siau and Shen 2006: 90). The results of the case study are used in the development of the Integration Model which illustrates a strategic approach to health informatics integration. The Model is intended to assist leaders not only in planning for the integration process, but also in foreseeing where obstacles are most likely to occur before the integration is completely derailed.

The purpose of the chapter will be threefold:

1. to explore how sociotechnical approaches to health communication studies can enhance health informatics knowledge;
2. to illustrate key issues with health informatics integration drawn from a recent case study research on the uses of mHealth technologies within an Ontario pediatric critical care unit; and
3. to explain how the Integration Model can be used as a tool to assist organizations in integrating health informatics.

Case Study

SITE DESCRIPTION

To investigate the extent to which the integration of health informatics influences interdisciplinary communication, a Pediatric Critical Care Unit (PCCU) in an Ontario children's hospital served as the site of a case study. The PCCU is a secular unit within a major Ontario hospital consisting of various disciplines working within one specialized unit including, but not limited to, nurses, respiratory and physical therapists, physicians, and pediatric specialists. In the critical care unit each nurse is responsible for only one patient during a shift; patients in the PCCU are in critical condition and require this specialized attention. However, other healthcare providers in the unit attend to multiple patients during a regular shift.

Electronic Medical Records (EMRs) have been used in the PCCU for several years. The organization uses electronic patient charting regularly. The children's hospital which houses the PCCU is an innovative organization which has an extensive history of health informatics integration and is at the forefront of health informatics innovation in Canada. In fact, the organization has an entire clinical informatics unit devoted solely to informatics. This unit works to ensure that all information technologies are effectively designed, integrated and maintained. The PCCU has a history of hosting pilot informatics projects for the organization and had recently integrated a mobile tablet option as an alternative method for patient charting. At the time of the study, only the staff in the PCCU were using mHealth to input patient information.

The mHealth application used in the PCCU is compact and can be carried from room to room. Alternatively, it can be attached to a keyboard outside the room to allow for additional methods of information input. The application allows the use of touch screens, a stylist pen, or an external keyboard to enter information into a patient's chart. The software used on the application is the same software used on desktop and laptop computers in the PCCU. All users are familiar with the computer software. Further, physicians working on the unit had other technologies at their disposal. For example, one physician used an iPhone to track patient information and a desktop computer to input patient information.

This case study looked at the integration of mHealth applications from an organizational top-level strategic perspective and from the perspective of the user. The following methodology section outlines the research design prior to presenting the study findings.

Methodology

Qualitative research methods were used in this case study to investigate the extent to which communication is influenced by the integration of health informatics. We followed Yin's (2003) three principles of case study research data collection to ensure adherence to proper case study protocol. The first principle of case study data collection as described by Yin is to use multiple sources of evidence, thus semi-structured interviews, document analysis and a literature review were used in this study. The second principle of case study research is to create a database of evidence and separate the evidence from researcher notes. During data analysis, we made notes of our initial thoughts and connections in a separate folder from the data in order to ensure separation from data. Third, Yin suggests maintaining a chain of evidence whereby researchers organize data collected and include the date and time of the collection, the source of the data, and situational context of the data collection. We kept a record of all documents received including the date, time, location and source as well as a record of all interviews with the same information.

Semi-structured interviews with 11 employees. Six interviewees were healthcare providers, five were administrators. Interviews ranged from 20 minutes to 45 minutes in length and were conducted face-to-face. One interview was conducted over electronic mail due to time and scheduling constraints. All face-to-face interviews were audio recorded and later transcribed verbatim, followed by transcription verification by interviewees to ensure accuracy. Ethical approval was received prior to data collection from the University of Ottawa Research Ethics Board. Each participant signed a consent form informing the interviewee that their information would be anonymized and used in further publications.

Organizational documents were collected from two main sources: those available online for public viewing and those supplied by organizational leaders. A total of 24 documents were collected. Six were internal documents; 18 were available to the public. All documents were written by employees of the organization. Documents ranged in length from four to 114 pages.

We used thematic analysis to analyze both the interviews and organizational documents on internal informatics strategy. Organizational documents were analyzed first in order to better understand the organization, followed by employee interviews. We engaged in an initial round of microanalysis, as detailed by Strauss and Corbin (1998), involving a word-by-word analysis to discover a variety of concepts in the data. In this case study, over 100 concepts were discovered through microanalysis. As we engaged in microanalysis, we also wrote analytic memos to separate the data from researcher-developed connections and contradictions (Yin 2003). These analytic memos were used to help us reflect on connections and to further understand the findings of the case study. With the help of our analytic memos, we found ten themes that helped us categorize the data. These categories from the findings of the case study were then compared to findings from literature on technology integrations in health. Using this comparison, an Integration Model was developed to translate the findings of the case study into a useable model for guiding health informatics integration.

The Integration Model

The findings from the case study illustrated many critical components required in successfully integrating health informatics, specifically mHealth technologies, into an organization, including: significant end user contribution to system design, an organizational culture open to technological change, creative internal communication practices, training and education, and the evaluation of training and education. The major finding from the case study was the fact that health informatics integration did not occur in a vacuum, but in an environment compounded with multidisciplinary decision-making, life and death situations, and strict care guidelines. Working in this environment has many pressures and integrating a new technology can put added pressures onto healthcare providers. As such, it is imperative that informatics be integrated purposefully, effectively, and efficiently.

Healthcare environments are complex communication systems, which require the coordination of several people and tools to function efficiently and effectively. As such, researching an information system in this environment requires a holistic view of both the social and technological components of the system. According to Coakes (2006), "Sociotechnical theory tells us we must importantly consider people, task, process, and environment (both internal and external) when considering how best to implement technology into our organizations" (591). Social subsystems can include, but are not limited to, organizational culture, politics, work-life issues, and other non-technical factors (Kaplan 1997, Pirnejad et al. 2007). For sociotechnical paradigms are rooted in communication, and without understanding and exploring communication in technological integrations, an adequate understanding of the impacts of the system on the organization cannot be uncovered (Herrmann, Loser, and Jahnke 2007).

Employee perspectives from this case study detailed the steps taken and opportunities missed during the implementation of the mHealth application in the PCCU. We discuss the procedures, intervening conditions, and pressures involved in the implementation of mHealth technologies as they emerged in the interviews and the document analysis. There are seven steps in this Integration Model and each step is described in sequence below: scanning the environment, choosing appropriate pilot site and technology, communicating organizational change, integration, adoption, evaluation of integration, and the decision stage.

SCANNING THE ENVIRONMENT

Scanning the environment was first described by Aguilar (1967) as the task of searching for information which will help to track the course for an organization's future. At the organization we investigated, information was gathered in both external and internal environments to provide insight into new and successful technologies as well as their viability within the organization. The information gathered was then used in combination with an internal scan of what the organization required and was ready for.

Pressures and lessons learned from past integrations influence the integration of a technology. As the organization is a teaching hospital, this type of healthcare organization is expected to employ the most innovative technologies and practices. However, this expectation is only one type of pressure among several within the Canadian healthcare environment. As indicated in a recent organizational strategy document, "key technology trends will also influence our information technology directions, financial struggles will continue as the government continues to reform healthcare and adjust to changes in demographics" (Hamilton Health Sciences 2006: 4–5). These multiple pressures illustrate the potential of external forces to influence the information gathering process as well as to steer the direction of the organization.

A second intervening condition is the institutional knowledge gained from past technological integrations. One participant explained, "we're a little bit limited by decisions we made back then, but always cognizant every time we get an upgrade, what those things are that we can do better" (Participant 1, personal communication, September 16, 2009). This statement implies that the internal environment, including institutional knowledge of past integrations inform the health informatics direction of the organization. Further, it demonstrates the value in learning from past decisions to be able to improve future health informatics integrations.

These intervening conditions guide the organization in deciding if technologies can solve issues, in choosing which technology to implement depending on external pressures, and how to implement it. After this information gathering, a pilot site and an appropriate technology are chosen.

CHOOSING THE APPROPRIATE TECHNOLOGY AND PILOT SITE

After the decision is made that integrating technology is required and the environments are scanned for information and organizational readiness, the organization then chooses the technology to integrate and the pilot site to integrate it. In this case study, the site chosen was the Pediatric Critical Care Unit (PCCU). The organization chose the pilot site first and then the users in the PCCU assisted in choosing the technology. It is well supported in the literature that user participation in early stages enhances user acceptance, encourages realistic user expectations, facilitates user ownership, and decreases resistance (Lorenzi et al. 1997, Aarts, Peel and Wright 1998, Kaplan 2001b, Tsiknakis and Kouroubali 2009). Another aspect of choosing the technology is the notion of "fit." Kaplan (2001b) and Aarts, Peel, and Wright (1998) agree that user needs and work routines should be major factors when choosing the appropriate technology. Each unit in a healthcare organization provides a unique service, and each therefore requires different technological systems, therefore the pilot site must first be chosen and then the users from that site should choose the technology.

The selection of a technology and a pilot site is a critical decision in the overall success of a technology; this selection is influenced by three factors: the organizational culture, employee characteristics, and resources available. Choosing the correct pilot site is important because the healthcare environment is constantly changing, and the users in the pilot group must be open to change and able to handle potential technical difficulties. The unique culture of the pilot group determines the viability of the technology. If users see technology as a tool that empowers and enables their work, they will accept the new technology; otherwise the technology will not be used (Lorenzi et al. 1997).

The current challenges faced by healthcare organizations in adopting new technologies may lessen as a younger generation joins the workforce. New employees expect technology to be implemented as they recognize that health informatics can improve their work routines and that these technologies are intrinsic to the delivery of quality healthcare services (Spitzer 2009). For example, the request for new technology is "coming from health care professionals and it is interesting; there wasn't this request for information technology ten years ago" (Participant 2, personal communication, September 15, 2009). In addition to younger employees, the existing staff who are more computer literate healthcare professionals are also more likely to accept the new technology. Computer literate employees are open to technology and possess the capabilities to assist the organization in choosing the appropriate technology. Therefore these users are critical in the technology selection process.

Human and financial resources are important conditions in deciding if, which, and to what extent health informatics technology can be integrated. In an organizational document, it was noted that financial resources are required to effectively integrate technology into the organization. The document also noted that insufficient investment in the past has led to inadequate integrations. The document said, "we have some of the technology partially implement but further investment is required more importantly in the area of staffing to support the implementation or the workflow changes" (Hamilton Health Sciences 2006: 12). The amount of human and financial resources available to the organization can influence the choice of technology and where the technology is integrated.

The decisions made in this step of the Integration Model are the foundation of the technological integration and are imperative to the overall success of health informatics technologies at the organization. Thus, the most time must be spent on this step because a mistake or wrong decision at this step has implications for every future step in the integration.

COMMUNICATING ORGANIZATIONAL CHANGE

Once the pilot site and technology have been chosen, the integration must be effectively communicated to affected employees. Communicating innovations is the foundation of the diffusion process, as it is "the information exchange by which one individual communicates a new idea to one or several others" (Rogers 2003: 18). Through this interaction, innovations are discussed and the diffusion process commences. According to Rogers, the degree of homophily (or perceived similarity) between the individuals implementing and the ones using the technology influences the effectiveness of communication. Rogers claims that, "One of the most distinctive problems in the communication of innovations is that the participants are usually quite heterophilous" (19), or that participants perceive little similarity to one another. This challenge shows the need for a common language or knowledge base between the two groups of individuals in order for diffusion to be effective. At the Organization, the department of clinical informatics is in charge of managing the process of integration, which includes communicating change to employees. This department, then, needs to cultivate shared language and shared knowledge to promote successful integrations of new technologies.

Training is a critical step in communicating change. Prior to training, employees may be informed of the changes coming and how it will affect his/her work routines. However, training is when users are first introduced to the technology and its system. In addition to communicating change, the clinical informatics department trains healthcare providers on new health informatics integrations. Kirkpatrick (1998) claims that evaluation of training justifies the future use of training, the training department, and investment in the improvement of training resources. The effectiveness of these training sessions is imperative to the eventual use and sustainability of the technology. Therefore, there is broad agreement in the organization that training procedures must be evaluated so that additional training needs can be identified.

Resistance is a constant challenge for the organization because "what we're asking them to do is to make lots of big changes" (Participant 2, personal communication, September 15, 2009). Resistance at this stage of the Integration Model is due to individuals feeling overwhelmed by change and by a loss of control over their work routines (Lorenzi et al. 1997). Although employee consultation in the "choosing" stage of the Integration Model reduces such resistance, the organization is large, and as such, there will always be resistance. Education and training sessions must address these concerns in order to reduce resistance and obtain broader support by users for the technological integration.

Communicating organizational change is the last step prior to the integration of health informatics technology within the organization. This step ends the planning stage of the Integration Model; it is in the next step that integration of the technology begins.

INTEGRATION

Integrating a technology requires the commitment of many individuals and resources within the organization. The physical act of integrating the technology, called "going live," only takes a matter of moments after the correct infrastructure is put in place. The integration step illustrates that the small amount of time invested in first going live must also have longer-term and consistent support in the initial weeks after going live. During this initial going live stage, it is imperative that users have continuous technical support for any questions or working out any issues. At the organization, the clinical informatics department is stationed at the pilot site at all times to assist in ameliorating technical difficulties.

Just as in the previous step, resistance is an intervening condition which affects the integration of the technology. The same anxieties (loss of control and being overwhelmed with change,) continue in this step of the Integration Model. What is different in this step is that technical difficulties feed into user resistance. Participant 3 (personal communication, November 17, 2009) highlighted that the transition from training and education to going live is not smooth because training cannot cover all possible situations. As a result, technical difficulties or situational uncertainties create resistance, resistance which influences the integration of the technology.

ADOPTION

In the Integration Model, adoption refers to the use of the technology after the initial integration. Integration and adoption are separated into two steps to differentiate the introduction of the technology and its use after the initial phase of integration ceases. Adopting the technology and using it purposefully in everyday work routines incorporates three intervening conditions: employee perceptions, resistance, and use.

Kaplan (2001a) suggests that conversations about technology influence the way the technology is viewed and, more importantly, how it is used. In other words, social interaction places importance on the users' conversations about technological integrations because these conversations create perceptions about the usefulness of the technology. This type of informal communication, a make-up of the organizational culture, frames the technology in a way which influences employee perceptions about health informatics integration. These perceptions do not directly affect adoption but encourage use of the technology or fuel resistance to the use of the technology. As participants highlighted throughout interviews, there will always be resistance to technological integrations, however as Kaplan suggests, these conversations assist to further drive understanding of health informatics.

EVALUATION OF INTEGRATION

It is well understood technological integration must be evaluated. Evaluation is important to understanding how to improve practices in the next project as well as ameliorating any barriers to current integration. The success or failure of a technological integration is difficult to determine in a small amount of time. If the organization is to expand the project to other units, decisions must be made before a longitudinal investigation into the effects of the technology on the overall workings of the users can be completed. What can be understood are the immediate benefits and challenges faced by the users of the technology. Two main evaluations must occur at this stage of the Integration Model: training re-evaluation and an evaluation of the immediate benefits and issues perceived when using the technology.

As was discussed earlier in the chapter, training evaluations are important tools in understanding the effectiveness of the training and where more support is required to improve training efforts. An evaluation of the training after the adoption stage allows users to better assess the adequacy of the training and highlight any educational gaps (Kirkpatrick 1998). Research suggests that the results of training are best measured after trainees are able to apply the skills and knowledge in their work situations (Kirkpatrick, 1998). As a result, pre- and post-adoption evaluations of training are most effective in measuring the changes and illuminating the gaps in trainee knowledge of the new technology.

The organization investigated in this chapter measured the success of a technological integration through the achievement of pre-determined milestones. While quantitative data is important when integrating a technology and ensuring that it is on time, it does little to understand the employees' perspectives on the effectiveness and usability of the technology in their work routines. During the integration stage, members of the clinical informatics department reported at a predetermined time every day to update the leaders and the Information Technology Department. These members discussed the successes and challenges with the new technology that were experienced that day. After the initial going live stage is over and the clinical informatics team leaves, there are meetings with managers of the pilot site to discuss successes, challenges, and opportunities for expansion with the newly integrated technology. A mix of qualitative and quantitative evaluation procedures assist in illustrating problems and allowing for an explanation of the quantitative data from the users' perspectives. From this data collected and evaluation conducted, the organization then decides how to progress on the integration.

DECISION

Once these technologies are introduced, research participants highlighted the changes in the way that information is charted using mHealth technologies, including what needs to be documented and when it is put into the patient's file. Healthcare organizations are all connected and require information sharing, thus a change in the way that one particular group of healthcare providers share information creates challenges and new communication policies for other providers within the organization. Participant 1 explains that "measurements of success are usually laid out in milestones because a lot of the projects depend on other projects being completed" (personal communication, September 16, 2009). Technological integration is constantly evolving and, in an interconnected organization, changes in one part have repercussions and create need in other areas. "HHS and ICT in particular has struggled to keep pace with the flood of new project and service requests and the demand for ICT services continues to grow significantly" (Hamilton Health Sciences 2006: 11). Thus, a realistic assessment of organizational resources is required to decide if the integration should continue, cease, and or expand to other units within the organization.

When these steps are completed, The Model begins anew. Each time the new technology is deployed to a new part of the organization, integration begins again. Our model is cyclical, as health informatics integrations with health are continuous, and previous implementations inform the next. In our view, it is important to consider the continuation of health informatics as technology drives the organization forward. It is clear that integration is not a one-time process. In addition, the linearity of previous models does not allow for backtracking where necessary. There is fluidity in the integration of health informatics which is better represented through a cyclical model, more so than a linear model as proposed by Golden (2006) and Aarts, Peel and Wright (1998).

The illustrated model incorporates intervening conditions which can impact the integration and eventual use of the technology; The Models of Golden (2006) and

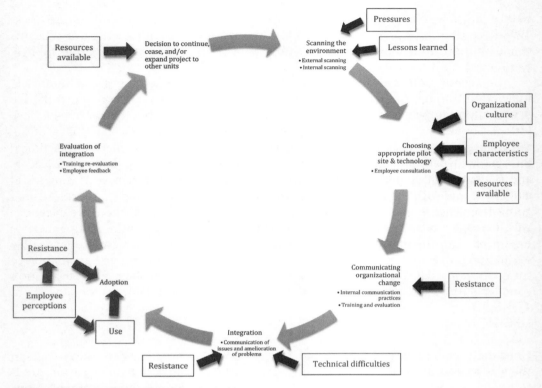

Figure 12.1 The Integration Model

Aarts et al. (1998) do not. Pressures, lessons learned from past integrations and employee perceptions have the potential to impact the extent to which and how a technology is implemented. Each of these conditions alters how the organization implements technology. These pressures are not static. For example, the changing demographics of the employee base are relieving one pressure from the organization while imposing a new challenge. In previous integrations, the Information Technology Department spent much of their time selling the importance of health informatics to employees and leaders. However, a younger and more computer literate generation of healthcare providers is entering the organization. These employees are encouraging new health informatics and "backdooring" these technologies themselves when necessary. This generational difference in user attitude and experience creates a new challenge for the organization that the organization strives to meet. Meeting such challenges is an ongoing process and represents important aspects in the Technology Integration Model because they inevitably influence the next health informatics integration.

Implications for Academics

This case study demonstrates the lack of knowledge about integrating health informatics, which should be viewed as a call to academics to conduct more thorough research on the topic. Further, this case study illustrates the importance of communication in health informatics integration and the role of socio-technology in the success and failure of an organization. Although this chapter provides some discussion on the role of social interaction, the role of organizational culture in health informatics integration requires further attention from academics.

Implications for Health Practitioners

For health practitioners this case study demonstrates the role of the internal and external environment in health informatics integration. It suggests that organizational culture has the potential to influence the success or failure of health informatics integration. This case study adds further understanding as to how communication can influence health informatics integration as well as illustrates the importance of communication in integration. It is imperative that health practitioners understand the influences of communication in integration as health informatics are to be adopted by healthcare organizations.

Conclusion

Assessing technological integrations is not about labeling various technologies as successes or failures, but, as Bijker (2010) suggests, should be focused on understanding the process not the product. If this is to be true, one should not investigate the technology directly but the extent to which technology is perceived by its users as positive. For example the changing work routines and information sharing patterns of employees and any other repercussions resulting from the integration can be seen as helpful to or hindering the organization. As previously mentioned, employee perceptions about health informatics are becoming more positive as the larger share of younger employees see the necessity of electronic integration. However, these same employees stress the importance of user consultation as to ensure the most appropriate technologies are implemented.

Once these technologies are introduced, research participants highlighted the changes in the way that information is charted using mHealth technologies, including what needs to be documented and when it is put into the patient's file. Health informatics integration alters organizational policies and procedures, creating repercussions for the entire organization, like changes in the work routines of healthcare providers. Healthcare organizations are all connected and require information sharing, thus a change in the way that one particular group of healthcare providers share information, creates challenges and new communication policies for other providers within the organization.

In reverse, one must look at how work routines inspire new technological integrations. Healthcare is a highly mobile environment, and as such mHealth technologies fit into the needs of the healthcare providers' work routines. Thus, as the employees become more technologically sound, they call for the technologies to be integrated. One participant (Participant 1) mentioned that it will not take very long before students will not want to come to learn at the organization if it does not integrate health informatics into healthcare service delivery. Kaplan's (2001b) notion of "fit" is important because the technology needs to fit the users' work routines and how they best communicate. If healthcare providers use information and manage their decisions through technology in ways unanticipated by developers, technology may have a poor fit (Heathfield and Wyatt 1993). Therefore, developers of the technology must first assess users' needs to choose the most appropriate technology to implement.

While this case study illustrates the role that communication plays in the integration of health informatics, there are other mitigating factors which may influence the integration of health informatics. This study focused solely on the Pediatric Critical Care Unit and thus the findings cannot be generalized to other units or hospitals. Nevertheless, the findings from the case study have shown that integration of new technology consists of many intervening conditions and complex processes. The proposed Integration Model accounts for these complexities better than existing linear models do. Previous research has focused on either the technology or the organization; however, as illustrated by this case study, the combination of social and technology contexts influence the integration of health informatics technology. Communication is a critical aspect of effective healthcare service delivery, and as such, the influence of communication in integration is important to consider. Future research should focus more closely on the role of communication in integration. One possibility would be to examine the Integration Model with respect to user consultation prior to integration.

References

Aarts, J., Peel, V., and Wright, G. 1998. Organizational issues in health informatics: A model approach. *International Journal of Medical Informatics*, 52, 235–42.

Aguilar, F.J. 1967. *Scanning the Business Environment*. New York: Macmillan.

Baker, G.R., Norton, P.G., Flintoft, V., Blais, R., Brown, A., Tamblyn, R. 2004. The Canadian adverse events study: The incidence of adverse events among hospital patients in Canada. *Canadian Medical Association Journal*, 170 (11), 1678–86.

Berg, M. 2001. Implementing information systems in health care organizations: Myths and challenges. *International Journal of Medical Informatics*, 64 (2–3), 143–56.

Berg, M., Aarts, J. and van der Lei, J. 2003. ICT in health care: Sociotechnical approaches. *Methods of Information in Medicine*, 42(4), 297–301.

Bijker, W.E. 2010. How is technology made? That is the question! *Cambridge Journal of Economics*, 34, 63–76.

Coakes, E. 2006. Storing and sharing knowledge: Supporting the management of knowledge made explicit in transnational organisations. *The Learning Organization*, 13(6), 579–93.

Coiera, E. 2003. *Guide to Health Informatics*, 2nd Edition. New York, NY: Oxford University Press.

Coiera, E. and Tombs, V. 1998. Communication behaviours in a hospital setting: An observational study. *British Medical Journal*, 316(7132), 673–6.

Glaser, B.G. and Strauss, A. 1967. *The Discovery of Grounded Theory: Strategies for Qualitative Research*. New York, NY: Aldine.

Golden, B. 2006. Change: Transforming healthcare organizations. *Healthcare Quarterly*, 10 (Special Issue), 10–20.

Hamilton Health Sciences. 2006. *Vision 2010: Future Priorities*. Hamilton, ON: Author.

Heathfield, H.A. and Wyatt, J. 1993. Philosophies for the design and development of clinical decision support systems. *Methods of Information in Medicine*, 26 (9), 910–34.

Herrmann, T., Loser, K. and Jahnke, I. 2007. Sociotechnical walkthrough: A means for knowledge integration. *The Learning Organization*, 14 (5), 450–64.

Kaplan, B. 1997. Addressing organizational issues into the evaluation of medical systems. *Journal of the American Medical Informatics Association*, 4, 94–101.

Kaplan, B. 2001a. Evaluating informatics applications – some alternative approaches: Theory, social interactionism, and call for methodological pluralism. *International Journal of Medical Informatics*, 62, 39–56.

Kaplan, B. 2001b. Evaluating informatics applications – clinical decision support systems literature review. *International Journal of Medical Informatics*, 64, 15–37.

Kirkpatrick, D.L. 1998. *Evaluating Training Programs*, 2nd Edition. San Francisco, CA: Berret-Koehler Publishers, Inc.

Layman, E.J. and Watzlaf, V.J. (eds). 2009. *Health Informatics Research Methods: Principles and Practice*. Chicago, IL: American Health Information Management Association.

Lorenzi, N.M., Riley, R.T., Blyth, A.J.C., Southon, G. and Dixon, B.J. 1997. Antecedents of the people and organizational aspects of medical informatics: Review of the literature. *Journal of the American Medical Informatics Association*, 4, 79–93. DOI:10.1136/jamia.1997.0040079.

Pirnejad, H., Bal, R., Stoop, A.P. and Berg, M. 2007. Inter-organisational communication networks in healthcare: Centralised versus decentralised approaches. *International Journal of Integrated Care*, 7, 1–10.

Plummer, A.A. 2001. Information systems methodology for building theory in health informatics: The argument for a structured approach to case study research, *34th Hawaii International Conference on System Sciences*. Maui, Hawaii, 1–10.

Rogers, E.M. 2003. *Diffusion of Innovations*, 5th Edition. New York, NY: Free Press.

Rose, A.F., Schnipper, J.L., Park, E.R., Poon, E.G., Li, Q. and Middleton, B. 2005. Using qualitative studies to improve the usability of an EMR. *Journal of Biomedical Informatics*, 38 (1), 51–60.

Siau, K. and Shen., Z. 2006. Mobile healthcare informatics. *Medical Informatics and the Internet in Medicine*, 31(2), 89–99.

Snyder-Halpern, R. 2001. Indicators of organizational readiness for clinical information technology/ systems innovation: A Delphi study. *International Journal of Medical Informatics*, 63(3), 179–204. DOI:10.1016/S1386-5056(01)00179-4.

Spitzer, R. 2009. Clinical information and sociotechnology. *Nurse Leader*, 7(3), 6–7.

Tsiknakis, M., and Kouroubali, A. 2009. Organizational factors affecting successful adoption of innovative eHealth services: A case study employing the FITT framework. *International Journal of Medical Informatics*, 78, 39–52.

Yin, R.K. 2003. *Case Study Research: Design and Methods*, 3rd Edition. Thousand Oaks, CA: Sage Publications, Inc.

Zinn, C. 1995. 14,000 preventable deaths in Australian hospitals. *British Medical Journal*, 310(6993), n.p.

PART 5

Health Communication and and Media Ethics

13 *Doing Good, Doing Right: The Ethics of Health Communication*

SEOW TING LEE

Introduction

Most exemplars in health communication in mass mediated contexts focus on message efficacy and ignore ethical dimensions. Such a worldview is grounded in the assumption that doing good is more important than doing right, as seen in the ascension of teleological beliefs emphasizing outcomes over deontological, duty-based approaches that accentuate the rightness of an action rather than the action's consequences. The limited discussion about ethics in health communication, however, is confined to philosophical or normative approaches with little systematic efforts in theory-building, empirical research, and practical applications. This chapter, with its foci in ethics and mass mediated communication, extends the health communication literature by applying an ethical lens to better understand the ethical values underpinning health messages by:

1. explicating the values and ethical dimensions such as truth telling, authenticity, respect, equity and social responsibility in mass mediated health messages;
2. connecting message ethicality to message attributes through an analysis of *thematic frames, tone, gain-loss framing, emotion appeals, source*, and target audience characteristics such as *age group, health status,* and *gender*; and
3. advancing an applied model for ethical health communication that includes practical recommendations for practitioners.

HEALTH COMMUNICATION AS A BENEVOLENT ENDEAVOR

Although health communication has developed over the last three decades into a dynamic and important field of study and practice with regard to the roles performed by mass mediated communication in creating, sharing, and disseminating health information for health promotion, little is understood about the values and ethical concerns embedded in persuasive messages to promote public health, disease prevention, and individuals' adoption of healthful behaviors. Ethics, as a branch of philosophy and applied inquiry that addresses the moral correctness of an action or conduct of individuals or groups, is rarely discussed in health communication practice and scholarship for several reasons.

As targeted, goal-driven communication that seeks to effect positive changes in people's lives by promoting health and preventing diseases, health communication efforts are taken for granted to be benevolent endeavors grounded morally in noble, altruistic justifications and beneficent regard for others (Andreasen 2001, Faden and Faden 1978, Guttman 1997, 2000, 2003, Kirklin 2007a, 2007b, Kozlowski and O'Connor 2003, Lee and Cheng 2010, Lee 2011, Rogers 1994, Salmon 1989, Seedhouse 1988, 2004). There is an implicit understanding that health communication, as a purposeful attempt to bring about desired changes in individuals' health-related behaviors or attitudes through messages of awareness, instruction and persuasion, is inherently and categorically moral, as it is a pursuit of a larger axiomatic good: individuals' and societies' well-being in health, a matter of fundamental import. Health communication sets itself apart from other mass communicated, persuasive messages. Advertising and public relations are seen as seeking to alter individuals' attitudes and behaviors, often to the detriment of their interests or well-being, with the goal of selling a product or service, or of satisfying organizational goals (Jaksa and Pritchard 1994). With health communication's historical associations with public service, lack of commercial motivations, and connections to the activities of governmental agencies, international and charitable organizations in public health interventions, as well as "a promise that scholarship, when applied to practice, can help individuals and groups with particular needs, or better society as a whole" (Guttman 2000: xii), health communication's values and motivations tend to attract little scrutiny.

In health communication, an applied area of research, scholars focus on studying how to make public health communication more strategic, an approach that appeals both to practitioners and researchers. They seek ways to enhance communication's impact in health promotion through tangible, measurable outcomes such as drops in smoking rates or reductions in the number of teenage pregnancies. Consistent with the strategic approach, health communication inquiry is usually problem-driven, focusing on identifying, examining, and overcoming obstacles to better health. In such a calculus, ethics is given little consideration, yet any form of communication that aims to change people's attitudes or behaviors by touching on deeply held personal preferences and values should be bound to raise many ethical questions.

Several health communication scholars (for example, Guttmann 1997, 2000, 2003, Salmon 1989, Guttman and Salmon 2004, Seedhouse 1988) have questioned the presumed ethicality or moral soundness of health communication. Seedhouse (1988), who suggested that "work for health is a moral endeavor," wrote: "It can be tempting to think that work for health is value free, that some endeavors are simply good and desired by all, and have no effects that can be described as bad or undesirable" (57). Salmon (1989) made an eloquent argument for examining the implicit and taken-for-granted values in public communication interventions such as health campaigns. According to Salmon, "Rather than passively accepting that all social engineering efforts described in the 'public interest' are actually so, one must examine the underlying assumptions of the campaigners as well as the values they are implicitly and explicitly promoting" (20). Guttman (2000) observed that health communication campaigns tend to bask in a sense of righteousness and virtue.

Seedhouse (2004) suggested that "[e]thics is rarely thought to be an issue in standard health promotion work." (53) Not surprisingly, the literature in public health communication, with few exceptions (Andreasen 2001, Faden and Faden 1978, Guttman 1997, 2000, 2003, Kozlowski and O'Connor 2003), has rarely discussed ethics, and most of the discussion is philosophical or normative in approach (for example, Guttman 1997, 2000, 2003). Ethical health communication is not only a moral prerequisite but has pragmatic significance. Considering the interplay of accountability, credibility, respect, and trust, a better understanding of public health messages could set forth a framework for testing the relationships between message ethicality and message efficacy, and for explicating the socially responsible behavior of health communicators.

Ethical Theories and Health Communication

Guttman (2000) observed that the central concerns in health communication ethics relate to persuasion and paternalism. In the context of speech acts, the communication activities in health communication include exposing, threatening, predicting, promising, encouraging, warning, and recommending, each with attendant ethical implications. Another set of concerns focuses on the infringement of autonomy. Manipulative or deceptive messages distort information, do not fully disclose all the facts, or make claims that deprive individuals of the ability to make autonomous decisions. Health messages seek to influence people's attitudes or behaviors. These attempts at influence interfere with personal freedom, if we accept the notion that all competent individuals have the intrinsic right of self-determination to make decisions for themselves insofar that such decisions do not bring harm to others. Health communication interventions can also create unintended harm through fear appeals or implicit values that stigmatize a particular group of individuals, such as unwed mothers, smokers or AIDs patients, or when preventive or treatment activities are communicated in a positive light highlighting only the good and downplaying the potential risks.

Two broad approaches in ethical thought – teleological and deontological – provide an important framework for understanding such ethical issues. Teleological theory posits that the consequences of an act determine whether the act is right or wrong. The teleological approach, in emphasizing outcomes, is best summed up by utilitarian valuation of efficiency and results through maximizing the greatest good for the greatest number. From a teleological perspective, tools of persuasion such as exaggeration, omission of information, and fear appeals in public health messages may be justified even if these strategies may be untruthful, disrespectful, harmful to individuals or play a role in fanning anxieties, labels or stigmas or triggering contradictory reactions (Earler 2000, Guttman 1997, 2000, 2003, Kirklin 2007a, 2007b, Kozlowski and O'Connor 2003, Lee and Cheng 2010, Lee 2011).

In contrast, the deontological approach suggests that some acts are bound by duty and must be executed regardless of consequences. The focus on the action rather than the consequences is evident in single-rule, non-consequentialist theories such as German philosopher Immanuel Kant's categorical imperatives. One example is the precept of truth telling; a lie is a lie and cannot be mitigated by the lie's benefits. Kant offered the strongest objection to deception. Kant (1785/1993), who defined a lie as any intentional statement that is untrue, considered lying to be an affront to human dignity. He famously argued that people have a moral duty to tell the truth, even to a would-be murderer who asks where his would-be victim is hiding. The Kantian approach is deontological, in that moral rightness depends on the act rather than its consequences. Based on the deontological perspective, health messages that employ exaggeration or untruths or questionable strategies would always be wrong (Earle 2000, Guttman 1997, 2000, 2003, Kirklin 2007a, 2007b, Kozlowski and O'Connor 2003, Lee and Cheng 2010, Lee 2011).

Public health communication's reliance on teleological ethics, by focusing on consequences as the main determinant of a message's ethicality, has been questioned by some scholars who_suggested that a health message should be assessed for its intrinsic moral worth rather than its outcome alone (for example, Guttman 1997, 2000, 2003, Kirby and Andreasen 2001, Kirklin 2007a, 2007b, Lee 2011). Others (for example, Baker and Martinson 2001, Cutlip 1994, Fagothey 1976) focused on the relative last end to distinguish it from more immediate instrumental ends such as improved fatality rates or drops in smoking rates. The final relative end of public health communication is open to debate, and involves complex variables including human values, education, advocacy, and freedom of choice. Seedhouse (2004) maintained that health promotion is fundamentally prejudiced and all initiatives held in the name of health promotion are ultimately based on human values rather than defensible, evidence-based theory.

THE TARES FRAMEWORK

Baker and Martinson (2001) acknowledged that professional persuasion is a means to an instrumental end but argued that ethical persuasion "must rest on or serve a deeper, morally based final (or relative) end" (172). Baker and Martinson offered the TARES as a deontological framework for assessing the ethicality of public health messages through five principles to serve this final end. TARES is an acronym based on the first letters of five interconnected principles: *Truthfulness* of the message, *Authenticity* of the persuader, *Respect* for the person being persuaded, *Equity* of the persuasive appeal, and *Social Responsibility* for the common good. The TARES, designed for mass mediated persuasive messages including advertising and public relations, is the first model to examine the notion of practitioner accountability toward the message receiver in persuasive communication.

In applying the TARES, this chapter focuses on tobacco control messages, a rich locus for understanding the ethics of health communication. Tobacco control messages, one of the earliest manifestations of public health messages, account for one of the largest and most visible bodies of public health communication messages. In the United States, tobacco control campaigns, or antismoking campaigns, first gained momentum after 1964 when the U.S. Surgeon General's Office released the findings of a 15-year study that provided indisputable evidence about the negative effects of smoking on health, leading to a surge in the dissemination of antismoking messages by state and federal agencies.

Testing the TARES

The first empirical testing of the TARES was conducted by Lieber (2005), who conducted an online survey of public relations practitioners to examine their conceptualization of ethics. However, methodologically, the TARES is more suited for content analyses. Taking a content analytic approach, Lee and Cheng (2010) applied the TARES to health messages and published the first study to test the TARES by directly examining the content of persuasive messages for the five principles of *Truthfulness*, *Authenticity*, *Respect*, *Equity*, and *Social Responsibility*. In a content analysis of 826 television ads from the CDC's Media Campaign Resource Center, Lee and Cheng (2010) identified and explicated relationships between the five values of the TARES and tobacco control message attributes such as thematic frames, emotion appeals, source, and target audience. The coding categories were based on prima facie duties toward the receiver according to the TARES through 19 items (Baker and Martinson 2001, Patterson and Wilkins 2008) (Appendix 13.1). For example, *truthfulness* was operationalized through eight questions related to verbal truthfulness, visual truthfulness, omission, exaggeration and intent to mislead or to deceive. Lee (2011) focused on explicating truth, a fundamental dimension of ethics and one of the five TARES principles, in health messages through a content analysis of 974 television antismoking ads.

ASSESSING THE ETHICALITY OF TOBACCO CONTROL MESSAGES

The TARES provides a means of measuring the ethicality of health messages based on its five dimensions. Previously, Lee and Cheng (2010) showed that the tobacco control messages scored highly on ethicality based on the TARES. Under the TARES, questions are asked about the characteristics of the message (see Appendix 13.1). To pass the TARES test, a message must fulfill all five values. The number 1 indicates a failure to meet a TARES principle, and 2 indicates a "pass." The *truthfulness* principle based on eight items averaged 1.95 (S.D.=.009); *Authenticity* based on two items averaged 1.96 (S.D.=.178); *Respect* based on two items averaged 1.96 (S.D.=.165); *Equity* based on two items averaged 1.94 (S.D.=.192); and *Social Responsibility* based on 5 items averaged 1.88 (S.D.= .142), The grand mean for the 19 TARES items is 1.94 (S.D.=.009). Overall message ethicality or TARES index based on 19 statements operationalizing the five ethical principles ranged from 29 to 38, with a mean of 36.67 and a standard deviation of 2.60. A reliability analysis showed that the 19 items have a good internal consistency, with Cronbach's alpha exceeding .85.

Of the 826 messages, more than 1 in 3 (37.8 percent) passed the TARES fully by meeting the expectations of all 19 items operationalizing the five values of *truthfulness, authenticity, respect, equity* and *social responsibility*. Nearly one-third (29.9 percent) or 247 messages met the expectations of 18 items of the TARES, followed by 133 messages (16.1 percent) that fulfilled 17 items; 55 messages (6.7 percent) on 16 items; 28 messages (3.4 percent) on 15 items; 23 messages (2.8 percent) on 14 items; 12 messages (1.5 percent) on 13 items; nine messages (1.1 percent) on 12 items; five messages (.6 percent) on 11 items; and finally two messages (.2 percent) that met the expectations of only 10 TARES items.

Although the messages scored well in overall ethicality, three items (in descending importance) appear more challenging than others. *Social responsibility*. Nearly half (397 messages or 48.1 percent) failed the item addressing the message's impact on the audience's level of trust for health messages in general. *Truthfulness*. Nearly a quarter of messages (200 or 24.2 percent) failed the item addressing visual exaggeration. However, of the 200 "failed" messages, only two were misleading in visual exaggeration. *Equity*. About 10 percent of messages (82) failed the item addressing the issue of health messages taking advantage of human weaknesses such as anxieties, fears, and self-esteem issues.

Of 826 messages analyzed in Lee and Cheng (2010), more than half of the messages, 458 or 55.4 percent were affiliated with state tobacco-control agencies and health departments, followed by 49 (6 percent) from the CDC, and 38 (4.6 percent) from the American Legacy Foundation.

FRAMING AS SCHEMA OF INTERPRETATION IN HEALTH COMMUNICATION

Framing offers an important theoretical framework for understanding health messages and ethics. Selective organization of information – thematically, stylistically and factually – is a means of interpretation that helps individuals make sense of the world. According to Entman (1993), "To frame is to select some aspects of a perceived reality and make them more salient in a communicating text, in such a way as to promote a particular problem definition, causal interpretation, moral evaluation, and/or treatment recommendation for the item described." (52) Discussing health message frames, Kirklin (2007b) observed that individuals consciously and subconsciously frame their arguments to achieve specific goals, and their choice of frames is determined by personal beliefs and values. Conveying information in this sense is "far more than choosing which facts to share; it is about the way in which those facts will be presented or framed, with the choice of frame in turn shaping the nature of the truth that is conveyed" (59). For example, doctors, worried about consequences of a measles outbreak, are more likely to emphasize the protection that MMR immunization offers rather than research findings connecting MMR and autism or otherwise.

Although there is evidence to suggest that different message appeal types influence people's attitudes and behavior differently (for example, Keller and Lehmann 2008, Leshner and Cheng 2009, Meyerowitz and Chaiken 1987, Rothman et al. 1993), the specific effects of message appeal types are neither consistent nor generalizable to other messages sharing those features (Beaudoin 2002, Leshner and Cheng 2009, Pechman et al., 2003, Wakefield et al., 2005).

The framing of health messages extends beyond *gain-loss* into other message attributes such as *thematic frames, emotion appeals, tone,* and *message source,* as well as audience characteristics such as *target age group, smoker status* and *gender.* Content analytic work to characterize and identify common elements of antismoking messages is relatively new. Studies that examined antismoking messages mostly focused on descriptive identification and classification of *thematic frames* (for example, Beaudoin 2002, DeJong and Hoffman 2000, Goldman and Glantz 1998, Teenage Research Unlimited 1999, Pechman and Goldberg Wakefield et al., 2005), with forays into *target audience, emotion appeals* and *gain-loss framing.*

Emotion appeals in persuasive messages (see Lang 1995, Donohew, Lorch and Palmgreen 1998, Keller and Block 1996, Witte 1992, Witte and Allen 2000) are grounded in health-behavioral theories that suggest that an expectancy of a negative outcome might reduce the likelihood of a behavior (for example, Fishbein and Middlestadt 1989, Glanz and Rimer 1997, Rosenstock, 1990). Other scholars postulate that negative emotions elicited by health messages, such as fear, may facilitate the persuasion process (for example, Janis and Feshbach 1953, Rogers 1983, Witte 1992). Cohen, Shumate and Gold (2007), who content-analyzed 399 TV messages from the CDC, found that messages use more informational and humor appeals rather than sadness, fear, or anger. Another important message attribute is *source.* Wakefield et al. (2005) found that tobacco-company messages tend to elicit positive emotions in youth than messages made by tobacco-control agencies.

In the body of research identifying and describing message attributes and audience characteristics of antismoking messages, evidence of efficacy of thematic frames, emotion appeals, source, and target audiences is still limited and contradictory (Pechman et al., 2003, Wakefield et al., 2005). One link worth exploring is the relationship between message framing and message ethicality.

MESSAGE ETHICALITY AND MESSAGE ATTRIBUTES OF TOBACCO CONTROL MESSAGES

Previous findings (Lee and Cheng 2010, Lee 2011) and the preliminary data from ongoing research in this area present compelling evidence about a link between ethicality and message attributes, suggesting that judicious framing of health messages is a necessary component in public health communication. Health messages are not value-free; they are inherently built on the underlying assumptions of communicators as well as the values that they consciously or unconsciously promote. Furthermore, these assumptions and values are closely intertwined with the framing choices made by communicators with regard to the message attributes and target audience characteristics. Based on chi-square and correlational analyses of 826 ads, message ethicality was significantly associated with message attributes such as *thematic frame, tone, gain-loss framing, emotion appeal,* and *source* (see Appendix 13.2). Intercoder reliability, based on Scott's pi, exceeded .85 for the coding categories.

Thematic frame   Messages that portrayed smoking as damaging to health and socially/ romantically unacceptable are found to be less ethical than messages that focus on tobacco industry manipulation, addiction, secondhand smoke and cessation. In particular, the social/romantic thematic frame is the least truthful.

Tone   Messages with a negative or neutral tone are less ethical than messages with a positive tone.

Gain-loss framing   Messages that framed the consequences as loss are less ethical than messages that framed the consequences as gain.

Emotion Appeal   Messages that used shame and humor appeals are less ethical than messages using anger, sadness or fear appeals. However, fear appeals score the lowest on equity and respect.

Source   Messages produced by state agencies, tobacco firms, or those without an identifiable source are less ethical than messages produced by the CDC and the American Legion Foundation.

Second, message ethicality is significantly associated with audience attributes such as *target age group* and *smoker vs. non-smoker.*

- *Target Age Group* – Messages targeting teens/youth are less ethical than messages targeting adults and general audiences. They score lower in truthfulness, equity, authenticity and respect than messages targeting adults and general audiences.
- *Smoker vs. Non-smoker* – Messages targeted at smokers are less ethical than messages targeting nonsmokers and general audiences, and score lower in equity and respect.
- *Gender* – There is no relationship between message ethicality and target gender.

Implications for Academics

The relationships between framing and ethical values have implications for framing theory. Theoretically, framing theory posits that persuasive mass communicators actively and deliberately deploy frames in advertising, public relations or political communication to achieve specific goals. Framing theory suggests, at the same time, that *news* framing is shaped unconsciously by journalistic routines, social norms and values as well as organizational culture, with journalists having little control over the framing process (for example, Gamson 1989, Shoemaker and Reese 1996, Tuchman 1978). This tension is worthy of exploration.

Health communication closely intersects public relations and advertising in terms of its persuasive bent. Health messages are planned, targeted and managed with specific goals to alter people's attitudes and behaviors in health. It is, however, unclear whether health messages are shaped by active intervention by communicators, as in the case of public relations or advertising messages, or unconsciously as in what is widely believed about journalists' framing of news. We must ask, to what extent do public health communicators consciously embed their values into health communication, which is widely presumed to be a value-free, objective endeavor? The link between health communicators' individual-level variables (for example, their personal values, belief systems, and socio-economic backgrounds) and media frames deserves more attention than it has received.

To paraphrase Salmon (1989), we need to look beyond the superficial framing of health messages by their proponents as "prosocial" or "congruent with public interest." (2) If health message framing is a conscious, active act by communicators, health communicators must directly confront their moral obligations to their audiences and can no longer seek refuge in vague presumptions of public interest and altruism.

Implications for Health Practitioners

The findings of Lee and Cheng (2010) and Lee (2011) and the ongoing content analytic work in this area offer several implications for the practice of health communication. There are underlying tensions between self-accountability and other-accountability, and between supportive and confrontational approaches.

Human beings are defined by a capacity for self-accountability (guilt) that keeps them functioning ethically and responsibly. Individuals may be accountable to others but they may not be as accountable to themselves when no one is watching or holding them responsible for their actions (for example, Shearer 2002, Passyn and Sujan 2006). However, the content analysis data suggests that self-accountability messages that directly confront individuals with evidence of their poor personal choices by spelling out the action's negative consequences are less ethical according to the TARES. In contrast, thematic frames that focused less on *self*-accountability (poor personal choice) but more on *other*-accountability – for example the negative impact of other people's behaviors (that is, tobacco company executives' roles in tobacco industry manipulation, or other smokers' addiction to cigarettes) or the action's negative impact on other people (that is, secondhand smoke) – are more ethical. The link between ethicality and accountability suggests that framing choices in public health messages should consider avoiding first-person-directed ("you") messages and "in your face" accusations of poor personal choices. Instead, messages should present smoking as a third-person conceptualization or problem for the generalized other, for example, how other people are smoking cigarettes and how this practice is impacting their health.

Another form of accountability centers on the relationship between the message and the source. Under the TARES explication of ethicality, messages without source are less ethical than messages that are clearly labeled as produced by the CDC, state agencies/health departments, or the American Legacy Foundation. Anonymity – with its implications of diminished accountability – plays an important role in ethics. In the context of persuasive communication such as public health messages, the moral agents – public health officials, communicators and organizations – are driven by specific motives and goals to communicate health messages to individuals or audiences. The very process of having to identify oneself in a health message, opening the message and source to public scrutiny and a test of publicity, is likely to alter the choices made about the framing of the message. It is suggested that health agencies clearly identify themselves as the source in health communication messages to foster communicator accountability toward the message receiver.

There also is a difference in ethicality between frames that support and those that censure. The cessation frame, by providing resource referrals and information, is more supporting than censuring, and does not force the message receiver to confront the consequences of his or her own action, unlike in the health damage theme that censures individuals directly for their poor personal choices. The claim that messages with a positive tone are more ethical than negative or neutral messages is consistent with the literature that suggests human beings react to a message differently if the same information is framed differently (for example, Kahneman and Tversky 1979). Based on the findings of the TARES, public health communication campaigns should be framed positively, supportively, and thematically to address *other*-accountability than adopt negative/neutral, confrontational frames and thematic frames that focus on *self*-accountability.

In addition, TARES findings suggest an unethical targeting of youth and smokers. It seems that the young are presumed to be less deserving of ethical treatment, as messages that target teens/youth were found to be less ethical than messages targeting adults and general audiences. Specifically, messages for teens/youth score lower in truthfulness, equity, authenticity and respect than messages targeting other age groups. Although a power imbalance is inherent because the messages for teens/youths are designed and created by adults and figures of authority, this imbalance does not mitigate the issue of unethical treatment of youth/teens and blatant paternalism. Messages targeting smokers are less ethical than messages targeting non-smokers, and score lower in respect and equity in the TARES. Although this approach may be justified under a teleological or utilitarian reasoning, the double standards are questionable. Antismoking messages for teens/youth and smokers must better reflect TARES principles such as truthfulness, authenticity, respect, equity, and social responsibility. Teens/youth and smokers should be involved in the campaign planning and message creation.

Finally, the findings show a link between emotional appeals and ethicality as conceptualized by the TARES. Anger and sadness are two appeals that scored the highest in message ethicality and do not compromise any of the five TARES dimensions. Although fear is also positively associated (to a lesser degree) with message ethicality, it scored low in *equity* – possibly because messages that elicit fear tend to overload on information that goes beyond reasonable audience comprehension, and exploit human weaknesses. This finding to some extent supports the literature critical of fear appeals (Benet et al. 1993, Hastings et al. 2004). The fear approach has adequate theoretical grounding in the teleological and utilitarian perspective that appears to drive public health communication work. Messages are a means to an end and are valued not for their intrinsic moral worth but for their outcome. Based on such a notion, it is reasonable to "harm" a few individuals to achieve a larger public good for society as a whole. The least ethical emotion appeal is humor, followed by shame. Humor pushes the borders of reality with depictions of the absurd and the funny side of life is easily understood, and rarely focuses on directly exploiting human weaknesses such as anxieties and fears. However, humor is a questionable appeal as it is negatively associated with *truthfulness, authenticity, respect* and *social responsibility*, and only slightly associated positively with *equity*. Another questionable emotion appeal is shame that scored poorly in *respect, equity* and *social responsibility*. Hence, the findings suggest that public health practitioners must proceed with caution when considering the use of humor, shame, and fear appeals.

Conclusion

This chapter, by focusing on a moral ground for health messages, offers an empirical contribution to a topic that has received mostly normative and philosophical discussion. It expands our understanding of message framing and provides a new ethics lens for investigating the interplay of truthfulness, respect, credibility, trust, social responsibility and effectiveness in public health communication. Health campaigns, despite their proponents' assertions of objectivity and claims of evidence-based theory, are fundamentally subject to human values, as seen in the sample of tobacco control messages analyzed. The dominance of teleological beliefs emphasizing outcomes over deontological duty-based approaches that focus on the moral worth of the message is evident in the messages analyzed. However, doing good cannot be separated from doing right. To be morally grounded, an ethical model of public health messages, such as that built upon the values of the TARES, needs to embrace both teleological and deontological perspectives.

References

Andreasen, A.R. 2001. *Ethics in Social Marketing*. Washington, DC: Georgetown University Press.

Baker, S. and Martinson, D.L. 2001. The TARES Test: Five principles for ethical persuasion. *Journal of Mass Media Ethics*, 16(2), 148–76.

Beaudoin, C.E. 2002. Exploring antismoking ads: Appeals, themes, and consequences. *Journal of Health Communication*, 7, 123–37.

Benet, S., Pitt, R.E. and LaTour, M. 1998. The appropriateness of fear appeal use for health care marketing to the elderly: Is it OK to scare granny? *Journal of Business Ethics*, 12(1), 45–55.

Bok, S. 1978. *Lying: Moral Choice in Public and Private Life*. New York: Pantheon Books.

Cohen, E., Shumate, M.D. and Gold, A. 2007. Anti-smoking media campaign messages: Theory and practice. *Health Communication*, 22(2), 91–102.

Cutlip, S. 1994. *The Unseen Power: Public Relations, a History*. Hillsdale, NJ: Erlbaum Associates.

Deaver, F. 1990. On defining truth. *Journal of Mass Media Ethics*, 5(3), 168–77.

DeJong, W. and Hoffman, K.D. 2000. A content analysis of television advertising for the Massachusetts Tobacco Control Program Media Campaign, 1993–1996. *Journal of Public Health Management and Practice*, 6(3), 27–39.

Donohew, L., Lorch, E.P. and Palmgreen, P. 1998. Applications of a theoretic model of information exposure to health interventions. *Human Communication Research*, 24, 454–68.

Earle, R. 2000. *The Art of Cause Marketing*. Chicago, IL: NTS Business Books.

Elliot, D. and Culver, C. (1992). Defining and analyzing journalistic deception. *Journal of Mass Media Ethics*, 7(2), 69–84.

Entman, R. 1993. Framing: Toward clarification of a fractured paradigm. *Journal of Communication*, 43(4), 51–8.

Faden, R. and Faden, A.I. 1978. The ethics of health education as public health policy. *Health Education & behavior*, 6(2), 180–97.

Fagothey, A. 1976. *Right and Reason: Ethics in Theory and Practice*. St Louis, MO: Mosby.

Fishbein, M. and Middlestadt, S.E. 1989. Using the theory of reasoned action as a framework for understanding and changing AIDS-related behaviors, in V.M. Mays, G.W. Albee and S.F. Schneider (eds), *Primary Preventions of AIDS*. Newbury Park, CA: Sage, 93–110.

Gamson, W.A. 1989. News as framing: Comments on Graber. *American Behavioral Scientist*, 33, 157–66.

Glanz, K. and Rimer, B.K. 1997. *Theory at a Glance: A Guide for Health Promotion Practice* (No. NIH Publication No. 97-3896): National Cancer Institute, National Institute of Health.

Goldman, L.K. and Glantz, S.A. 1998. Evaluation of antismoking advertising campaigns. *Journal of American Medical Association*, 279(10), 772–7.

Guttman, N. 1997. Ethical dilemmas in health campaigns. *Health Communication*, 9(2), 155–90.

Guttman, N. 2000. *Public Health Communication Interventions: Values and Ethical Dilemmas*. Thousand Oaks, CA: Sage Publications.

Guttman, N. 2003. Ethics in health communication interventions, in T.L. Thompson, A.M. Dorsey, K.I. Miller and R. Parrott (eds), *Handbook of Health Communication*. Mahwah, NJ: Lawrence Erlbaum, 651–79.

Guttman, N. and Salmon, C.T. 2004. Guilt, fear, stigma and knowledge gaps: Ethical issues in public health communication interventions. *Bioethics*, 18, 531–52.

Hastings, G., Stead, M. and Webb, J. 2004. Fear appeals in social marketing: Strategic and ethical reasons for concern. *Psychology and Marketing*, 21, 961–86.

Hill, D., Chapman, S. and Donovan, R. 1998. The return of scare tactics. *Tobacco Control*, 7, 5–8.

Jaksa, J.A. and Pritchard, M.S. 1994. *Communication Ethics: Methods of Analysis*. Belmont, CA: Wadsworth.

Janis, I.L. and Feshbach, S. 1953. Effects of fear-arousing communication. *Journal of Abnormal and Social Psychology*, 48, 78–92.

Kahneman, D. and Tversky, A. 1979. Prospect theory: An analysis of decisions under risk. *Econometrica*, 47, 313–27.

Kant, I. 1785/1993. *Grounding for the Metaphysics of Morals: On a Supposed Right to Lie because of Philanthropic Concerns*. 3rd Edition. Translated by James W. Ellington [1785] (1993). Indianapolis, IN: Hackett.

Keller, P.A. and Block, L.G. 1996. Increasing the persuasiveness of fear appeals: The effect of arousal and elaboration. *Journal of Consumer Research*, 22, 448–59.

Keller, P.A. and Lehmann, D.R. 2007. Designing effective health communications: A meta analysis. *Journal of Public Policy & Marketing*, 27(2), 30–45.

Kirby, S.D. and Andreasen, A.R. 2001. Marketing ethics to social marketers: A segmentation approach, in A.R. Andreasen (ed.), *Ethics in Social Marketing*. Washington, DC: Georgetown University Press, 160–83.

Kirklin, D. 2007a. Truth telling, autonomy and the role of metaphor. *Journal of Medical Ethics*, 33(1), 11–14.

Kirklin, D. 2007b. Framing, truth telling and the problem with non-directive Counseling. *Journal of Medical Ethics*, 33(2), 58–62.

Kozlowski, L.T. and O'Connor, R.J. 2003. Apply federal research rules on deception to misleading health information: An example on smokeless tobacco and cigarettes. *Public Health Rep*, 118(3), 187–92.

Lang, A. 1995. The effects of emotional arousal and violence on television viewers' cognitive capacity and memory. *Journal of Broadcasting Electronic Media*, 39(3) 13–327.

Lee, S.T. and Cheng, I.-H. 2010. Assessing the TARES as an ethical model for antismoking ads. *Journal of Health Communication*, 15(1), 55–75.

Lee, S.T. 2011. Understanding truth in health communication. *Journal of Mass Media Ethics*, 26(4), 263–81.

Leshner, G. and Cheng, I. 2009. The effects of frame, appeal, and outcome extremity of antismoking messages on cognitive processing. *Health Communication*, 24(3), 219–27.

Meyerowitz, B.E. and Chaiken, S. 1987. The effect of message framing on breast self-exam attitudes, intentions, and behavior. *Journal of Personality and Social Psychology*, 52(3), 500–510.

Mieth, D. 1997. The basic norm of truthfulness: Its ethical justification and universality. In C. Christians and M. Traber (eds), *Communication Ethics and Universal Values*. Thousand Oaks, CA: Sage, 87–104.

Passyn, K. and Sujan, M. 2006. Self-accountability emotions and fear appeals: Motivating behavior. *Journal of Consumer Research*, 32(1), 583–9.

Patterson, P. and Wilkins, L. 2008. *Media Ethics: Issues and Cases*, 5th edition. Boston, MA: McGraw-Hill.

Pechman, C. and Goldberg, M. 1998. *Evaluation of Ad Strategies for Preventing Youth Tobacco Use*. San Francisco, CA: California Tobacco-Related Disease Research Program.

Rosenstock, I.M. 1990. The health belief model: Explaining health behavior through expectancies, in K. Glanz, F.M. Lewis and B.K. Rimer (eds), *Health Behavior and Health Education: Theory, Research, and Practice*. San Francisco, CA: Jossey Bass, 39–62.

Rothman, A.J., Salovey, P., Antone, C., Keough, K. and Martin, C.D. 1993. The influence of message framing on intentions to perform health behaviors. *Journal of Experimental Social Psychology*, 29(5), 408–33.

Salmon, C.T. 1989. *Information Campaigns: Balancing Social Values and Social Change*. Newbury Park, CA: Sage.

Seedhouse, D. 1988. *Ethics: The Heart of Health Care*. London: John Wiley and Sons.

Seedhouse, D. 2004. *Health Promotion: Philosophy, Prejudice and Practice*. Chichester: John Wiley and Sons.

Shearer, T. 2002. Ethics and accountability: From the for-itself to the for-the-other. *Accounting, Organizations and Society*, 27(6), 541–73.

Shen, L. 2010. The effect of message frame in anti-smoking public service announcements on cognitive response and attitude toward smoking. *Health Communication*, 25(1), 11–21.

Shoemaker, P. and Reese, S. 1996. *Mediating the Message: Theories of Influences on Mass Media Content*, 2nd edition. White Plains, NY: Longman.

Teenage Research Unlimited. 1999. *Counter-tobacco Advertising Exploratory. The States of Arizona, California, and Massachusetts Public Health Anti-tobacco Media Campaigns: Summary Report, January-March 1999*. Northbrook, IL: Teenage Research Unlimited.

Toll, B.A., Salovey, P., O'Malley, S.S., Mazure, C.M., Latimer, A., McKee, S.A. 2008. Message framing for smoking cessation: The interaction of risk perceptions and gender. *Nicotine & Tobacco Research*, 10(1), 195–200.

Tuchman, G. 1978. *Making News: A Study in the Construction of Reality*. Beverly Hills, CA: Sage.

Wakefield, M., Balch, G.I., Ruel, E., Terry-McElrath, Y., Szczypka, G., Flay, B., Emery, S. and Clegg-Smith, K. 2005. Youth responses to anti-smoking advertisements from tobacco control agencies, tobacco companies, and pharmaceutical companies. *Journal of Applied Social Psychology*, 35(9), 1894–910.

Witte, K. and Allen, M. 2000. A meta-analysis of fear appeals: Implications for effective public health campaigns. *Health Education and Behavior*, 27, 591–615.

Witte, K. 1992. Putting the fear back into fear appeals: The extended parallel process model. *Communication Monographs*, 59(1), 329–49.

Appendix 13.1

Coding Categories for TARES

Values	Truthfulness	– Are the verbal claims truthful?
		– Are the visual claims truthful?
		– Is there important information omitted?
		  • (If yes, is the omission deceptive?)
		– Are the verbal claims exaggerated?
		  • (If yes, is the claim misleading?)
		– Are the visual claims exaggerated?
		  • (If yes, is the claim misleading?)

	Authenticity	– Is there a sincere need for this message within the range of goods and services available in our society? – Would the reason(s) presented in the message be convincing equally to the audience member and the creator of the ad?
	Respect	– Is the creator of the message showing respect to the audience? – Is the creator of the message willing to take full, open, public and personal responsibility for the content of this ad?
	Equity	– Must the audience be unusually well-informed and bright to understand the message? – Does the ad take advantage of human weaknesses such as anxieties, fears, low self-esteem etc.?
	Social Responsibility	– If everyone changes his or her attitude or behavior about smoking, would society as a whole be improved, keeping in mind that recreation, entertainment and self-improvement are worthy societal goals? – Are there some groups in society who could benefit from attitude or behavior change after viewing this message? – Are there some groups in society that could be harmed by the message? – Does this message increase or decrease the trust the average person has for health messages in general? – Does this message take the notion of social responsibility seriously?

Appendix 13.2

Coding Categories for Message Attributes and Audience Characteristics

Category	Item	Description
Message Attributes		**The message ...**
Message Theme	*Health*	Mainly conveys that smoking/tobacco use damages health (for example cause illnesses, or negative effects on pregnancy).
	Addiction	Mainly conveys that cigarettes/tobacco products are addictive.
	Secondhand smoke	Is mainly about the dangers of second-hand smoke.
	Cessation	Is mainly about quitting smoking (for example benefit of quitting).
	Social/Romantic	Mainly conveys that smoking/tobacco use is socially unacceptable (for example among peers or in social/romantic settings).
	Family	Mainly depicts a smoker who quits smoking for the sake of family members.
	Tobacco Industry manipulation	Mainly conveys that the tobacco industry manipulatively market/sell their products.
	Access	Mainly about making it more difficult (esp. for youth) to gain access to cigarettes.
	Parents	Is mainly about parents needing to talk to their child about tobacco use.
Tone	*Positive*	Gives an overall pleasant feeling by using bright colors, uplifting music to convey a sense of cheerfulness.
	Negative	Gives an unpleasant feeling by showing a dark setting, scary or sad music to convey a sense of gloom
	Neutral	Neither of the above.
Gain-Loss Framing	*Gain*	Frames consequences of not smoking as gain.
	Loss	Frames consequences of not smoking as loss.
Emotion Appeals	*Fear*	Aims to frighten the audience or elicit feelings of fear (for example, shows a dissected/blackened lung or organ of a smoker, imagery of morgue and cemetery).
	Sadness	Aims to elicit sad feelings (for example, an emotionally negative scene that induces heartache, anguish, loneliness, such as smoking alone in the rain).
	Guilt	Aims to elicit feelings of guilt (defined as recognition that one's smoking behavior has violated a standard/value important to others, or that others may have been hurt by the choice; for example, discovering that your child has picked up smoking after you).

Category	Item	Description
Message Attributes		**The message …**
Emotion Appeals (continued)	Shame	Aims to elicit shameful feelings (defined as negative feelings about being a smoker and a desire to keep others from discovering that one is a smoker; for example, hiding in the bathroom to smoke).
	Humor	Features a humorous situation or dialogue that makes the audience smile/chuckle/laugh.
	Anger	Elicits feelings of anger or hostility toward someone (for example, tobacco industry; legislators).
Source	State Agencies	Identifies a state agency as the source of the message.
	Tobacco Companies	Identifies a tobacco company as the source of the message.
	CDC	Identifies CDC as the source of the message.
	American Legacy Foundation	Identifies the American Legacy Foundation as the source.
	Unidentified	Does not name the source.
Audience Characteristics		
Target Age Group	Teens/Youth	Targets teens/youth as the intended audience.
	Adults	Targets adults as the intended audience.
	General Audiences	Targets general audiences.
Smoker vs. Nonsmoker	Smokers	Is targeted at smokers.
	Non-smokers	Is targeted at non-smokers.
	General audiences	Does not differentiate in terms of the smoking status of the audience.
Gender	Female	Is targeted at females.
	Male	Is targeted at males.
	General Audiences	Targets general audiences.

14 Eating Disorders and Obesity: Conflict and Common Ground in Health Promotion and Prevention

HUNNA WATSON AND JULIE MCCORMACK

Introduction

Communication of information through health promotion initiatives, health campaigns, health education, and other forms of mediated health messaging has a significant role in improving health and preventing disease by shaping the knowledge and behaviors of community members. Unfortunately, for the spectrum of obesity, eating disorders, and related eating and weight problems, the messages given – despite utmost positive intent – can inadvertently create harm. Jointly aligning health communication initiatives and integrating best practice in health promotion across the weight-related spectrum are essential to optimize our capacity to reduce risk. Ensuring consistency and reach of health messaging is a particular challenge in this field, due to the diversity of mediated contexts whereby people obtain health information about weight, bodies, and eating.

This chapter describes conflicting and common ground in health communication for the broad spectrum of weight-related problems, including obesity, eating disorders, and disordered eating. The discussion is intended to assist with safe and effective communication of health information and implementation of health promotion initiatives. The information has relevance for a range of contexts (that is, interpersonal, family, group, school, community, and society) and communication channels (that is, members of healthcare teams, government, academia, and mass media).

Background

Worldwide obesity has more than doubled in the last three decades (Finucane et al. 2011), with over 60 percent of adults and one in four children overweight or obese (National Preventative Health Taskforce 2009). Eating disorders and disordered eating are also on the rise (Hay et al. 2008). Around one in ten in the general population has current disordered eating and around 16 percent of women will experience an eating disorder in their lifetime (Hay et al. 2008, Wade et al. 2006). Given the prevalence and significance of these issues, and challenges of treatment provision such as high costs and poor outcomes, clear, integrated health communication initiatives targeted to the prevention of these problems is vital. The next section outlines problems that may arise when communication initiatives to change attitudes and behaviors are not integrated.

Friendly Fire: Collateral Damage?

People today are inundated by messaging about health, bodies, food, and eating. Most alarming are the contributions made to our understanding by the food, diet, and cosmetic industries; industries that may profit from the vulnerability of people wanting to be healthier, thinner, or more attractive. However, even when messaging on these topics is provided by well-intentioned sources aiming to reduce the risk of obesity and/or eating disorders, there is potential for collateral damage to occur. This harm plausibly results from a failure to understand the full range of risk and protective factors across the broad spectrum of weight-related problems and when messaging is not well-integrated. The following cases exemplify how health communication messages designed to improve health knowledge and/or behaviors may inadvertently create harm. Each case is a composite narrative of clinical experience.

Twelve-year-old Sally is dressed in baggy clothes to cover and warm her body as she answers the doctor's questions about her rapid weight loss. "In class, the teacher was talking about healthy bodies and got us to weigh ourselves and put all the numbers up on the blackboard and...I was one of the highest", she sobbed. "When my friends found out that I was upset they told me I should skip lunch", Sally recalled. Her mother interrupted, "I explained to her that it was because she is one of the tallest, but you know, kids of that age don't understand". Following this event, Sally became increasingly worried about her weight, started to skip meals, cut out different foods, and was now barely eating anything.

Thirteen-year-old Tom had been the "most improved" football player last season and had been trying hard all summer to become super fit for the new season. He had taken all of his coach's, Mr Jones, advice about eating healthy food very seriously and he had decided to eat only "good" foods and not allow himself any "bad" foods at all. At first it was hard to eat healthy all the time, because his friends kept asking him to hang out with them and they always had tasty foods like pizza or chips, so he decided not to go to their houses. Initially he ran faster and this success encouraged him to keep being healthy, but as it got closer to the season starting, Tom's running time was getting slower no matter how hard he tried. At first, his parents has been pleased with his new interest in health and made him lots of salads and vegetables, but after a while they became concerned as he would not eat meat "because of the fat in it", would no longer eat previously enjoyed foods, such as chips, and his physical appearance had changed from lean to bony. Tom was in tears after coming home from football practice after summer break. Confused, he said to his dad, "What does Mr Jones mean? He told me I can't play - that I am too thin and not strong enough." Tom's parents thought he was going through a "phase" and would "snap out of it". However, Tom had developed a serious eating disorder and within weeks was hospitalised for medical problems associated with malnutrition.

These cases illustrate the overlap between problems on the weight-related spectrum, whereby education and interventions concerning nutrition and weight can backfire to trigger problems. They also highlight the range of contexts where information about eating and bodies is available outside typical health settings. To develop insight into the types of miscommunications that can occur, it is important to have a comprehensive understanding of the broad range of eating- and weight-related problems.

The Broad Spectrum of Weight-Related Problems

There are a range of eating and weight issues that are typically described as discrete entities, but may usefully be considered as part of the same spectrum (Neumark-Sztainer 2005) (see Figure 14.1). These issues are outlined below as background to the discussion.

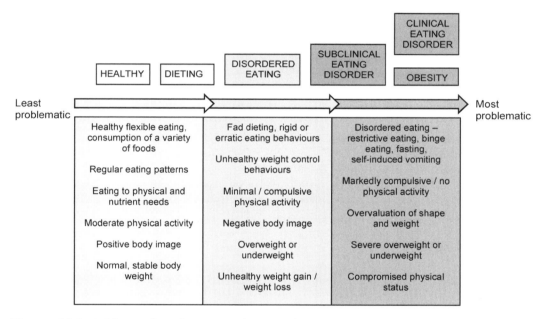

Figure 14.1 A Dimensional Approach to Eating- and Weight-Related Problems

OVERWEIGHT AND OBESITY

Overweight and obesity are defined as weight that exceeds an established criterion threshold value. The World Health Organization uses Body Mass Index (BMI), a measurement of weight relative to height, to define overweight in adults as a BMI between 25 kg/m² and 30 kg/m², and obesity as a BMI > 30 kg/m² (World Health Organization 1998). In youth, BMI age- and sex-specific percentile distributions are used. Raised BMI is not a disease, but is a major risk factor for cardiovascular diseases, musculoskeletal disorders, diabetes, and some cancers.

DIETING AND DISORDERED EATING

"Dieting" as defined in this chapter refers to a broad range of eating behaviors and cognitions that are unhealthy and potentially harmful from a physical and psychological standpoint. Overly restrictive eating, such as low caloric intake and cutting out entire food groups, strict and rigid food rules, and dietary changes that are not practical or sustainable long-term, such as seen in Tom's case, are examples. Dieting can be distinguished from healthful dietary practices and cognitions, such as having a balanced diet, eating the recommended serving of fruits and vegetables, and sustainable dietary practices. In Western countries, approximately one half of women and one third of men report having dieted to lose weight at some point in their life (Hill 2002). Dieting is linked to numerous negative health consequences.

Disordered eating behavior affects many youth and adults (Croll et al. 2002, Hay et al. 2008) and is a major risk factor for eating disorders (Patton et al. 1999). Disordered eating describes unhealthy, extreme, and dangerous dietary and weight control practices, including restrictive eating, fasting, skipping meals, self-induced vomiting, excessive exercise, misuse of laxatives and diet pills, and binge eating. Skipping meals and fasting – as in Sally's case – is a common pathway into other forms of disordered eating, because when sustained long enough, self-starvation triggers innate survival mechanisms, such as a dramatic increase in food preoccupations and binge eating. This was famously illustrated in a 1950s military experiment which recruited healthy conscientious objectors to an experiment to determine optimal refeeding methods after a period of prolonged famine-like semi-starvation (Keys, Borzek, Henschel, Mickelson, and Taylor, 1950).

One in 10 adults engages in one or more forms of disordered eating at least weekly (Hay et al. 2008) and one-third of male and over one-half of female adolescents report disordered eating in the previous 12 months (Croll et al. 2002). Even in the absence of an acute eating disorder, disordered eating is linked to problems in mental, physical, and social functioning (Herpertz-Dahlmann et al. 2008).

EATING DISORDERS

Eating disorders are chronic, complex and serious life-threatening illnesses with significant psychiatric and medical morbidity. They involve intense concern about body image, weight, and eating. Anorexia nervosa and bulimia nervosa are the two most commonly understood eating disorders. A third category is "eating disorders not otherwise specified," a residual diagnostic category which includes binge eating disorder and syndromes that do not meet full criteria for anorexia nervosa or bulimia nervosa (American Psychiatric Association 2000). Eating disorders are more prevalent in females but can affect males too, and for binge eating disorder the gender distribution is approximately equal. Although they can develop at any age, eating disorders commence most frequently in adolescence. Anorexia nervosa and bulimia nervosa are leading causes of disease and injury in female youth (Australian Institute of Health and Welfare 2007). Physical problems associated with eating disorders include gastrointestinal illnesses, osteoporosis, kidney failure, heart failure, dental and gum diseases, Type 2 diabetes, and anemia.

Two Sides of the Same Coin?

Obesity and eating disorder health communication initiatives, including health promotion strategies, policy, mass mediated campaigns, and school-based programs, tend to be designed and implemented separately. The segregation of professionals in these sectors, and limited cross-sector pollination, is largely to blame. There is a strong rationale for a multisectorial and co-ordinated approach.

Firstly, comorbidity studies and prospective research highlight patterns of concurrent and successive comorbidity, providing a further rationale for co-ordinated health communication initiatives. Above average weight in childhood elevates risk for future overweight, obesity, and eating disorders (Jacobi et al. 2004, Singh et al. 2008) and is associated with higher use of disordered weight control practices and lower use of healthy weight control practices (for example, eating breakfast; vegetable, grain, low-fat dairy consumption; regular physical activity) (Boutelle et al. 2002, Tanofsky-Kraff et al. 2004). Overweight and obese women are at elevated risk of disordered eating and eating disorders (Darby et al. 2007). Women with a lifetime history of bulimia nervosa and binge eating disorder have higher rates of overweight and obesity (Hudson et al. 2007). The prevalence of comorbid obesity and eating disorder behaviors in females quadrupled from the 1990s to 2000s – rising more than the prevalence of either alone (Darby et al. 2009).

Secondly, health communication about obesity and about eating disorders commonly target the same issues; body image, dietary practices, physical activity, nutrition, self-esteem, weight, and physical status. There are many shared risk and protective factors for obesity and eating disorders across these themes representing viable targets for collaborative interventions (Haines et al. 2010; Neumark-Sztainer et al. 2007).

Proposed modifiable shared risk factors include:

a) dieting and disordered eating;
b) being overweight in childhood;
c) weight-related bias, stigma, and teasing;
d) parent weight concern and weight-related behaviors;
e) parental teasing of child weight or eating behaviors;
f) hours of screen time (TV/internet/videogames);
g) media and marketing exposure;
h) poor body image; and
i) depression and anxiety.

Proposed modifiable shared protective factors include:

a) enjoyable physical activity;
b) positive body image;
c) high self-esteem;
d) eating breakfast, lunch, and dinner every day;
e) family modelling of healthy behaviors, (for example, avoiding unhealthy dieting, engaging in physical activity); and
f) regular and enjoyable family meals.

Not all risk or protective factors for eating disorders and obesity are shared. For example, being female and having a perfectionistic personality increases risk for eating disorders (Stice 2002) but not obesity, and low socioeconomic status and an inactive lifestyle increases risk for obesity (Parsons et al. 1999) but not for eating disorders. In addition to shared risk and protective factors at an individual or family level, the common ground becomes more striking when considering shared environmental or sociocultural risk and protective factors.

A Food and Weight Disordered World?

Our modern culture and environment make it easy for people to develop disturbances in weight, eating and exercise behavior, and body image; these disturbances are hard to modify. From a population perspective, weight and eating-related conditions occur in a macrosocial context that delivers ambiguous and opposing demands and messages; for instance, "taking diet pills will help you lose weight and are therefore good for your health" is juxtaposed with warnings of "diet pills are unhealthy and dangerous." "Downstream" approaches emphasize the individual taking personal action to protect his or her health (Dorfman and Wallack 2007). Whilst important, this emphasis on individual factors and personal responsibility for falling into unhealthy patterns, and for changing these patterns when identified, props up the diet and food industries and inhibits real change. There is a growing push to shift health promotion "upstream" to create more supportive physical, social, economic, and policy environments. Upstream approaches may also have the potential to affect downstream factors.

Contemporary urban food environments have been labelled "obesogenic." The food environment (for example, fast food outlet density, high cost of fresh food, availability of soft drinks) combined with the built environment (for example, lack of walkways, bike paths, and recreation spaces) and other population level trends (for example, increased working hours, decreased leisure time, decreased active work roles) may contribute to higher BMIs in modern urban populations and increase the risk for disordered eating by making healthy weight control practices more costly and difficult compared with disordered weight control practices. Binge eating is reliant upon the availability of excessive food, and as such did not become common until the 1960s, when food availability increased and rates of obesity also began to rise.

Stigmatization in Western culture is rife, and though significant progress has been made in addressing race and gender bias, the same cannot be said for weight and shape bias. Weight-based teasing at school and broader societal discrimination is prevalent. The mass media sometimes perpetuate this prejudice, for example, by presenting obese people in a biased, stereotyped manner and presenting unrealistic and digitally enhanced images of beauty (Sandberg 2007). Media guidelines and codes of conduct are constructive avenues to reduce stigmatization and idealization of narrow beauty ideals; examples include the "Guidelines for the Portrayal of Obese Persons in the Media" developed by the Rudd Center for Food Policy and Obesity at Yale University and The Obesity Society, and the "Victorian Voluntary Media Code of Conduct on Body Image" developed by the Victorian state government of Australia. Weight and appearance-based bias, including teasing, stereotyping, and discrimination, can activate shape and weight concerns, poor body image, and negative emotional states, which may increase vulnerability to eating disorders and weight-gain behaviors such as overeating (Brownell 2005). Those who internalize this stigmatization show a reluctance to exercise in public settings and avoid health care settings (Almeida et al. 2011; Puhl and Heuer 2009). Some health promotion initiatives for obesity have been criticized for increasing stigmatization.

Marketing, advertising, and media contexts play a significant role in propagating unrealistic beauty ideals, unhealthy food and beverage preferences, obesity stereotypes, negative content around body image, and the glamorization of eating disorders. The glamorization and normalization of an unrealistically thin feminine body or overly muscular masculine body is common, and sends negative and possibly destructive messages about the social unacceptability of normal bodies. As sociocultural vehicles, these media have significant scope for improving messaging around food, bodies, health, and weight, and health communication professionals and governments have a ripe ground available for facilitating large-scale improvements.

Conflict and Miscommunication in Health Promotion

Occasionally, despite our best efforts in the communication of health-related messages, unanticipated harmful effects occur. A concern with implementation of health promotion programs, for example, is "boomerang effects," whereby attitude and behavior change occurs in the direction opposite to that intended. In the drug and alcohol field, boomerang effects have been noted, with one study finding that one third of public service announcements aimed to prevent illicit drug use increased adolescent drug use and experimentation (Fishbein et al. 2002). Through research we now know that early efforts to prevent eating disorders, which involved classroom-based psychoeducation via a recovered eating disorder patient or other person, could paradoxically increase eating disorder symptoms and normalize and glamorize aspects of eating disorders (Carter et al. 1997, Mann et al. 1997). In addition to boomerang effects, messaged may inadvertently cause other harmful effects in other mental and physical domains. Very little research has been done in the eating and weight fields to ascertain whether obesity prevention programs may be harmful in relation to eating disorders, and vice versa (Carter and Bulik 2008). For instance, in Sally's case, although the health promotion lesson implemented by the teacher was based on good intentions, there was unanticipated risk. Traditionally, the eating disorder and obesity fields have been so separated that the necessary cross-sector outcomes have not been measured.

In the absence of scientific data, our understanding of the potential harm of weight-related health communication and associated initiatives is informed by public and community reactions, clinical observations, and the expertise of health specialists. The leading areas of concern with obesity-related messages and initiatives include the possibility for weight bias and stigmatization, food fears and unhealthy dieting, and body dissatisfaction, dieting, and use of unhealthy weight control practices (Ikeda et al. 2006 O'Dea 2005).

For eating disorder initiatives there has been concern about the promotion of size acceptance (that is, motivation may be lost to maintain or seek a healthy weight if people accept and are satisfied with their bodies), glamorization of eating disorders, suggestive information about unhealthy weight control practices that could promote longer-term weight gain, and dietary guidance that may promote a varied diet which includes enjoying sweet or fatty foods to the extent that people will not restrict their intake sufficiently to maintain or achieve a healthy weight range (O'Dea 2000). Again, there are very little data to clarify the risks associated with eating disorder prevention communication and initiatives.

The place where the two fields have most visibly been at opposite ends of the debate is the anchoring of weight to messaging and interventions. The eating disorders field aims to decouple identity and behavior from size and weight, even as the obesity field tries to intensify focus on weight loss or prevention of weight gain. For example, engaging in regular physical activity could be framed as a method to achieve a "healthy weight" and "healthy waist circumference" or to promote enjoyment and participation in community activities. The rationale for emphasizing weight is based on early health behavior change theories. The 'knowledge-attitude-behavior" (KAB) approach assumes that accumulation of knowledge will translate into changes in attitudes and behaviors; however, human behaviors are often not "objectively" rational, and for obesity no research has demonstrated that KAB initiatives change behavior (Baranowski et al. 2003). Fear-based communication emphasizing the negative consequences of overweight are based on the "health belief model" (Janz, Champion, and Strecher, 2002), which aims to modify perceptions of risk and the personal impact of the outcome (Baranowski et al. 2003). At the broader level, fear-based campaigns are only modestly successful (Witte and Allen 2000). Fear-based messages could inadvertently encourage weight and shape concerns, a simplistic view of weight and health, and weight stigma. Being overweight or obese is often linked unquestionably to poor health and disease onset, whereas weighing in the normal and "healthy" range is equated to good health. However, being thin does not guarantee health; thin people may engage in unhealthy eating and exercise behaviors and experience poor health. An overfocus on weight in messaging may perpetuate the cultural stereotype and stigma that "thin is good and fat is bad."

BMI screening in schools is controversial due to the unknown impacts, positive and negative. BMI screening is distinct from BMI surveillance. There is a robust rationale for surveillance, which is measurement at the population level, to determine weight status trends, groups at risk, population responsiveness to school-based health programs and policy, and progress toward health policy objectives (Nihiser et al. 2009). For surveillance, weight data are collected anonymously and parents are not informed of their child's weight status, whereas for screening the weight status of individual students is evaluated and parents are informed of the results, typically in the form of a written report containing a BMI-for-age percentile, an explanation of the results, and recommended follow-up strategies. The Center for Disease Control and Prevention (CDC) in the United States found that one quarter of States required school measurement of students' body mass, and three in four of those required parent notification of results (Nihiser et al. 2009). While the purpose of the measurements was not determined, many schools have adopted screening as an anti-obesity measure. Only a few studies have tested for benefits of use of BMI report cards, and findings are mixed (MacLean et al. 2010). Concerningly, diet-based weight control strategies, which are not typically medically recommended for youth, were common parental responses, rather than gradual changes in lifestyle behaviors. The current consensus is that BMI should not be used for individual screening unless a suitable clinical intervention is available for the individuals whose health may be at risk and these treatments are unavailable in most school settings. Anecdotes from clinical practice suggest that school weigh-ins can trigger eating disorder onset in those who are vulnerable. When BMI screening is medically necessary, it can be done sensitively to minimize harm, such as in a private space, with an experienced health professional mediating the impact through interpretation of BMI in the context of other clinical findings and providing appropriate recommendations. However in practice, there are reports of children being weighed in groups, with public display of weights and with labeling of children as overweight or obese without context or intervention.

Whilst most dietary guidance developed by experts in nutrition emphasizes a positive attitude to a variety of foods with regular healthful eating, the everyday translation of dietary advice is often negative. This situation, combined with marketing by the "diet" industries has contributed to far reaching food fears and an epidemic of dieting. Popular "low-carb" weight loss programs are a prominent example of how food fears can be propagated by industry, with large numbers of people now fearful of carbohydrates, and those with clinical eating disorders avoiding carbohydrates in the same way that sugar, and then fat, became feared in the 1990s. In Australia, the national education curriculum teaches children as young as four to dichotomize foods into "good" and "bad" foods. Clinical observations at the workplace suggest that some children adopt the healthy eating messages in extreme ways and develop food fears and restrictive eating practices. People at risk of eating disorders are vulnerable to this messaging, as they have a dispositional tendency to be perfectionistic, morally concerned, and socially compliant, as seen in the case of Tom. Tom progressed to cutting out all forms of "bad foods" until his diet was a limited composition of "safe" foods (for example, salad, vegetables, non-fat dairy). Such actions lead to the drastic malnutrition that is observed in restricting eating disorders, as bodies require a range of vitamins, minerals, and other nutrients that can only be derived from varied food sources. Unfortunately, the expert dietary guidance is often obscured, either in its translation by laypeople or by commercially driven diet and food propaganda. It is not surprising that most people report obtaining their dietary advice from the mass media, given the advertising budgets of food companies far outweigh the financial resources of dieticians and good quality health communication initiatives.

The negative portrayal of higher weight people in the media and in health communication initiatives has fuelled concerns about weight-based discrimination and stigma (Hilbert et al. 2008). In 2011, the government of Georgia, United States, launched an anti-obesity campaign in which pictures of overweight children were shown on billboards and in online videos with campaign messages such as "Big bones didn't make me this way. Big meals did" and "Fat kids become fat adults"; the campaign attracted controversy for the above reasons. Health communication methods that foster weight bias and stigmatization are generally contraindicated and seen as unhelpful from the perspective of both eating disorder and obesity prevention. Regardless of size or weight, health for the whole community can be promoted through healthful nutrition and meaningful physical activity; portrayal of obese persons in a positive and fair light, rather than in a pejorative, dehumanizing, or stereotypical manner, is recommended in both health communication initiatives and in media portrayals.

Understanding the full range of eating- and weight-related problems, the shared risk and protective factors, and the types of harms that may occur in the communication of information intended to promote health and prevent disease onset offers the strongest foundation for positive, co-ordinated intervention strategies.

Common Ground for Health Communication, Health Promotion, and Prevention

A viable path forward for co-ordinated eating disorders and obesity health communication, health promotion, and prevention is to focus messaging and interventions on shared risk and protective factors. As well as initiatives at the personal level (that is, "downstream"), environment and culture (that is, "upstream") provide a fruitful area for health promotion and prevention. Initiatives that have the potential to be unsafe at any point on the weight-spectrum are best avoided.

Practical key messages and strategies that exemplify an informed collaborative approach to health promotion and prevention follow, with progression from "downstream" to "upstream" approaches. These key messages were formed from a review of the limited international evidence, peer-reviewed publications, and resources developed by authoritative experts. They are relevant to a range of audiences, including members of health teams who give information to the community, parents, school teachers and administrators, policy-makers, researchers, and community members.

KEY MESSAGES AND STRATEGIES

Fat diets don't work Given that dieting is the single greatest risk factor for eating disorders, and that it leads to weight gain in the majority of people, a key message is the discouragement of fad and restrictive dieting (Haines and Neumark-Sztainer, 2006). An Australian Victorian government health promotion campaign named "Fad Diet's Won't Work" ran social marketing campaigns with one caption reading, "Fad dieting helped me go from a size 14 to a size 12, back to a size 16."

Nourish your body Emphasize a positive, healthful approach to nutrition including eating a variety of quality, fresh foods from across the food pyramid or plate emphasized in dietary guidelines (Russell and Ryder 2001). Focus messages on what to eat, not what not to eat (O'Dea 2010); for example, eat seven fruit and vegetables everyday, and keep the messages from being judgmental or blaming (O'Dea 2010).

Eat well Highlight regular, healthy patterns of eating (breakfast, lunch, and dinner), social eating (fun and enjoyable meals with family and friends), mindful eating (slow rather than fast), and ethical eating (local and sustainable) including growing food and buying local (for example, count miles, not calories) (Irving and Neumark-Sztainer 2002). Provide accurate information about healthy nutrition, including required daily intake, consequences of eating nutrient-poor energy-dense foods, and the perils of unhealthy weight loss (Irving and Neumark-Sztainer 2002).

Be physically active Ensure a positive approach to activity by accentuating the benefits (social, recreational, health and well-being) and enjoyment of physical activity and play, and help children in particular to pursue play and physical activity that boosts their self-esteem and friendships (O'Dea 2010). Provide balanced information as per physical activity guidelines about recommended activity levels and types of activity (resistance, cardiovascular), including information about overuse syndrome. Remove barriers to participation; for instance, in the school setting provide privacy in change rooms and sports uniforms that are comfortable and not too revealing (O'Dea 2010).

Health at every size   Eating well and being physically active is important for *everybody*, no matter their size or weight. The whole community can benefit from initiatives promoting healthy body image, nutrition, and physical activity.

Become media smart   Promote critical thinking about food marketing, the media, and corporate communications, particularly those that involve messaging and images about beauty, food, and diet preferences (Thompson and Heinberg 1999, Irving and Neumark-Sztainer 2002, Durkin et al. 2005).

Unplug and play   Encourage reduced screen time (TV, computer, video games) and involvement in more active leisure (Haines and Neumark-Sztainer 2006).

Positive parenting   Encourage parents to build children's self-esteem, model assertive communication, and model appropriate methods to deal with unpleasant emotions like stress, anxiety, and boredom rather than through comfort or controlled eating. Promote the message that teasing in general by any person is unhelpful and harmful (Keery et al. 2005, Haines and Neumark-Sztainer 2006).

Throw the "good" out with the "bad"!   Avoid labelling foods as "good" or "bad" in public messages (Russell and Ryder, 2001; Schwartz and Henderson, 2009) – food isn't moral, it's not immoral either, it's morally neutral! Simplistic terms may encourage food fears and avoidances.

Avoid fat talk   Use positive language about bodies and eating, and discourage "weight talk" "fat talk" (Durkin et al. 2005) and extremes (for example, war on obesity, battle of the bulge, fighting fat).

A family affair   Encourage families to adopt and role model helpful behaviors (that is, eating regular enjoyable family meals, eating breakfast, physical activity) and to reduce less helpful behaviors (for example, "fat" talk; sedentary behaviors). Encourage whole family change, like taking a walk together or planting a vegetable garden. Provide practical, realistic, and positive advice, for instance, ideas for physical games and activities the family can enjoy and small steps to healthful eating including recipe suggestions (Borra et al. 2003).

Responsible fashion   Promote a positive and responsible fashion industry that supports availability of larger clothing sizes, mannequins of healthy shapes and sizes, and use of healthy weight models. These key messages largely originated from grassroots ecological movements (Piran and Mafrici 2011).

Make it easy   Establish food and activity policies which enable healthy dietary and activity practices such as availability of healthy food choices in vending machines, increased access to affordable healthy foods including fruits and vegetables, curriculum requirements for physical education/sport, and adequate supervision of play areas and playground anti-bullying policies which are linked to more physical activity at school (Garrard 2009).

Health by design   Engage urban design to make activity and healthful eating accessible, for example by providing safe and shaded neighborhood recreational and exercise areas, walkable neighborhood streets, safe roads for pedestrian and cycle use, reduced density of fast-food outlets, mixed land-use zones, and access to supermarkets and grocery stores (Garrard 2009). Ensure parks are aesthetically pleasant, safe, with shade and amenities such as water fountains, bicycle racks, and fixed equipment (for example, basketball hoops). Create attractive neighborhood open spaces and environments (with natural, cultural and creative features) (Garrard 2009).

Regulate or legislate   Establish policies and laws that reduce the risk of harm such as school and workplace policy around weight-based teasing (Haines et al. 2006), bullying and discrimination, and codes of conduct that provide guidance for the media, fashion, and advertising industries. Examples include the Australian government *Voluntary Industry Code of Conduct on Body Image* which provides practice principles including promotion of a diversity of images, use of natural and realistic images and healthy weight models. The *Responsible Children's Marketing Initiative* developed by the Australian food and beverage industry which provides guidance on the marketing of food and beverage products to children, with the aim of reducing exposure to marketing of nutrient poor, energy-dense foods and beverages to young children.

These strategies and messages are integrated, and according to the extant evidence and literature, targeting shared evidence-based and theoretical risk and protective factors (implicit in these messages and practical strategies) represents a valuable direction for simultaneously working toward the prevention of eating disorders and obesity (Haines et al. 2010, Neumark-Sztainer et al. 2007).

Implications for Academics

More knowledge, methods, and communication channels than ever before are available to support researchers' efforts to reduce the incidence of eating disorders and obesity. A collaborative, inter-sectoral approach to future research is essential. Practical applications of health communication practices require evaluation for safety and efficacy across the weight-related spectrum and direct comparisons of different approaches will help to enumerate the most important risk and protective factors to target. More attention ought to be diverted to applied approaches at the upstream level and to the methodology that can capture change at this level.

Implications for Health Practitioners

Through an understanding of shared risk and protective factors, and integrated positive approaches to obesity and eating disorder prevention, health professionals are charged with translating this evidence to practice. Health professionals need to extend their reach into diverse mediated contexts, embracing the new technologies to deliver healthful information about nutrition and physical activity. When communication about obesity and eating disorders is combined, a more effective health message will ensue. Further, effort is required to ensure all frontline health professionals deliver messages in a coordinated way. There is also significant scope for prevention, not just of obesity and eating disorders, but of other diseases, with the population, especially families, in having access to consistent, life enhancing health messages and strategies about nutrition, activity and body image. Health professionals also have a responsibility to communicate with government and industry, to ensure this knowledge is available to other sectors who plan and fund aspects of the environment, such as urban design, that have implications for community health.

Conclusion

Not a single person in our modern world is exempt from the endeavors to communicate about health, food, and bodies. Rates of obesity and eating disorders are at an all-time high, and are escalating. Do no harm is paramount in contemporary medicine and it is incumbent upon the fields of eating disorders and obesity to join forces in the delivery of positive health communication messages that promote healthful behaviors and attitudes, whilst minimizing the risk of damage. A commitment from both sides needs to be made, not just to eliminate harm, but to develop constructive messages and programs that promote the health of the entire population. Central to this responsibility is an obligation to evaluate the iatrogenic affects of both eating disorder and obesity prevention initiatives, as we develop them and ascertain their effectiveness.

A first step to reducing the risks is for the currently disconnected fields of studies to begin a conversation and recognize that we all aspire to the same end point: a healthy, disease-free population who eat well, are physically active, and are satisfied with their bodies.

Downstream approaches are one option for health promotion, though care must be taken not to do harm or create a "narrative of the failed citizen" (Elliott 2008). For instance, some campaigns have used "scare tactics" which are not only often ineffective but may also escalate anxiety, shame, body hatred, fears of food, nutritional deficits, and uptake of unhealthy and extreme weight loss methods. Rather than censuring individuals for unhealthy behaviors or becoming unwell, we need to make it easy for people to live well. Upstream initiatives that focus on supportive environments have widespread potential and can impact downstream factors. These approaches may occur in the background of the individual's life, without him or her necessarily having a strong understanding of the environmental modifications that have taken place. A public health exemplar is the use of fluoride in public drinking water supplies to protect teeth against dental decay. Rather than educating the population on the importance of fluoride and placing the onus of action for fluoride exposure onto the individual (for example, mouth rinse, dietary supplements, dental products), legislation on mandatory public water fluoridation has been introduced in many parts of the world (Watt 2007). Analogous upstream initiatives that may lower the risk of eating disorders and obesity, such as standards of conduct for the mass media or altering "obesogenic" community environments and urban planning to encourage uptake of healthy weight control behaviors may be safer and more effective than individualistic approaches which can risk harm and may occur too late.

Health communication, promotion, and prevention across the weight-related spectrum is poised on an exciting, new frontier, where dialogue, cross-pollination, and sharing of knowledge between sectors has the potential to enhance community health and well-being in creative and previously unimagined ways.

Acknowledgments

We wish to thank Professor Dianne Neumark-Sztainer for her helpful feedback on an earlier draft of this chapter.

References

Almeida, L., Savoy, S. and Boxer, P. 2011. The role of weight stigmatization in cumulative risk for binge eating. *Journal of Clinical Psychology*, 67(3), 278–92.

American Psychiatric Association 2000. *Diagnostic and Statistical Manual of Mental Disorders. Fourth Edition Text Revision.* Washington, DC: American Psychiatric Press.

Austin, S.B., Field, A.E., Wiecha, J., Peterson, K.E. and Gortmaker, S.L. 2005. The impact of a school-based obesity prevention trial on disordered weight-control behaviors in early adolescent girls. *Archives of Pediatrics and Adolescent Medicine*, 159(3), 225–30.

Australian Institute of Health and Welfare 2007. *Young Australians: Their Health and Wellbeing 2007. Phe 87.* Canberra.

Baranowski, T., Cullen, K.W., Nicklas, T., Thompson, D. and Baranowski, J. 2003. Are current health behavioral change models helpful in guiding prevention of weight gain efforts? *Obesity Research*, 11 Suppl, 23S–43S.

Borra, S.T., Kelly, L., Shirreffs, M.B., Neville, K. and Geiger, C.J. 2003. Developing health messages: Qualitative studies with children, parents, and teachers help identify communications opportunities for healthful lifestyles and the prevention of obesity. *Journal of the American Dietetic Association*, 103(6), 721–8.

Boutelle, K., Neumark-Sztainer, D., Story, M. and Resnick, M. 2002. Weight control behaviors among obese, overweight, and nonoverweight adolescents. *Journal of Pediatric Psychology*, 27(6), 531–40.

Brownell, K.D. 2005. *Weight Bias: Nature, Consequences, and Remedies.* New York: Guilford Press.

Carter, F.A. and Bulik, C.M. 2008. Childhood obesity prevention programs: How do they affect eating pathology and other psychological measures? *Psychosomatic Medicine*, 70(3), 363–71.

Carter, J.C., Stewart, D.A., Dunn, V.J. and Fairburn, C.G. 1997. Primary prevention of eating disorders: Might it do more harm than good? *International Journal of Eating Disorders*, 22(2), 167–72.

Croll, J., Neumark-Sztainer, D., Story, M. and Ireland, M. 2002. Prevalence and risk and protective factors related to disordered eating behaviors among adolescents: Relationship to gender and ethnicity. *Journal of Adolescent Health*, 31(2), 166–75.

Darby, A., Hay, P., Mond, J., Quirk, F., Buttner, P. and Kennedy, L. 2009. The rising prevalence of comorbid obesity and eating disorder behaviors from 1995 to 2005. *International Journal of Eating Disorders*, 42(2), 104–8.

Darby, A., Hay, P., Mond, J., Rodgers, B. and Owen, C. 2007. Disordered eating behaviours and cognitions in young women with obesity: Relationship with psychological status. *International Journal of Obesity*, 31 (5), 876–82.

Dorfman, L. and Wallack, L. 2007. Moving nutrition upstream: The case for reframing obesity. *Journal of Nutrition Education and Behavior*, 39 Suppl 2, S45–50.

Durkin, S.J., Paxton, S.J. and Wertheim, E.H. 2005. How do adolescent girls evaluate body dissatisfaction prevention messages? *Journal of Adolescent Health*, 37(5), 381–90.

Finucane, M.M., Stevens, G.A., Cowan, M.J., Danaei, G., Lin, J.K., Paciorek, C.J., Singh, G.M., Gutierrez, H.R., Lu, Y., Bahalim, A.N., Farzadfar, F., Riley, L.M., Ezzati, M. and Global Burden of Metabolic Risk Factors of Chronic Diseases Collaborating Group 2011. National, regional, and global trends in body-mass index since 1980: Systematic analysis of health examination surveys and epidemiological studies with 960 country-years and 9.1 million participants. *Lancet*, 377(9765), 557–67.

Fishbein, M., Hall-Jamieson, K., Zimmer, E., Von Haeften, I. and Nabi, R. 2002. Avoiding the boomerang: Testing the relative effectiveness of antidrug public service announcements before a national campaign. *American Journal of Public Health*, 92(2), 238–45.

Garrard, J. 2009. *Taking action on obesogenic environments: Building a culture of active, connected communities: An options paper prepared by Dr Jan Garrard for the national preventative health taskforce.* Canberra.

Haines, J., Kleinman, K.P., Rifas-Shiman, S.L., Field, A.E. and Austin, S.B. 2010. Examination of shared risk and protective factors for overweight and disordered eating among adolescents. *Archives of Pediatrics and Adolescent Medicine*, 164(4), 336–43.

Haines, J. and Neumark-Sztainer, D. 2006. Prevention of obesity and eating disorders: A consideration of shared risk factors. *Health Education Research*, 21(6), 770–782.

Haines, J., Neumark-Sztainer, D., Eisenberg, M.E. and Hannan, P.J. 2006. Weight teasing and disordered eating behaviors in adolescents: Longitudinal findings from Project EAT (Eating Among Teens). *Pediatrics*, 117(2), e209–15.

Hay, P.J., Mond, J., Buttner, P. and Darby, A. 2008. Eating disorder behaviors are increasing: Findings from two sequential community surveys in South Australia. *PLoS ONE*, 3(2), e1541.

Herpertz-Dahlmann, B., Wille, N., Holling, H., Vloet, T.D., Ravens-Sieberer, U. and Bella Study Group 2008. Disordered eating behaviour and attitudes, associated psychopathology and health-related quality of life: Results of the Bella Study. *European Child and Adolescent Psychiatry*, 17 Suppl 1, 82–91.

Hilbert, A., Rief, W. and Braehler, E. 2008. Stigmatizing attitudes toward obesity in a representative population-based sample. *Obesity*, 16(7), 1529–34.

Hudson, J.I., Hiripi, E., Pope, H.G., Jr. and Kessler, R.C. 2007. The prevalence and correlates of eating disorders in the national comorbidity survey replication. *Biological Psychiatry*, 61(3), 348–58.

Ikeda, J.P., Crawford, P.B. and Woodward-Lopez, G. 2006. BMI screening in schools: Helpful or harmful. *Health Education Research*, 21(6), 761–9.

Irving, L. and Neumark-Sztainer, D. 2002. Integrating the prevention of eating disorders and obesity: Feasible or futile? *Preventive Medicine*, 34(3), 299–309.

Jacobi, C., Hayward, C., De Zwaan, M., Kraemer, H. and Agras, W. 2004. Coming to terms with risk factors for eating disorders: Application of risk terminology and suggestions for a general taxonomy. *Psychological Bulletin*, 130(1), 19–65.

Janz, N.K., Champion, V.L. and Strecher, V.J. 2002. The health belief model, in *Health Behavior and Health Education: Theory, Research, and Practice*, 3rd Edition, edited by K. Glanz, B.K. Rimer and F.M. Lewis. San Francisco, CA: Jossey-Bass, 45–66.

Keery, H., Boutelle, K., Van Den Berg, P. and Thompson, J.K. 2005. The impact of appearance-related teasing by family members. *Journal of Adolescent Health*, 37(2), 120–27.

Keys, A., Borzek, J., Henschel, A., Mickelson, O. and Taylor, H.L. 1950. *The Biology of Human Starvation* (2 vols). Minneapolis, MN: University of Minnesota Press.

Maclean, L.M., Meyer, M., Walsh, A., Clinton, K., Ashley, L., Donovan, S. and Edwards, N. 2010. Stigma and BMI screening in schools, or 'Mom, I hate it when they weigh me', in *Childhood Obesity Prevention: International Research, Controversies, and Interventions*, edited by J. O'Dea and M. Eriksen. London: Oxford University Press.

Mann, T., Nolen-Hoeksema, S., Huang, K., Burgard, D., Wright, A. and Hanson, K, 1997. Are two interventions worse than none? Joint primary and secondary prevention of eating disorders in college females. *Health Psychology*, 16(3), 215–25.

National Preventative Health Taskforce 2009. *Australia: The Healthiest Country by 2020: A Discussion Paper*. Canberra.

Neumark-Sztainer, D. 2005. Preventing the broad spectrum of weight-related problems: Working with parents to help teens achieve a healthy weight and a positive body image. *Journal of Nutrition Education and Behavior*, 37 Suppl 2, S133–40.

Neumark-Sztainer, D.R., Wall, M.M., Haines, J.I., Story, M.T., Sherwood, N.E. and Van Den Berg, P.A. 2007. Shared risk and protective factors for overweight and disordered eating in adolescents. *American Journal of Preventive Medicine*, 33(5), 359–69.

Nihiser, A.J., Lee, S.M., Wechsler, H., Mckenna, M., Odom, E., Reinold, C., Thompson, D. and Grummer-Strawn, L. 2009. BMI measurement in schools. *Pediatrics*, 124 Suppl 1, S89–97.

O'Dea, J. 2000. School-based interventions to prevent eating problems: First do no harm. *Eating Disorders*, 8, 123–30.

O'Dea, J. 2005. Prevention of child obesity: 'First, do no harm'. *Health Education Research*, 20(2), 259–65.

O'Dea, J. 2010. Developing positive approaches to nutrition education and the prevention of child and adolescent obesity: First, do no harm, in *Childhood Obesity Prevention: International Research, Controveries*, edited by J. O'Dea and M. Eriksen. New York: Oxford University Press, 31–41.

Parsons, T.J., Power, C., Logan, S. and Summerbell, C.D. 1999. Childhood predictors of adult obesity: A systematic review. *International Journal of Obesity and Related Metabolic Disorders*, 23 Suppl 8, S1–107.

Patton, G.C., Selzer, R., Coffey, C., Carlin, J.B. and Wolfe, R. 1999. Onset of adolescent eating disorders: Population based cohort study over 3 years. *British Medical Journal*, 318(7186), 765–68.

Piran, N. and Mafrici, N. (2011). Ecological and activism approaches to prevention, in *Body Image: A Handbook of Science, Practice, and Prevention*, edited by T.F. Cash and L. Smolak. New York: Guilford Press, 451–9.

Puhl, R.M. and Heuer, C.A. 2009. The stigma of obesity: A review and update. *Obesity*, 17(5), 941–964.

Russell, S. and Ryder, S. 2001. BRIDGE (Building the relationship between body image and disordered eating graph and explanation): A tool for parents and professionals. *Eating Disorders*, 9(1), 1–14.

Sandberg, H. 2007. A matter of looks, the framing of obesity in four swedish daily newspapers. *European Journal of Community Research*, 32(4), 447–72.

Schwartz, M.B. and Henderson, K.E. 2009. Does obesity prevention cause eating disorders? *Journal of the American Academy of Child and Adolescent Psychiatry*, 48(8), 784–6.

Singh, A.S., Mulder, C., Twisk, J.W.R., Van Mechelen, W. and Chinapaw, M.J.M. 2008. Tracking of childhood overweight into adulthood: A systematic review of the literature. *Obesity Reviews*, 9(5), 474–88.

Stice, E. 2002. Risk and maintenance factors for eating pathology: A meta-analytic review. *Psychological Bulletin*, 128(5), 825–48.

Tanofsky-Kraff, M., Yanovski, S.Z., Wilfley, D.E., Marmarosh, C., Morgan, C.M. and Yanovski, J.A. 2004. Eating-disordered behaviors, body fat, and psychopathology in overweight and normal-weight children. *Journal of Consulting and Clinical Psychology*, 72(1), 53–61.

Thompson, J.K. and Heinberg, L.J. 1999. The media's influence on body image disturbance and eating disorders: We've reviled them, now can we rehabilitate them? *Journal of Social Issues*, 55(2), 339–53.

Wade, T., Bergin, J., Tiggemann, M., Bulik, C. and Fairburn, C.G. 2006. Prevalence and long-term course of eating disorders in an adult australian cohort. *Australian and New Zealand Journal of Psychiatry*, 40(2), 121–8.

Watt, R.G. 2007. From victim blaming to upstream action: Tackling the social determinants of oral health inequalities. *Community Dental and Oral Epidemiology*, 35(5), 1–11.

Witte, K. and Allen, M. 2000. A meta-analysis of fear appeals: Implications for effective public health campaigns. *Health Education and Behavior*, 27(5), 591–615.

World Health Organization 1998. *Report of a WHO Consultation on Obesity – Obesity: Preventing and Managing the Global Epidemic*. Geneva: World Health Organization.

15 *The Ethics of Disability Representations on Television*

TRACY R. WORRELL

In 2010, former Alaska Governor Sarah Palin criticized the show *Family Guy* for the portrayal of a character with Down's syndrome accusing the show of making fun of her young son, Trig. The voice actor of the character, who has Down's syndrome, said that the show was not making fun of Trig but his mother and that the former governor doesn't "get the joke" (Itzkoff 2010). What followed was an interesting, and sometimes heated, public discussion between Palin and *Family Guy* producers. Down's syndrome advocates such as Gail Williamson, executive director of the Down's syndrome Association, argue that asking for, "full inclusion in the world, we should appreciate full inclusion with other genres. Even if those genres are not what we appreciate" (Itzkoff 2010). Could Itzkoff's argument indicate a case of "any publicity is good publicity" for disabilities in the media? Fortunately for *Family Guy* producers, this discussion waged on and further explanation was given regarding the character, but not all television shows have the ability to explain their side to the general public. So, what if there are other portrayals where viewers do not "get the joke?" What are the ethical implications of these 'inclusive' portrayals in the media?

Introduction

Hundreds of studies have surveyed thousands of hours of television, concerned about the effects on viewers. The majority of these studies have focused on violence and sex and how people may become more violent or promiscuous from watching the media. Much less research is being done to examine representations of disabilities in the media (there is substantial research into the health *messages* of the media but little on individuals with disabilities [see Kline 2003 for further discussion]). Aside from the intrinsic value of examining trends in the portrayal of disabilities in the media and the lack of complete examinations of disabilities in American television, important social changes have occurred recently. Changes such as federal and state budget freezes and decreases have impacted disability services and programs. The United Nations Convention on the Rights of Persons with Disabilities came into force in 2008. And, recently the popularity of characters with disabilities on highly rated television programs (that is, *Glee* and *Dancing with the Stars*) may have begun to impact the number of and portrayal of individuals with disabilities on television.

If all of the characters with disabilities on television were "positively" portrayed (as perhaps Artie, a wheelchair-using character on *Glee*, is) there may be very little need to examine the ethicality of the representation of disabilities on television. Unfortunately, the much more common portrayal is of characters like Floyd Feylinn Ferell, a mentally ill young man on *Criminal Minds* (*Lucky*; 2007–08 season) released from an institution and who goes on to be a cannibalistic serial killer who eats his live victims piece by piece until they finally expire. Many researchers would focus on the violent, cannibalistic aspects of this episode, particularly the ethics of showing such material and its potential effects. There should also be (and arguably more importantly be) a thorough examination of the ethical considerations when airing this representation of a disability, in this case mental illness.

Before delving into these ethical considerations, one must try to understand exactly how individuals with disabilities are portrayed within television programming. Television's portrayal of disabilities is important for a number of reasons including the implications for general disability knowledge, the potential of stigmas (for example, of mental illness [Signorielli 1989]), attitude change towards disabilities (for example, Elliott and Byrd 1983), and the portrayal's potential to impact how individuals in the real world with said disability are treated by others (Zoller and Worrell 2006). This chapter examines the ethics of disability representation on primetime television by focusing not only on the representation of health in the media but also the accuracy of such portrayals. This understanding can help generate knowledge and further research.

In line with the objectives of this book, this chapter provides an example of current research being conducted in the portrayal of health issues in the media. In doing so the chapter offers a practical application of health communication research in that it can be used to directly educate individuals on what the general primetime television viewing public is exposed to (regarding disability). If the public is receiving misinformation regarding a disability, aside from the ethical considerations, it is possible that those creating health campaigns would be able to combat this information with Public Service Announcements (PSAs) or other materials to generate knowledge. As mentioned previously, there have been several changes to federal and state budgets including freezing or cutting disability services. Generating more knowledge on how disabilities are portrayed and the ethics of these portrayals can only help to educate policymakers and voters on any discrepancies that may be affecting their decision-making.

The examination in this chapter is multidisciplinary in that it combines media and health communication research. Some information is also drawn from sociological research as the potential impacts to society may be discovered. By examining previous research looking at the media's portrayal of disability one can see if there are changes in representation and accuracy. If positive changes in accuracy of messages are seen, one may argue that these changes are based (at least in part) on efforts from those in the health field communicating their informational messages to the public.

This chapter focuses on the ethical implications of the portrayal of disabilities in the media. After a brief examination of media ethics, previous research is examined to see how disability has been portrayed in the past. Then, a current analysis which examines the portrayals of disability in the media is discussed. This analysis is followed by brief implications for academics and health practitioners. Finally, the ethical implications of these representations of disability on television are discussed. In examining this information the following questions are answered: What are media ethics? What are the previous portrayals of disabilities on television? What are the current portrayals of disabilities on television? How do some of these portrayals compare to reality? What are the ethical implications of the portrayals of disabilities?

Mass Media Ethics

The discussion of media ethics does not frequently extend into examining fictional television programming content (Brown and Singhal 1990). Much ethical concern is directed at the news and journalists (see Starck 2001). Early journalism was criticized for potential negative effects on attitudes, beliefs, and behaviors (Ferré 2009). There has, however, been an increase in discussion regarding media ethics as a whole (for example, Christians 2000), expanding to include fictional portrayals of behaviors and minorities. Much of these conversations begin by looking at early ethical theorists.

One can examine several common ethical theorists and apply these principles to the media (specifically in this report, television). Aristotle's principle of the "Golden Mean" looks at the desirable middle between two extremes. Accordingly, the media should present a balanced view of society and the characters within those societies. An argument might exist that the extreme views are what makes for good television. If this is the case then the balance would be in providing both sides of an issue or topic. With extreme portrayals, the inclusion of more temperate portrayals should be able to balance any potential effects.

If the storyline precludes the opportunity for a balanced view, there are other ethical principles that may be useful. The Utilitarian principle judges ethicality by what produces the greatest amount of good for the greatest number of people (Shaw 1999). The media should be concerned with reflecting the lives of the majority of viewers. Further, if only a few individuals are adversely affected by portrayals in the media and the majority of others are entertained, the utilitarian principle would likely be more concerned with the people being entertained versus harmed. Klobas (1988), however, mentions the potential for "us" versus "them" mentalities when individuals are presented as being different in the media. This disparity could lead to problems for the majority as their society becomes fractured. Of course, potential adverse effects would likely be unintended.

When looking at unintended effects, one can use violence as an example. Many ethical theorists would view excessive violence in the media as unethical. Specifically, the Kantian view of ethics (1780) would argue that violence violates the idea where the person is the end versus the means to an end. This ethical viewpoint would suggest that individuals should receive beneficial media messages, and not those that would cause harm. If previous research is correct, then some violence in the media would indeed cause many viewers harm and this ethical principle would be violated. Therefore, media practitioners would have a moral obligation to not show violent media. The same could be said for negative representations of individuals in the media. After all, research has found that negative representations of illness can cause negative repercussions on those individuals that have that illness (for example, Zoller and Worrell 2006).

Previous Research

DEFINING DISABILITY IN THE MEDIA

Before delving further it is important to define disability. The World Health Organization uses "disability" as an umbrella term to describe impairments, activity limitations, and participation restrictions. Disability refers to the negative aspects of the interaction between individuals with a health condition (such as cerebral palsy, Down syndrome, depression)and personal and environmental factors (such as negative attitudes, inaccessible transportation and public buildings, and limited social supports) (World Report 2011).

Others have defined disability as portrayals of blindness, wheelchair use, deafness, amputees, developmental disabilities, and small stature (Klobas 1988). Research has varied on what constitutes physical disabilities. Gardner and Radel (1978) defined physical disability as physical impairments including paraplegia, quadriplegia, blindness, deafness, cerebral palsy, epilepsy, diabetes, and physical deformation. Other research has relied simply on the use of orthotic or prosthetic devices to determine physical disability (Warzak, Majors, Hansell, and Allan 1988). Some definitions of mental illnesses have included everything from attention deficit disorder to schizophrenia (Diefenbach 1997). Some researchers (for example, Signorelli 1989) require verbal confirmation of a mental illness diagnosis in the portrayal, whereas others look at the specific verbal labels as well as character behavior (for example, Diefenbach 1997). For example, a character discussing hearing voices telling him to kill does not need to be verbally labeled as schizophrenic for this portrayal to count as mental illness. For this chapter, both explicit and implicit portrayals of disability will be examined.

PREVIOUS DISABILITY FINDINGS

Previous research was examined to determine what types of disabilities have been portrayed in the media and how often they were portrayed. This examination also included whether the portrayal was deemed positive or negative (when reported by the authors). Brief comparisons were then made between fictional representations and reality.

Some early analyses of disability in the media and on television show distinctly limited and negative portrayals (for example, Head 1954, Signorelli 1989, Turowand Coe 1985). Many early studies also found that much of the information provided was misleading or inaccurate (for example, Gerbner 1980, Gerbner and Tannenbaum 1961, Heeter, Perlstadt and Greenberg 1984, Wahl and Roth 1982). In one of the earliest studies looking at disability in the media, Head (1954) examined over 1,700 characters in the media and found very few portrayals of illness. One character had a physical illness and 12 others portrayed serious mental illness. He found that fewer than 1percent of characters shown had a disability. Head concluded that crucial events in life (that is, birth, death, illness) are almost completely ignored within the sample.

Later works found more variety in the number of programs featuring disability and the number of characters portraying disabilities. Some studies focused on overall programs versus characters, finding diverse ranges of the number of programs that included disabilities (disability was often included when examining overall health information in the media). In 1968, 149 television programs depicted some type of disability. Ten years later, in 1978, there were 256 programs depicting disability (Byrd, McDaniel and Rhoden 1980). Smith, Trivax, Zuehlke, Lowinger and Nghiem (1972) found that 7.2 percent of programming content examined contained health-related information, and Wahl and Roth (1982) found that one in 11 shows contained mental illness (physical illness was not examined).

When focusing on individuals within programs, a number of studies from 1950–2000 were examined. The range of characters with a disability was between 0.4 percent and 8 percent of all characters. Donaldson (1981) found the low 0.4 percent of characters with disabilities after examining over 900 characters. The 1982 Cultural Indicators Project found that 8 percent of major characters experienced physical illness (mental illness was not included). Other studies found that 1.5 percent of characters were disabled (Leo 1993), 2.9 percent of characters experienced mental illness (Diefenbach 1997), and 3 percent of major adult characters were identified as mentally ill (Signorelli 1989).

The types of disabilities found in the aforementioned studies were both physical and mental. Physical disabilities included paraplegia, deafness, blindness, and other physical handicaps (Byrd et al. 1980) to name a few. Mental disabilities included psychosis, schizophrenia, obsessive compulsive disorder, and many others (Diefenbach 1997). Some programs contained main characters (such as *Ironsides*) with a physical disability. Other programs brought in guest or minor characters for a one or multi-episode arc. Few programs contained characters with long-term mental illness.

While there is a wide variety in the types of disabilities portrayed, characters are overwhelmingly portrayed in a negative light. Heeter et al. (1984) found the portrayals of disability in the media to be not informative; Smith et al. (1972) found that 70 percent of the health information provided was inaccurate, misleading, or both. Wahl and Roth (1982) found that people with disabilities were portrayed negatively and frequently stereotyped. Signorielli (1989) and Diefenbach (1997) both found that mentally ill individuals were more likely to be portrayed as criminals. Signorielli, found that individuals with disability were also portrayed as victims or overall failures.

When comparing these portrayals to reality two aspects become clear, individuals with disabilities are both under- and mis-represented on television. Contrary to the portrayal of disabilities from 1950–2000 (0.4–8 percent), the number of Americans who possess some type of disability has ranged from 10 to the current high of just over 19 percent (Americans with Disabilities 2005, 2008). It is clear that individuals with disabilities have historically been vastly underrepresented on television. Not only are individuals with disabilities underrepresented, but the limited portrayals typically present inaccurate depictions of individuals with disability being violent, dangerous, and insignificant criminals. These portrayals also suggest that individuals with disabilities are and should be marginalized within society. In fact, individuals with disabilities do not commit any more crimes than the general population (Diefenbach 1997). It appears that by and large, past television programs have portrayed disability inaccurately and negatively. However, there is little information on more current presentations of disabilities on television.

Primetime Television Analysis

Due to the fact that very few recent publications have examined disability on American television it was important to gather more current data for comparison and discussion purposes. Television programs airing from 2006–2011 were examined for their portrayals of disability. Specifically, the analysis examined if a disability was present in a given episode, the type of disability, the demographics of the character with the disability, the character's role (main or minor), and any symptoms, difficulties, or side effects displayed by the character. Finally, the overall portrayal was deemed positive, negative, or neutral and the outcome of the character's life in the episode was examined as either positive or negative. For the purpose of this analysis, the aforementioned definition from the World Health Organization will be used and both explicit and implicit portrayals of disabilities will be examined.

A total of 195 episodes were examined. Three episodes (randomly selected) from the top ten fictional[1] programs of each season between 2006–2011 from network programming and the top 15 programs from cable were selected. The top shows were chosen based on Nielsen ratings for the years sampled. If a show was rated highly in multiple seasons, that show was chosen only once and removed from the pool for other seasons (therefore, some of the shows sampled were below the "top 10" mark for the year to give a solid 50 program sample of primetime broadcast programming).[2] For example, the show *House* was rated in the top 10 for multiple years but was examined only once. A few significant findings are highlighted below.

FINDINGS

Of the episodes, 24 percent portrayed an individual with a disability with a total of 11 percent of characters displaying a physical or mental disability. There were 498 total "regular" characters on the programs examined (characters were deemed as regulars if they appeared in at least 75 percent a program's episodes in the given season). Only 27 percent of the characters shown with a disability were main characters; the remaining 73 percent were guest stars on for one or two episodes in the season. Some of these main characters were, however, the title characters of their programs (for example, Adrian Monk on *Monk*). Entire series might revolve around an individual with a disability such as Samantha on *Samantha Who*, a show that revolves around Samantha's amnesia and her difficulties remembering her sordid past.

The most frequent type of disability portrayed was mental illness, specifically, psychosis. Programs within the crime genre most often showed individuals with disabilities which were almost exclusively some type of psychosis. While an occasional diagnosis was provided (schizophrenia, paranoia) the labels of "crazy" or "psychotic" were more commonly used. Physical disabilities were also present in the sample; these were usually found within medical dramas. *ER*, *House* and *Grey's Anatomy* all had at least one character with some type of physical disability. Within the medical dramas, one main character (Gregory House of *House*) displayed a physical disability, and the remaining characters were confined to one episode. In the same subsample, of the individuals with physical disabilities, 80 percent were seemingly cured by the end of the program (the other 20 percent either died or bravely carried on with their disability). While physical

---

1   Reality programs were not included in the sample of programming. While individuals with disabilities do appear in some reality programming (for example, *Dancing with the Stars*) as these are *real* people whose disabilities are not being manufactured or significantly altered by program producers such as in fictional television.

2   In the 2007–2008 season, there was a writer's strike which led to the inclusion of many of the top programs of the year in the reality genre. This inclusion allowed many lower ranked programs to be a part of the sample for this season.

disabilities were less common in other genres, a few main characters did display permanent disabilities (for example, the aforementioned Artie from *Glee* and Auggie, a character with visual impairment on *Covert Affairs*).

As was previously mentioned, the majority of the characters with a disability had a mental illness. Of these portrayals roughly half of characters with disabilities were portrayed as criminals. This finding is not too surprising when one notes that almost half of the sample programs were crime dramas (for example, *CSI*, *Law and Order: SVU*, *Criminal Minds*). Those with a disability were also portrayed as suspects, victims, patients, and the more positive (and rare) doctor, detective, student, and business executive. Almost all of the characters with disabilities were portrayed in a negative or neutral manner. Even those individuals with good jobs (that is, the non-criminals) were seen as surly, troubled, socially awkward, mean, or incredibly silly. Fortunately, the outcome for some of the characters with disabilities did turn more positive. For example, the aforementioned characters with temporary physical disabilities that were "cured" by the end of the program or the person suffering from amnesia learns a valuable lesson by the end of the half hour.

A small increase in the percentage of individuals shown was found (previous highs fall around 8 percent, whereas this study found 11 percent, which is still an under representation compared to current figures of 19 percent), these more recent findings are not far removed from much of what was discussed in the previous research. The information provided is not usually accurate (cures in 30 minutes), is often misleading (not all criminals have a disability and vice versa), and is predominantly negative. Characters with disabilities do not fit into a normative role and they exemplify the "them" that Klobas (1988) was referring to.

DISCUSSION

What do these findings mean for viewers? What do they mean for people have a disability? Studies reveal that the mass media are a primary source of health information for the public, particularly for individuals who do not have direct experience with an illness or disability (Sharf, Freimuth, Greenspon and Plotnick 1996). Dutta-Bergman (2004) found that television was a primary resource of health information for people who are not health-oriented. If people continually turn to and believe what they see about disabilities in the media they may believe that these portrayals are accurate. Based on media theory and previous research findings, these false representations have the ability to negatively impact not only viewers but real people with a disability.

Cultivation theory (Gerbner et al. 2002) states that heavy viewers of television will believe that the "real" world more closely resembles what they see on television. If Gerbner is correct, then television fills a void in one's direct experience. Under- and mis-representation of disabilities can lead to three potential issues: television viewers may not have any knowledge that such a disability exists; if the prevalence is well below the number of individuals with such a disability in the real world then this representation can affect the attitudes of viewers; or, this underrepresentation could lead viewers to believe that all individuals with a disability are like the few they see on television.

Further, studies have found that the media's portrayal of disabilities influences people viewing as well as those who have a disability (for example, Glauberman 1980, Zollerand Worrell 2006). These effects have been found to be negative and potentially damaging to individuals. Negative portrayals do little to reduce already negative perceptions of disabilities held by the public. Farnall and Smith (1999) found that viewing positive portrayals of characters with disabilities reduced feelings of anger, fear, or concern regarding encounters with individuals with disabilities. However, even the positive portrayals of disability did not reduce discomfort at the thought of interacting with such individuals.

Implications for Academics

As previously mentioned, one of the first steps in examining the ethical representation of disability in the media is by examining the portrayal of disabilities. If characters with disabilities are non-existent in the television landscape, then this underrepresentation will be problematic based on what we know from cultivation theory. If the portrayal does exist but is inaccurate or implausible or even heroic, there are potential negative implications. While the negative implications of inaccurate or implausible portrayals are more obvious (see previous section). The heroic or "super crip" portrayals (see Nelson 1994) can also diminish the lives of those in the real world living (the majority less heroically) with disability. Therefore, it is important to examine all types of disability portrayals.

The lack of current research looking at the portrayal of disabilities in the media needs to be remedied in order to more fully examine the scope of the ethical nature of these representations. Research focusing on the potential effects of negative disability portrayals on the general population as well as those diagnosed with disability can provide great heuristic value to academic research. These studies can also provide valuable information for health practitioners.

Implications for Health Practitioners

Media practitioners have a moral obligation to show accurate or at the very least balanced representations of disability in the media. How can this be accomplished? One way to show accuracy is by using actors and actresses who actually have a disability to play the character. While this practice will not change the role of the character ("crazy criminal" or socially awkward obsessive compulsive), at least the disability itself will be accurately represented. Health practitioners can encourage media producers to utilize organizations such as the Media Access Office (MAO) in Los Angeles, which was founded in 1980 to help producers provide more realistic and responsible representations of people with disabilities. The MAO encourages producers to hire people with disabilities to play the role of a character with disabilities. This practice would create the most realistic representation of disability in the media.

If utilizing an individual with a disability in this capacity is not possible health practitioners should encourage media producers to follow the "Golden Mean" and provide balance. An option to create balance would be to have multiple characters with the same disability. For example, if there is a need for someone with a mental illness to be portrayed as a cannibalistic maniac, perhaps another family member with the same mental illness can be portrayed as living a more "normal" lifestyle. Providing a balance across time may also be a more viable option due to the constraints of a 30 to 60 minute television program. If all else fails, the friendly PSA at the end of the episode better explaining the disability in question can also help to create a balance to the messages received.

Health campaigns related to disabilities may also take note of such representations. If the public is receiving misinformation regarding a disability, it is possible that those creating health campaigns may be able to combat this information with PSAs or other materials to generate knowledge. As mentioned previously, there have been several changes to federal and state budgets including freezing or cutting disability services. Generating more knowledge on how disabilities are portrayed can only help to educate policymakers and voters on any discrepancies that may be affecting their decision – making.

Conclusion

If we look back on the early theorists again, we can see how false representations would be seen as unethical. While the media may present a balanced view of society for the majority what about for minorities? The underrepresentation of disability in the media does a disservice to those that have a disability in reality. Gerbner et al. (2002) might argue that if someone is not represented on television not only do they not exist in the eyes of many individuals but when encountering someone with a disability the "cultivated" individual will not know how to react leading to possible marginalization of individuals. Aristotle might also be concerned with the extreme representation of those with a disability. That the majority of televised individuals with a disability are seen in a negative light (as criminal, victim, stigmatized) without the same number of individuals being shown in a positive light causes a great imbalance of disability representations. Fictional television does not show both sides to a disability. Even without removing the "crazy criminal" element on television highlighting the other side of the story (for example, information about the disability itself, what it does to a person) might provide the balance needed to offset some of the potential negative effects.

Of course, the Utilitarian principle might actually account for why there are so limited portrayals of disabilities in the media. The 10 to 19 percent of Americans with a disability are still a minority. The media may just be reflecting the lives of the majority of its viewers (Plaisance 2009). Do these negative portrayals, however, reflect a "harmonious" social life? Possibly, if Klobas's (1988) "us" versus "them" mentality holds true then the false representations of people with disabilities may unite the "us" of society to more adequately marginalize the "them" or those with disabilities.

According to Kant's principles, however, the lack of disabilities in the media as well as the overall negative portrayal are unethical and not beneficial to viewers and may in fact cause harm for those with a disability. The entertainment does not justify the potential harm. One example of an area of disability research that is important is that of shame. Shame has been found to be related to discrepancy between one's ideal self and their perceptions of actual self (Sidoli 1988). More importantly, in media research, shame is related to the fear of being negatively evaluated by others (Gilbert, Pehl and Allan 1994). If viewers are most often exposed to negative representations then those with the disabilities shown may believe that others perceive them in the same light as the televised portrayal.

The media has the power to shape and facilitate lives and societies; at the very least, the images it portrays should not harm either. The under- and mis-representations of disabilities in the media are problematic and potentially harmful. Continuing research into disability portrayals and their potential effects may help individuals and organizations working to improve Hollywood's representations of disabilities and the lives of people affected by those representations.

References

Brown, W.J. and Singhal, A. 1990. Ethical dilemmas of prosocial television. *Communication Quarterly*, 38(3), 268–80.

Byrd, E.K., McDaniel, R.S., and Rhoden, R.B. 1980. Television programming and disability: A ten year span. *International Journal of Rehabilitation Research*, 3(3), 321–6.

Christians, C. 2000. Social dialogue and media ethics. *Ethical Perspectives*, 7(2), 182–93.

Diefenbach, D.L. 1997. The portrayal of mental illness on prime-time television. *Journal of Community Psychology*, 25(3), 289–302.

Donaldson, J. 1981. The visibility and image of handicapped people on television. *Exceptional Children*, 47(6), 413–16.

Dutta-Bergman, M.J. 2004. Primary sources of health information: Comparisons in the domain of health attitudes, health cognitions, and health behaviors. *Health Communication*, 16(3), 273–88.

Elliott, T. and Byrd, E.K. 1983. Attitude change toward disability through television portrayal. *Journal of Applied Rehabilitation Counseling*, (14)2, 35–7.

Farnall, O. and Smith, K.A. 1999. Reactions to people with disabilities: Personal contact versus viewing of specific media portrayals. *Journalism and Mass Communication Quarterly*, 76(4), 659–72.

Ferré, J.P. 2009. A short history of media ethics in the United States, in *Mass Media Ethics*, edited by L. Wilkins and C. Christians. New York: Taylor and Francis, 15–27.

Gardner, J.M. and Radel, M.S. 1978. Portrait of the disabled in the media. *Journal of Community Psychology*, 6(3), 269–74.

Gerbner, G. 1980. Dreams that hurt: Mental illness in the mass media, in *The Community Imperative*, edited by R.C. Baron, I.D. Rutman, and B. Klaczynska. Philadelphia: Horizon House Institute, 19–23.

Gerbner, G., Gross, L., Morgan, M., Signorielli, N., and Shanahan, J. 2002. Growing up with television: Cultivation processes, in *Media Effects: Advances in Theory and Research* (2nd edition), edited by J. Bryant and D. Zillmann. Hillsdale, NJ: Lawrence Erlbaum Associates, Inc., 43–68.

Gerbner, G. and Tannenbaum, P.H. 1961. Regulation of mental illness content in motionpictures and television, *Gazette*, 6, 365–85.

Gilbert, P., Pehl, J. and Allan, S. 1994. The phenomenology of shame and guilt: An empirical investigation. *British Journal of Medical Psychology*, 67, 23–36.

Glauberman, N.R. 1980. *The Influence of Positive TV Portrayals on Children's Behavior and Attitude Toward the Physically Disabled*. Unpublished doctoral dissertation at Columbia University, New York, NY.

Head, S. 1954. Content analysis of televised drama programs. *Quarterly of Film, Radio, and Television*, 9, 175–94.

Heeter, C., Perlstadt, H. and Greenberg, B.S. 1984. *Health Incidence, Stages of Illness and Treatment on Popular Television Programs*. Paper presented at the annual convention of the International Communication Association, San Francisco, CA.

Itzkoff, D. 2010 'Family Guy,' Palin and the Limits of Laughter. NYTimes.com, February 19. Available at: http://www.nytimes.com/2010/02/20/arts/television/20family.html?scp=1sq=%22seth%20 macfarlane%22&st=cse

Kant, I. 1780. *The Metaphysical Elements of Ethics*.

Kline, K.N. 2003. Popular media and health: Images, effects, and institutions, in *Handbook of Health Communication*, edited by T.L. Thompson, A.M. Dorsey, K.I. Miller and R. Parrott. Mahwah, NJ: Lawrence Erlbaum Associates, Inc., 557–8.

Klobas, L.E. 1988. *Disability Drama in Television and Film*. Jefferson, NC: McFarland and Co.

Nelson, J.A. 1994. *The Disabled, the Media and the Information Age*. Westport, CT: Greenwood Press.

Plaisance, P.L. 2009. Violence, in *Mass Media Ethics*, edited by L. Wilkins and C. Christians. New York: Taylor and Francis, 162–76.

Sharf, B.F., Freimuth, V.S., Greenspon, P. and Plotnick, C. 1996. Confronting cancer on *Thirty Something*: Audience response to health content on entertainment television. *Journal of Health Communication*, 1, 157–72.

Shaw, W.H. 1999. *Contemporary Ethics: Taking Account of Utilitarianism*. Oxford: Blackwell Publishers.

Sidoli, M. 1988. Shame and the shadow. *Journal of Analytical Psychology*, 33, 127–42.

Signorielli, N. 1989. The stigma of mental illness on television. *Journal of Broadcasting and Electronic Media*, 33, 325–31.

Smith, F.A., Trivax, G., Zuehlke, D.A., Lowinger, P., and Nghiem, T.L. 1972. Health information during a week of television. *The New England Journal of Medicine*, 286(10), 516–20.

United States Census. 2008. *Americans with Disabilities: 2005*. [Online]. Available at: http://www. census.gov/prod/2008pubs/p70-117.pdf [accessed: 1 September 2011].

Warzak, W., Majors, C., Hansell, A. and Allan, T. 1988. An analysis of televised presentations of disability. *Rehabilitation Psychology*, 33, 106–12.

World Health Organization. 2011. *World Report on Disability*. [Online]. Available at: http://whqlibdoc. who.int/publications/2011/9789240685215_eng.pdf [accessed: 1 September 2011].

Zoller, H. and Worrell, T.R. 2006. Television illness depictions, identity, and social experience: Responses to multiple sclerosis on *The West Wing* among people with MS. *Health Communication*, 20(1), 69–79.

Index

If you have found this book useful you may be interested in other titles from Gower

Gower Handbook of Internal Communication
Edited by Marc Wright
Hardback: 978-0-566-08689-2
e-book: 978-0-7546-9097-9

Knowledge Management in Health Care
Edited by Lorri Zipperer
Hardback: 978-1-4094-3883-0
e-book: 978-1-4094-3884-7

Mediating Mental Health
Contexts, Debates and Analysis
Michael Birch
Hardback: 978-0-7546-7474-0
e-book: 978-1-4094-2501-4

Liberalizing, Feminizing and Popularizing
Health Communications in Asia
Edited by Liew Kai Khiun
Hardback: 978-0-7546-7839-7
e-book: 978-0-7546-9660-5

GOWER